The
Reference Shelf ®

Conspiracy Theories

Edited by
Paul McCaffrey

The Reference Shelf
Volume 84 • Number 1
H. W. Wilson
A Division of EBSCO Publishing, Inc.
Ipswich, Massachusetts
2012

The Reference Shelf

The books in this series contain reprints of articles, excerpts from books, addresses on current issues, and studies of social trends in the United States and other countries. There are six separately bound numbers in each volume, all of which are usually published in the same calendar year. Numbers one through five are each devoted to a single subject, providing background information and discussion from various points of view and concluding with an index and comprehensive bibliography that lists books, pamphlets, and articles on the subject. The final number of each volume is a collection of recent speeches, and it contains a cumulative speaker index. Books in the series may be purchased individually or on subscription.

Library of Congress has catalogued this serial title as follows:

Conspiracy theories / editor, Paul McCaffrey.
    p. cm. -- (The reference shelf ; v. 84, no. 1)
  Includes bibliographical references and index.
  ISBN 978-0-8242-1115-8
  1. Conspiracy theories. I. McCaffrey, Paul, 1977–
  HV6275.C663 2012
  001.9--dc23

                    2011050295

Cover: Kennedys and Connally in Limousine. © Bettmann/CORBIS

Visit: www.salempress.com/hwwilson

Printed in the United States of America

Contents

1

"The Paranoid Style": An Introduction to Conspiracy Theories

2

The Twin Towers and the Truthers: 9/11 Conspiracy Theories

After Hofstadter: Conspiracy Theories in America

By Paul McCaffrey

Most authorities agree that the modern study of conspiracy theories began in 1964, when the historian Richard Hofstadter published his seminal essay "The Paranoid Style in American Politics" in the October issue of *Harper's Magazine*. Though Hofstadter's thesis has endured its share of criticism over the years, with some contending that the ideas he enunciated have since been overapplied, it remains one of the essential texts in understanding conspiracy theories and their various components. Written in the long shadow of the John F. Kennedy assassination, "The Paranoid Style" is very much a product of its time and place, yet the issues and themes it illuminates continue to resonate in the present day. Moreover, through his survey of conspiracy theories throughout American history, Hofstadter draws powerful parallels between the past and the present, suggesting that the so-called "paranoid style" is a common and enduring historical current, one that comes in "waves of different intensity, [but] appears to be all but ineradicable."

While Hofstadter's modern examination focuses on right-wing political movements in the United States—Senator Joseph McCarthy's Red Scare and the John Birch Society, for example—he explores antecedents going back to the 1700s that do not fall so neatly on one side or the other of the Left-Right divide, such as anti-Catholic and anti-Masonic movements. Hofstadter stresses that the patterns of conspiratorial thinking he discusses are evident on the political left as well the right, and while he emphasizes American examples of the phenomenon, the paranoid style is by no means unique to the United States.

Hofstadter's use of the term "paranoid" was qualified as well. He did not mean that those espousing such views were paranoid in the clinical sense. He observed, rather, that "it is the use of paranoid modes of expression by more or less normal people that makes the phenomenon significant." Despite this distinction, the "paranoid" in paranoid style evokes something else about conspiracy theories: They carry with them a pejorative undertone that is probably unavoidable. As a form of stigmatized knowledge, conspiracy theories often exact a social cost from those espousing them. The conspiracist is frequently seen as mentally unhinged or otherwise to be avoided. Hofstadter does not shy away from such characterizations and can be openly dismissive of the conspiracy theorist. He is careful to point out, however, that "there are conspiratorial acts in history, and there is nothing paranoid about taking note of them."

Beyond the "more or less normal" characterization, the major difference between clinical paranoia and the paranoid style is one of emphasis. According to Hofstadter, the political paranoiac and the clinical paranoiac "tend to be overheated, oversuspicious, overaggressive, grandiose, and apocalyptic in expression." The clinical paranoiac, however, "sees the hostile and conspiratorial world in which he feels himself to be living as directed specifically *against him*," while the political paranoiac believes the target is not himself, but rather "a nation, a culture, a way of life whose fate affects not himself alone but millions of others."

As an example of the paranoid style in action, Hofstadter describes a group of men from Bagdad, Arizona, who drove all the way to Washington, D.C., in 1964 to testify against proposed gun control legislation championed by Connecticut senator Thomas E. Dodd. The measure sought to tighten the rules regulating the purchase and sale of mail-order firearms. Given that Lee Harvey Oswald, Kennedy's alleged assassin, had purchased his rifle through the mail under an alias, the Dodd bill, whatever its shortcomings, had the "color of conventional political reasoning," in Hofstadter's words, and could be viewed as a rational reaction to a demonstrable problem. Nevertheless, one of the Arizonans failed to see the issue in such a light. Testifying before the US Senate, he registered his opposition to the measure, declaring that the Dodd bill represented "a further attempt by a subversive power to make us part of one world socialistic government." He alleged the measure would "create chaos" and embolden the enemies of the United States in their plot to gain control over the levers of government.

Even today, nearly fifty years after this testimony, the fears it expresses are familiar. Trepidation over a one-world government remains a common theme in conspiracy theories of the current era, as demonstrated by belief in the alleged New World Order (NWO) or the North American Union (NAU) plots. So, too, is the tendency to perceive the most modest of measures as a potential Trojan horse, a subterfuge designed by conspirators as a means of seizing power.

To Hofstadter, the Arizonan's testimony reflected the larger paranoid style at work and recalled conspiracy theories from earlier in American history. Of particular importance is the alleged conspiracy's "central image," in this case a subversive plot to establish "a one world socialistic government." Within the paranoid style, according Hofstadter, this central image is "a vast and sinister conspiracy, a gigantic and yet subtle machinery of influence set in motion to undermine and destroy a way of life."

To the conspiracist, Hofstadter observes, "history is a conspiracy, set in motion by demonic forces of almost transcendent power." Given the size and influence of these forces, the conspiracy theorist believes that only an apocalyptic struggle—a crusade—is capable of thwarting the nefarious plot.

Along with the apocalyptic warnings, there is an undercurrent in the paranoid style of a feeling of powerlessness. As Hofstadter observes, "Time is forever running out." As a witness to the conspiracy, the conspiracist is one of the elect, one of the few who understands the insidious and overarching might of the conspirators. Confronted by the vast plot, however, conspiracists know that they probably lack the influence to counteract it, to rally the necessary crusade to defeat it. The docile public remains largely aloof from the conspiracy theorists' dire warnings, paying them little heed or ignoring them altogether. According to Hofstadter, the conspiracy theorist "has little real hope that his evidence will convince a hostile world." The plotters, meanwhile, continue to accumulate power, manipulating the media, the educational system, and other levers of power, moving with single-minded intensity toward the realization of their scheme. Thus, Hofstadter notes, the "apocalypticism of the paranoid style runs dangerously near to hopeless pessimism, but usually stops short of it."

Within this sense of hopelessness is another element of the paranoid style: a profound and grudging respect for the conspirators. Though their aims are sinister, the conspirators are admirably clever, even brilliant, and worthy of emulation. As Hofstadter observes, "A fundamental paradox of the paranoid style is the imitation of the enemy." Two important examples of this phenomenon, Hofstadter notes, can be found in Joseph McCarthy and the Ku Klux Klan (KKK). As an anti-Communist who often targeted the intellectual elite, McCarthy nevertheless couched his denunciations in the terms of academia, including extensive footnotes to give his work a scholarly air. The KKK, similarly, began as an anti-Catholic organization, but in opposing the church took on some of its most obvious attributes, placing a heavy emphasis on ritualized ceremonies.

Though some behaviors of the conspirators are worthy of imitation, conspiracists spare nothing when characterizing the plotters' crimes. "Much of the function of the enemy," Hofstadter writes, "lies not in what can be imitated but in what can be wholly condemned." In the paranoid style, the Mason, the Roman Catholic, the Communist, the enemy in whatever form, is both bloodthirsty and sexually licentious. Rape and butchery are employed without qualm. The practices are so brutal that there would seem to be no hope for the conspirator's redemption. Their sins are too great to be purged.

Except when they repent. Another paradox in the paranoid style is the value placed on defectors. As awful as the agents of the conspiracy are, those who abandon the cause, whatever their past sins, are embraced by the conspiracists. Hofstadter points out how the anti-Masons and anti-Catholics relied on former Masons or supposed runaway nuns and excommunicated priests, whether credible or not, to describe the inner workings of the underlying plot to which they formerly contributed. Who better to reveal the conspiracy than a former conspirator? In Hofstadter's time, the accounts of ex-Communists were eagerly accepted and disseminated by anti-Communists, while in today's politics, where the paranoid style flourishes, the accounts of apostate liberals or conservatives are held up as proof positive of the other side's malevolence. "Such converts," Hofstadter states in speaking of these defectors, "remind one of those ancient converts from paganism to Christianity of whom it is told that upon their conversion they did not entirely cease to believe in their old gods but converted them into demons."

Lastly, one of the paranoid style's foremost qualities, according to Hofstadter, is its reliance on the factual record, on real evidence. The veracity of the defrocked priest, the ex-Communist, or the former Mason may be subject to doubt, but it cannot be completely discounted. McCarthy did not abandon the art of deduction and inference when he authored his assaults on alleged Communist conspiracies. "Paranoid writing," Hofstadter observes, "begins with certain defensible judgments." From these logical starting points, the paranoid style leaps from one inference to the next until a grand conspiracy that neatly divides the world in two is revealed. Hofstadter notes, too, that much as the paranoid style rests, however awkwardly, on actual evidence, the conflicts it evokes are equally real.

Anti-Catholic agitation served in one measure as a reaction to immigration. It also raised a probing question as to whether the religion was compatible with republican government. Given its hierarchical structure and the influence of ecclesiastical authority, this question may have had some legitimacy in a nineteenth-century context. To some, the values of Catholicism and democracy were not perfectly in sync and were hard to reconcile. But in the paranoid style, more rational concerns were drowned out by breathless talk of lecherous nuns, murderous priests, and a papal plot to turn the United States into a monarchy under the thumb of Rome.

The anti-Masons raised concerns of similar import. The ranks of the Masons were filled with society's elite, and according to their oaths they were, in Hofstadter's words, "bound by special obligations" to one another. Such arrangements, secret as they were, could be conceived as a threat to more democratic relationships and to civil society. Of course, again, these concerns were not openly expressed, but were channeled into tales of Masonic orgies and ritual murders. So while the conflicts that motivate conspiracy theories may be real, how they are presented can stretch the bounds of credibility. As Hofstadter remarks, "We are all sufferers from history, but the [conspiracist] is a double sufferer, since he is afflicted not only by the real world, with the rest of us, but by his fantasies as well."

Conspiracy Theories: An Overview

By Micah Issit
Points of View: Conspiracy Theories, 2011

A conspiracy theory seeks to explain a disputed event as a plot by a secret group or alliance rather than an individual or isolated act. Conspiracy theories of various kinds have been part of human culture for centuries. The struggle against conspiracies, whether real or imagined, has become a standard model in literary fiction, while the belief in actual conspiracies is a type of social phenomenon.

Conspiracy theories serve a number of functions. In some cases, conspiracy theories can be used to express suspicion and anger toward a dominant social group or to express frustration with perceived powerlessness within society. Conspiracy theories have been used by those in power to justify the persecution of targeted groups. In a more fundamental sense, conspiracy theories express a basic desire to uncover mysteries and secrets hidden within the generally accepted explanations of historical events.

History

In Western society, the fascination with conspiracy theories became pronounced during the seventeenth and eighteenth centuries. There is some debate over when the term conspiracy theory was coined, but it is generally believed to have arisen in the early twentieth century. According to historian Daniel Pipes, most Western conspiracy theories were created between 1815 and 1945, a period during which numerous conspiratorial ideas and theories proliferated. During this time, popular historians spawned a number of theories that sought to explain many of history's major events, including wars, genocide, and shifts in political power, in light of conspiracies enacted by secret societies.

However, some of history's most persistent conspiracy theories originated before the eighteenth century. Some historians have suggested that fear of a plot by the Jewish elite to seize control of Christian Europe played a role in motivating citizens to take part in the Crusades (1095–1291). The theory was later used by the Nazis to justify the Holocaust; it has also been used in the twenty-first century by some extreme anti-Semitic groups to justify mistrust or hatred of Jewish people.

During and after the French Revolution (1789–1799), it was suggested that several powerful groups were instigating revolutionary violence in order to benefit from the resulting shifts in power. It was during this period that two groups, the Freemasons and the Illuminati, gained infamy as two of the world's most powerful secret societies.

Conspiracy theories express a basic desire to uncover mysteries and secrets hidden within the generally accepted explanations of historical events.

The Freemasons are one of the oldest known and most mysterious fraternal organizations in the world. The society's history is shrouded in uncertainty; some claim that the group originated as early as the tenth century CE, while other historians place the society's origins closer to the sixteenth century. Membership in the Freemasons is closed to all but those nominated by other members. Masonic meetings and rituals were a closely guarded secret for centuries. Masonic society is based on the belief in a supreme being, and is dedicated to upholding just laws. As of 2007, the Masonic order had thousands of members operating in chapters around the world.

The Bavarian Illuminati, founded in 1776 by law professor Adam Weishaupt, was a fraternal society of intellectuals dedicated to rational analysis of politics and society. The organization drew its members from the intellectual elite and counted a number of prominent politicians and philosophers among its members. Because meetings of secret societies were prohibited in Bavaria (a German state), the Illuminati were considered a criminal organization. The Bavarian Illuminati were involved in a number of movements to alter the balance of political power in Bavaria.

Because the Freemasons and the Illuminati were extremely secretive and counted a number of influential political and social figures among their membership, many people believed that both groups were capable of exerting tremendous influence on societal development. Throughout the eighteenth century, both groups were the subject of hundreds of fictionalized stories. In such stories, the secret societies were described as villainous organizations involved in a plot for global domination or personal benefit until foiled by a heroic character or group.

In the eighteenth and nineteenth centuries, the American political landscape was rife with conspiracy theories. From the American Revolution until the Civil War, many politicians and citizens believed that European governments were attempting to infiltrate and cause the downfall of the American government. Some Americans also likened the Catholic Church to a foreign monarchy, in which the pope served as a sovereign. Many Americans opposed Catholic immigration; they believed that Catholics, acting on the behalf of the pope, would undermine or try to overthrow the government, which was dominated by Protestant officials. Belief in the Catholic conspiracy led to the development of several anti-Catholic political parties, the most prominent of which, the Know Nothing Party, had a substantial impact on politics during the mid 1800s.

During the Cold War (1940s–1980s), many Americans believed that there was a plot among communist leaders to gain control of the United States government through covert agents functioning as US citizens. During the 1940s and 1950s, Senator Joe McCarthy prompted a number of Senate hearings aimed at uncovering communist activity in the United States. Thousands of US citizens were detained and questioned on suspicion of involvement in anti-American activities. Years later, the McCarthy trials became symbolic of how conspiracy theories can lead to paranoia and persecution.

In the 1960s, the United States and rival nations, such as the Soviet Union, raced to be the first country to successfully explore space and land an astronaut on the moon. In the 1990s, some conspiracy theorists began to propose that the 1969 US moon landing never occurred. It was suggested that the National Aeronautics and Space Administration (NASA), in conjunction with the federal government, filmed the moon landing in a movie studio in order to convince foreign governments that the United States had won the race into outer space. The moon landing theory has persisted into the twenty-first century.

Between the 1960s and the 1990s, the focus of conspiracy theories arising within the United States shifted from the belief that foreign agents were trying to influence US politics to the notion that the US government was manipulating the populace to fuel the advancement of individual politicians or political lineages. In some polls, American trust in the government fell from close to 80 percent in the 1950s to less than 25 percent in the late 1990s.

The 1963 assassination of US President John F. Kennedy became the basis for one of the most famous conspiracy theories in American history. Numerous books, films, and journalistic investigations attempted to illustrate key points that either supported or refuted the conspiratorial angle. This conspiracy theory is especially notable in that theorists often accuse the US government and its operative organizations of carrying out the assassination.

Historically, conspiracy theories are more common in periods of social unrest or change. During times of political or social crisis, conspiracy theories may arise among groups that believe they are at a political or social disadvantage in comparison to other groups judged to have a superior social status. In other cases, conspiracy theories may be used to justify the persecution of a group that has been politically or militarily targeted. Though conspiracy theories persist, in the twenty-first century, a majority of Americans consider most conspiracy theories to be a product of fiction or paranoia rather than a viable explanation for political or social events.

Conspiracy Theories Today

The 2000 election was one of the most closely-contested presidential races in American history. Because of numerous voting irregularities, some suggested that George W. Bush and his supporters in the conservative political community conspired to rig the election in his favor. Allegations of conspiracy with regard to Bush and his political allies occurred again after the terrorist attacks of 2001, when they were accused of having prior knowledge of the attacks. Most political analysts view these conspiracy theories as little more than an example of paranoia and increasing distrust of the government on the part of some segments of the American populace.

Though many feel that modern conspiracy theories represent extreme cynicism and skepticism and are generally based on apocryphal beliefs, history is punctuated with evidence of verified conspiracies aimed at influencing political developments. Evidence suggests that secret or covert groups around the world remain engaged in conspiratorial enterprises with the goal of influencing political, economic, or social change. Whether modern conspiracies can be linked to secret societies such as the Freemasons or other sociopolitical conglomerations is a matter of debate and investigation.

Historians have suggested that conspiracy theories are a natural outgrowth of a human desire to explore and uncover facets of experience that remain unexplained. Others suggest that such theories are the product of frustrations related to the secretive nature of some political, social and historical organizations and operations. In addition, conspiracy theories have had an enduring aesthetic appeal as a plot device for fiction and as an expression of the mythic struggle between good and evil. Whether in reference to actual conspiracies or fictional accounts of secret covenants, the perpetuation of conspiracy theories reflects both the human desire to pursue and untangle any mystery and the uneven distribution of power and influence within society.

Bibliography

Barkun, M. *A Culture of Conspiracy: Apocalyptic Visions in Contemporary America*. Berkeley: University of California Press, 2003.

Basham, Lee. "Living with the Conspiracy." *Philosophical Forum* 32.3 (Fall 2001): 265.

Berlet, Chip. "Siren song—conspiracy!" *New Internationalist* (Oct. 2007): 12.

Bethell, Tom. "Conspiracy Talk." *American Spectator* 30.2 (Oct. 1997): 18.

Burnett, Thom. *Conspiracy Encyclopedia: The Encyclopedia of Conspiracy Theories*. Essex (UK): Chamberlain Brothers, 2005.

Camp, G. S. *Selling Fear: Conspiracy Theories and End-Times Paranoia*. Grand Rapids: Baker Books, 1997.

Fenster, Mark, and Philip Rosen. *Conspiracy Theories: Secrecy and Power in American Society*. Minneapolis: University of Minnesota Press, 2001.

Hari, Johann. "Conspiracy theories: a guide." *New Statesman* 131.3 (16 Dec. 2002): 27.

Hidell, A., and D'Arc, J. *The conspiracy reader: From the deaths of JFK and John Lennon to government-sponsored alien cover-ups*. Secaucus, NJ: Carol, 1999.

Irvine, Simon, and Natasha Beattie. "Conspiracy Theory, Pre-Millennium Tension and the *X-Files*: Power and Belief in the 1990s." *Social Alternatives* 17.4 (Oct. 1998): 31–34.

Keeley, B. L. "Nobody Expects the Spanish Inquisition! More Thoughts on Conspiracy Theory." *Journal of Social Philosophy* 34.1 (Spring 2003): 104–110.

Knight, P. (Ed.) (2002). *Conspiracy nation: The politics of paranoia in postwar America*. London: New York University Press, 2002.

Pipes, Daniel. *Conspiracy: How the Paranoid Style Flourishes and Where It Comes From*. New York: Free Press, 1997.

Skelton, Ike. "Don't Let Truth Be Next Casualty of 9/11." *FDCH Press Releases* (04/12/2002).

Swann, Julian. "Conspiracy Theories." *History Today* 51.2 (May 2001): 5.

Tuckett, Kate. *Conspiracy Theories*. New York: Berkley Books, 2005.

Conspiracy Theories Probe the Dark Side of Life

By Sally Driscoll and Laura Finley
Points of View: Conspiracy Theories, 2011

Conspiracy theories offer many benefits to society. Some conspiracy theories attempt to offer explanations to perplexing questions and unsolved mysteries, while others are a natural reaction to denial or a valuable tool to demand government accountability. More importantly, conspiracists often take up where investigative journalists leave off, and in some cases, their theories turn out to be true. Nonetheless, conspiracy theories stir up evidence and questions that can provoke important discussions and debates in a democratic society, whether it concerns the terrestrial intrusion of alien beings or the involvement of the United States government in infamous assassinations and terror plots; to a conspiracist, the only implausibility is the refusal to believe.

Searching for Answers

Conspiracy theories attempt to offer explanations, most often educated ones, to the questions that perplex humans the most, however bizarre the solutions or outcome may seem. For example, in the 1970s, author Charles Berlitz and others picked up on earlier accounts of ships and planes vanishing at seemingly unusual rates in or above the Atlantic Ocean between Florida, Bermuda, and Puerto Rico. Berlitz put forth his theories in the bestseller, "The Bermuda Triangle." One of these theories proposed that aliens from outer space were abducting the passengers as they traveled to and from the islands, and as a result, the authorities were covering up the matter because they were working with the aliens.

Other conspiracy theories are rooted in denial, an understandable human trait present during the first stage of Elisabeth Kübler-Ross's five stages of grief. The theories serve to offer hope and explanation for those who are grieving. For instance, Kurt Cobain, singer and guitarist with the alternative rock band Nirvana, would never have taken his own life so early in a promising career; Elvis Presley would never have betrayed his fans by allowing drugs to ruin his life; and John Lennon was too much of an icon to have succumbed to the senseless act of violence committed by a mentally disturbed fan. Instead, they must have been the victims of something bigger, perhaps the Central Intelligence Agency (CIA) or organized crime.

While the aforementioned conspiracies may seem baseless or emotionally-charged, it is important to understand that conspiracy theorists provide a valuable service, no matter how illogical, imaginative, or desperate their theories sometimes are. The individuals behind conspiracy theories don't accept "No" as the final answer; they question authority and demand answers. They often relish the role of "devil's advocate," and may uncover overlooked or hidden evidence that provokes important discussions in society. In many cases, these conspiracies deal with the greatest conspirer: the government.

Media is an important purveyor of conspiracy theories, so much so that an entire film, *Conspiracy Theory*, starring Mel Gibson and Julia Roberts, was devoted to the topic in 1997. Although the film was fictional, it did address some legitimate concerns, including CIA-perpetrated mind-control. Many decades earlier, J. D. Salinger authored *The Catcher in the Rye*, now a classic that is widely assigned to high school students. The book has been associated with numerous conspiracy theories, including the assassinations of Robert Kennedy and John Lennon. It was featured in the 1997 film as well.

The Kennedy Assassination

The playwright George Bernard Shaw once stated that it was the inherent nature of a government to tell lies. This statement rings true when one considers that former US president Lyndon B. Johnson allegedly manipulated intelligence over the Gulf of Tonkin incident to justify attacking North Vietnam, and that the government then allegedly covered up the dangers of the herbicide Agent Orange that sickened thousands of Vietnam War soldiers. Major deceptions such as these have incited a general mistrust of government, just as perjury committed routinely by police officers and other witnesses that implicate innocent people have resulted in a general mistrust of the judicial system.

These sentiments form the conspiracy theories that surround the assassination of former US president John F. Kennedy. On November 22, 1963, Kennedy was shot by Lee Harvey Oswald, an ex-Marine who had, at one time, defected to the Soviet Union. Oswald also had ties to right-wing organizations and anti-Castro groups, which would motivate an independent investigation conducted later by the district attorney of New Orleans. Most Americans had a difficult time believing that a gunman acted alone in taking the life of such a popular president, yet Oswald did not live long enough to negate or confirm the disbelief. While being transferred while in custody, he was shot by Jack Leon Ruby, who had ties to organized crime. Soon after, a number of mysterious deaths occurred, often involving those who had ties to Oswald, Ruby, or Kennedy. The Warren Commission investigated these deaths, but could not find any evidence of a conspiracy.

Fifteen years later, the US House Select Committee on Assassinations, after studying a home movie of the assassination taken by an amateur, stated that Kennedy might have been shot by two gunmen, and not one as was earlier indicated. Other evidence included a recording that depicted one more gunshot than the three known to have been fired by Oswald.

In 1991, director Oliver Stone attempted to sort out much of the conspiracy surrounding the assassination in his movie *JFK*, which promoted the theory that the shooting was undertaken by the CIA, with a cover-up conducted by the US Federal Bureau of Investigation (FBI). The motive was grounded in Kennedy's plan to promote peace with North Vietnam and Cuba rather than following the CIA's and Pentagon's desire to go to war. A recent investigation by David Kaiser detailed in *The Road to Dallas: The Assassination of President John F. Kennedy*, promotes a link to the Mafia, supported in part by Kennedy's persistent efforts to dismantle this illegal organization.

A variety of polls conducted over the past several decades shows that Americans overwhelmingly support one of the Kennedy assassination conspiracy theories. In fact, some polls have shown that over 80 percent of the population believes that Oswald did not act alone. In addition, conspiracy theories that link the CIA, the FBI, or the Ku Klux Klan, a white supremacist organization, to the assassination of Martin Luther King, Jr. also continue to be supported by many Americans.

> *The individuals behind conspiracy theories don't accept "No" as the final answer; they question authority and demand answers.*

Bin Laden, 9/11, and the Bush Administration

The immediate decision to bomb Afghanistan after the terrorist attacks of September 11, 2001, followed by the war on Iraq, confused many Americans. Why would the US not attack Saudi Arabia, the country of origin for fifteen of the attackers? In fact, none of the terrorists were from either Afghanistan or Iraq, and an investigation conducted by the US Pentagon confirmed earlier suspicions by many Americans that Saddam Hussein had no links to al-Qaeda, the terrorist organization behind the terrorist attacks. To make matters more complicated, no weapons of mass destruction were ever found in Iraq, as claimed by the administration of President George W. Bush.

These alleged deceptions are just some of the points raised by conspiracy theorists, who believe the administration of George W. Bush knew in advance of the attacks on September 11, but did nothing to stop them. Thierry Meyssan, author of *The Big Lie*, speculates that the terrorist attacks were undertaken in part by the US government to justify war and bring vast financial rewards to the defense-related industries, to which the Bush family and US vice president Dick Cheney reportedly have financial connections.

Among the evidence cited is the close business relationship shared between the Bush and bin Laden families; supporters point to the fact that Osama bin Laden's half-brother, Shafiq, and his family were in the US conducting business with former US president George H. W. Bush and members of the Carlyle Group on the morning of the attacks. The bin Ladens were subsequently allowed to leave the country only two days later, a period of time when air space was closed to all other air travel. Furthermore, many believe the reason why Osama bin Laden, the reputed leader of al-Qaeda, is still on the loose after seven years of pursuit during the Bush administration and additional years during the Administration of former US president Bill Clinton, can be attributed to "special orders" given to the military and the CIA.

Understandably, this conspiracy theory has not generated nearly as much support as the Kennedy assassination theories, but is valid if only for its ability to generate discussion among the general public and to demand accountability from the government. It gained some mainstream popularity through Michael Moore's *Fahrenheit 9/11* in 2004.

Flying Saucers and Alien Invaders

In 1947, just two weeks after a pilot sighted "flying saucers" over Mt. Rainier in Washington, an unidentified flying object (UFO) supposedly crashed near Roswell, New Mexico. A farmer, Mac Brazel, found pieces of a silvery, aluminum-like substance scattered on his property. Witnesses claimed to have seen dead, alien bodies miles away from where the UFO actually crashed, yet were allegedly ordered to remain silent.

On July 7, Army Major Jesse Marcel retrieved some of the tinfoil-like wreckage and was commanded to deliver it to Wright-Patterson Air Force Base for inspection. At that time, the Air Force confirmed it had recovered "a crashed flying disc," but later changed the story to a weather balloon. For the next several decades, the Air Force stood by the weather balloon explanation, though they later admitted that it was a cover-up. The weather balloon had actually been a surveillance balloon used in the top-secret Project Mogul.

Nuclear physicist Stanton T. Friedman, an ufologist, or those who study UFOs, investigated the incident and co-wrote *Crash at Corona: The US Military Retrieval and Cover-Up of a UFO*, which disputed the military's explanation and planted the seed that the cover-up was intended to protect citizens from an alien invasion.

Reports of UFOs have surfaced hundreds, if not thousands, of times since the Roswell incident. In fact, on July 19, 1952, an air traffic controller at Washington National Airport sighted several UFOs traveling at a high speed towards the capital. Air Force jets pursued, but the mysterious objects disappeared. In 1967, a security guard at Malstrom Air Force Base in Montana noticed a glowing disc-shaped object hovering near the missile launch area. At the same time, some of the missiles became mysteriously disabled, and no one ever issued a logical explanation for either case.

A UFO sighting in 2007 over O'Hare International Airport in Chicago was followed up in January 2008 with a sighting over Stephenville, Texas. Several people spotted one or more aircraft with bright lights, speeding silently across the sky over Stephenville, and two military jets were seen pursuing the objects. At first, the military denied there were jets in the area, but weeks later, changed their story and stated they were, in fact, conducting military operations. The earlier cover-up, as well as hundreds of unexplained sightings over the past several decades, provides an understandable grounding for theorists who believe the military knows more about UFOs than they have acknowledged.

Conspiracy theories run the gamut from the outrageous to the highly reasonable. Those who support conspiracy theories tend to do so because they understand that it is human nature to cover up uncomfortable situations. Conspiracists also base many of their theories on the fact that many things are indeed secretive, such as covert military operations and political scandals. In turn, the general public is often left speculating. Regardless of the outcome, conspiracy theories play an important role, especially in a democratic society where they serve as an extension of our fundamental right to ask questions, and to keep those in power accountable.

Bibliography

Bale, Jeffrey M. "Political paranoia v. political realism: on distinguishing between bogus conspiracy theories and genuine conspiratorial politics." *Patterns of Prejudice* 41.1 (Feb. 2007): 45-60.

Burnett, Thom, et al. *Conspiracy Encyclopedia*. New York: Chamberlain Bros/Penguin, 2005.

Carey, Thomas J. *Witness to Roswell: Unmasking the 60-Year Cover-Up*. Franklin Lakes, NJ: New Page Books, 2007.

CBC News. "Conspiracy Theories: Uncovering the Facts Behind the Myths of September 11, 2001." The Fifth Estate: Conspiracy Theories. Web. 29 October 2003.

Donskis, Leonidas. "The Conspiracy Theory, Demonization of the Other." *Innovation: The European Journal of Social Sciences* 11.3 (Sep. 1998): 349–360.

Dutton, Edward. "Devil Fervour: Conspiracy Theories, Ground Zero and the Religion of the Dispossessed." *Contemporary Review* 290.8 (Spring, 2008): 52.

Friedman, Stanton T. *Top Secret/Majic: Operation Majestic-12 and the United States Government's UFO Cover-Up*. Emeryville, CA: Marlowe/Avalon, 2005.

Kaiser, David. *The Road to Dallas: The Assassination of President John F. Kennedy*. Cambridge, MA: Belknap Press, 2008.

Marcus, George E., and Michael G. Powell. "From Conspiracy Theories in the Incipient New World Order of the 1990s to Regimes of Transparency Now." *Anthropological Quarterly* 76.2 (Spring, 2003): 323–334.

Meyssan, Thierry. *9/11: The Big Lie*. New York: Carnot U.S.A. Books, 2003.

Moore, Michael. *Fahrenheit 9/11*. Web. 28 October 2011.

Newton, Michael. *The Encyclopedia of Conspiracy Theories*. New York: Facts on File, 2006.

Ray, James Earl. *Who Killed Martin Luther King, Jr.?: The True Story by the Alleged Assassin*. 2nd ed. New York: Westview Press/Perseus, 1997.

Simmons, William Paul, and Sharon Parsons. "Beliefs in Conspiracy Theories Among African Americans: A Comparison of Elites and Masses." *Social Science Quarterly* (Blackwell Publishing Limited) 86.3 (Sep. 2005): 582–598.

Sullivan, Will, Aamir Latif, and Dan Morrison. "Viewing 9/11 from a Grassy Knoll." *U.S. News & World Report* 141.2 (Sep. 2006): 39.

Conspiracy Theories Are Fodder for the Gullible

By Beverly Ballaro and Chuck Goodwin
Points of View: Conspiracy Theories, 2011

Conspiracy theories purport to explain historical and social phenomena as the results of elaborate, behind-the-scenes machinations by mysterious and powerful manipulators. In doing so, they affront logic, probability, historical precedent, rational evidence, and even common sense. Moreover, whereas some of the more outlandish conspiracy theories in circulation offer a certain benign entertainment value, such as the belief that the Apollo 11 moon landing was a fabricated hoax, others dangerously fuel cycles of prejudice and conflict. An example of a dangerous conspiracy theory is the September 11, 2001, terrorist attacks, which were said to be orchestrated by Israeli intelligence operatives acting in conjunction with American Jewish government officials. This may play into preconceived prejudices, by providing a scapegoat with no evidence or logical links for individuals who are scared and seeking answers to a devastating event. It is because of this instigated prejudice, and the discouragement of critical thinking and lack of moral accountability, that these conspiracy theories need to be taken seriously and debunked whenever and as often as possible.

Popular conspiracy theories include the belief that the Holocaust never happened; that Amelia Earhart was captured and executed by the Japanese for her secret role as Franklin Roosevelt's spy; that Princess Diana's fatal car crash was the work of British intelligence agents fulfilling royal orders; that the AIDS epidemic was deliberately unleashed by the US government as part of its genocidal plans for the African American population; and that the Freemasons' sponsorship of the MasoniCHIP is really a plot, cleverly disguised as an abduction awareness campaign, to implant microchip tracking devices in the children of unsuspecting parents.

These kinds of theories do not hold up; instead, they fly in the face of logic, probability, historical precedent, expert analysis, concrete evidence, and common sense. Yet, despite mountains of credible evidence to the contrary—including, for example, entire museums dedicated exclusively to documenting the Holocaust through films, photographs, artifacts, and eyewitness accounts—people persist in clinging to conspiracy theories. The popularity and power of such theories highlight the need to debunk them whenever possible, in the interest of promoting logic and critical thinking, as well as human harmony and dignity.

Occam's Razor

Conspiracy theorists would do well to take a lesson from modern scientists and philosophers who rely, with good results, on a principle articulated in medieval times. "Occam's Razor" is an approach to problem-solving named for the fourteenth century English theologian William of Occam. The theory states that "of a group of plausible but different explanations for any one outcome, the simplest theory is likely to prove the most accurate."

Conspiracy theories, by their nature, favor complicated explanations, such as secret organizations, convoluted plots, and twisted motives. In doing so, they consistently stack the odds against the probability of the scenarios they propose. The mere possibility of all these complex variables being able to coordinate together at precisely the right time to create or cause the event increases the very odds against its occurrence. Beyond the tremendous odds against any of these forces being able to coordinate themselves to take some type of action, the possibility of success for any of these theories is substantially decreased. Therefore, "Occam's Razor" would suggest that the greater probability is that the simplest variables come into play, resulting in the event.

As such, while it is theoretically possible that the British royal family, incensed at the prospect that the future king's mother might marry a Muslim, could have hatched a plot to use secret agents to tamper murderously with the car in which she was being driven, the mundane likelihood is that Princess Diana simply died because her chauffeur was driving drunk. The variables supporting this conclusion are far more statistically credible and mathematically more likely.

The approach is based on the premise that the more factors involved, the greater the chance that something will go awry to change the intended outcome. Advocates of conspiracy theories however, assign meaning to what is sometimes random, and attribute an extraordinary, yet unsubstantiated, degree of power and organization to the forces they firmly believe responsible for engineering history.

Is it possible that the same federal government that demonstrated such an inept response to Hurricane Katrina, despite the billions of dollars poured into the emergency response system created by the Department of Homeland Security (DHS), is aware of alien spacecraft landings and complicit in a massive deception? Is the United Nations (UN), which is notorious for its financial dependence on the United States, a feared epicenter and mastermind of a covert scheme to absorb the US as part of an ominous New World Order?

Faulty Powers

Despite their outlandishness, many conspiracy theories succeed in gaining traction among some sectors of the population. Some theories are coordinated to appeal to the paranoia borne of legitimate historical grievances. If one incorporates a real and substantiated event (or events) such as the horrors of institutionalized racism endured by generations of African Americans in the South, a conspiracy theory may attempt to use this event as a foundation to build its pretense of a current conspiracy against African Americans. This allows conspiracy theory architects to create

> *The cherry-picking of facts, or focusing only on anec-dotal evidence, to lend an air of credibility to precon-ceived conclusions is yet another common tactic of conspiracy theories.*

fertile ground for the urban legend that certain fast food franchises are controlled by the Ku Klux Klan (KKK). Allegedly, these KKK-owned fast food franchises deliberately lace their fried chicken with a chemical designed to render African American men either impotent or sterile. Viewed through a critical lens, such a conspiracy is preposterous, but theories such as these exploit a real discriminatory past. There is a lack of scientific literacy and logical reason among those who believe in this theory, such as the simple fact that African American ownership of these franchises is proof that counters this conspiracy. Advocates of such conspiracies introduce them to others with such passion and commitment; the average person can begin to think the conspiracy may be plausible to exist regardless of reason. They are aware of the two legitimate elements of the theory (there was institutionalized racism and there is a Ku Klux Klan), and possibly then take the conspiracy at face value, regardless of the logic and how unlikely such a conspiracy could occur. Another dubious way in which conspiracy theories attempt to make their case is by the use of fixating upon a perceived inconsistency and using it as a narrative to create doubt over the explained cause of the event. Some conspiracy buffs have claimed, for example, that the US government was fully aware of the intention of Japanese imperial forces to attack Pearl Harbor and permitted the tragedy to occur as of way of rallying American support for entry into World War II. Human error, coincidence, inability to acquire legitimate intelligence and miscalculation are discounted in this theory. The conspiracy theorists are seeking some other reason that the American military was caught unprepared for this attack, and their answer is a massive government plot.

As evidence, they offer anecdotal accounts of how then-president Franklin Roosevelt, during a White House dinner held the night before Pearl Harbor's attack, remarked that war was inevitable, despite the staunchly isolationist mood of the country at the time. They cite other events that occurred to prove complicity with this conspiracy, such as the defensive measures taken by the base commanders, or how certain other events were ignored. It is unlikely that Roosevelt had foreknowledge of the attack, as some historians have pointed out, and had let his culpability slip at a dinner party knowing the potential carnage to come and its effect on his legacy.

The cherry-picking of facts, or focusing only on anecdotal evidence, to lend an air of credibility to preconceived conclusions is yet another common tactic of conspiracy theories. According to some speculations, the as-yet-unsolved 2007 disappearance of British toddler Madeleine McCann from a Portuguese holiday resort must be the work of an international pedophile ring targeting blonde European children and smuggling them into North Africa. Proponents of this theory point out, correctly, that Morocco is but a short boat ride from the Portuguese coast and that child exploitation is a tragically common aspect in some quarters of Moroccan culture. Unfortunately, they fail to take into account other relevant facts, including the reality that no other similar abductions or attempted abductions by North African of children fitting such a profile have been documented in the area in question. Logic would suggest that it would likely be the case, if such abduction rings were in operation.

A Need to Believe

The tendency to spin and believe in conspiracy theories is as old as human culture itself; although contemporary conspiracy theories focus on manmade plots, they are not far removed from those of our ancient ancestors, who firmly believed in the ability of divine, unseen powers to manipulate the outcomes of battles or the occurrence of natural disasters. While inhabitants of the modern world can turn to science to explain many phenomena once thought to be subject to the whims of the gods, the fundamental uncertainties of human existence persist, as does the hardwired human impulse to make sense of a world that frequently fails to operate in either a logical or predictable manner.

For some people, conspiracy theories provide an oddly comforting way to cope with the anxiety of living in an uncertain and often inexplicable universe. The prospect of puppeteers, even sinister ones, shaping the course of human events must seem less frightening to some people than the possibility that some events are either random, a result of human error, beyond our comprehension, or a combination of all the above.

Comforting though they may be to some believers, conspiracy theories are frequently anything but harmless. These theories can become dangerous, helping to perpetuate cycles of prejudice and conflict. Conspiracy theories that argue that the Holocaust was a hoax enable Holocaust deniers to deflect moral responsibility, while theories that shift any number of terrorist attacks away from the actual perpetrators absolve all people within a culture from the critical task of self-consciously examining the social pathologies that can lead to mass murder. For this reason, skeptics must consistently challenge conspiracy theories and the ignorance that cloaks them.

Even the most convincing critical appraisal of the most farfetched theory will, inevitably, fail to convince the most deluded. Yet, not subjecting conspiracy theories to sharp scrutiny is a serious threat to society. Because they discourage critical thinking and moral accountability, and instigate the most pernicious human instincts, conspiracy theories must be resisted in a world already ravaged by the consequences of fundamentalist mindsets.

Bibliography

Barkun, Michael. *A Culture of Conspiracy: Apocalyptic Visions in Contemporary America.* Berkeley: University of California Press, 2006.

Basham, L. "Malevolent Global Conspiracy." *Journal of Social Philosophy* 34.1 (Spring 2003): 91–103.

Bratich, Jack Z. *Conspiracy Panics: Political Rationality and Popular Culture*. Albany: SUNY Press, 2008.

Critchlow, Donald T., John Korasick, and Matthew C. Sherman. *Political Conspiracies in America: A Reader*. Indianapolis: Indiana University Press, 2008.

Crook, Clive. "One Evil Conspiracy Is Missing." *National Journal* 33.1 (Nov, 2001): 3540.

Dunbar, David, and Brad Reagen, eds. *Debunking 9/11 Myths: Why Conspiracy Theories Can't Stand Up to the Facts*. New York: Hearst, 2006.

Gainer, Dan. "New Conspiracy Theory: Cheaper Gas." *Human Events* 62.0 (Sep, 2006): 18.

Gettelman, Elizabeth. "Conspiracy Watch: The Wisest Guys in the Room." *Mother Jones* 34.0 (Jan, 2009): 14.

Gilson, Dave. "Conspiracy Watch: You Are Getting Verrry Hopeful." *Mother Jones* 34.0 (Mar, 2009): 14.

Goldberg, Robert Alan. *Enemies Within: The Culture of Conspiracy in Modern America*. New Haven: Yale University Press, 2001.

Hawn, Carleen. "Conspiracy Theory." *Forbes* 168.2 (Dec, 2001): 42.

McConnachie, James, and Robin Tudge. *The Rough Guide to Conspiracy Theories 2*. London: Rough Guides, 2008.

North, Oliver. "Liberal Conspiracy Theories." *Human Events* 60.0 (Jan, 2004): 14.

Roeper, Richard. *Debunked!: Conspiracy Theories, Urban Legends, and Evil Plots of the 21st Century*. Chicago: Chicago Review Press, 2008.

Rothschild, Matthew. "Enough Conspiracy Theories, Already." *Progressive* 70.5 (Oct, 2006): 39.

Sullivan, Will, Aamir Latif, and Dan Morrison. "Viewing 9/11 from a Grassy Knoll." *U.S. News & World Report* 141.2 (11 Sep. 2006): 39.

The Truth Is Out There ... Way Out There

By George Case
Skeptic, 2005

The peak popularity of the television series *The X-Files*, and the initial Internet-boosted acceleration of the Information Revolution are behind us, but their legacies live on, in the pervasive familiarity of the conspiracy theory. Indeed, the trust-no-one phenomenon is today so much a part of our culture that it has become an object of suspicion: recent books such as Daniel Pipes' *Conspiracy: How the Paranoid Style Flourishes and Where It Comes From*, Robert Anton Wilson's *Everything Is Under Control: Conspiracies, Cults, and Cover-Ups*, and Devon Jackson's *Conspiranoia! The Mother of All Conspiracy Theories*, dissect the history, nature, and function of phobic fantasies in all their sprawling interconnectedness. Yet conspiracy theories—let's call them CTs—remain almost routine elements of our socio-political discourse, even if few of their exponents would describe them as such, and even if fewer of us recognize one when we see it. Why?

A lot of CTs' attractiveness, logicians will say, is in their dexterity at skirting the basic rules of deduction and inference. The world is complicated; many arguable factors contribute to events; CTs simplify things enormously and with great flair. Psychologists might add that the sheer randomness of modern life is so distressing that CTs offer a weirdly reassuring "master narrative" no longer provided by religion. No matter how malevolent the alleged String-Pullers are said to be, they are perhaps less scary than the thought of no String-Pullers at all. And rhetoricians may remind us that CTs are a kind of all-purpose argument winner, inevitably shutting down further debate by invoking sinister, shadowy agents whose very elusiveness confirms their existence and influence. Through all of these—supposition, evasion, innuendo—CTs work, in journalism, education, political activism, and ordinary conversation. But they aren't infallible: studied carefully, they form patterns, fall into categories, and hide errors of reason and common sense. A brief field guide to their habits may help detect them before they turn dangerous.

Hidden Connection CTs

George H. W. Bush and Osama bin Laden have shared interests in a Saudi oil company. Lee Harvey Oswald was seen in his future killer Jack Ruby's Dallas nightclub. A numerical translation of Bill Gates' full name adds up to 666. Or, the synchronicities found in any daily newspaper, e.g. "Unexpected Shutdown of Corruption

Inquiry" on page one, and "Lawyer's Death Called Foul Play" on page ten. As *Hidden Connections*, such links are essentially twisted chains of circumstantial evidence, whereby any tenuous overlaps of time, place, and incident become proof of deliberate collusion. But all of us are never more than a few relationships removed from everyone else (the so-called "six degrees of separation"), and putative causes and effects are always happening around each other, especially in hindsight; a really compelling *Hidden Connection* would accurately predict a future event, rather than employing the hindsight bias by stringing together a disparate assortment of dots after the fact. Chance, simultaneity, and accidents are never conceded by *Hidden Connection* spotters, and their only conclusion is the ultimate hanging question, "Coincidence? You be the judge." In the court of *Hidden Connection CTs*, a verdict of "Guilty" is never in doubt.

Manipulated Media CTs

At their most sensible these might reflect the view that print and broadcast news and entertainment outlets have an interest in maintaining a stable, none-too-critical audience of pliant consumers. But towards the fringe the *Manipulated Media* message is less "Don't believe *everything* you hear," and more "Don't believe *anything* you hear," with the straightforward truth—that trivial material can distract people from serious matters—embellished into a scenario where all information is mere propaganda that obscures government or corporate misdeeds. Implicit here is the assumption of a single entity called "the media" that can be wholly hijacked by a single body, giving us deathless slurs like "The Jews control Hollywood" (did they steal it from the Amish?). Thus the inconvenient responsibility of informing oneself through one or many of the thousands of publicly available news and opinion sources is dismissed. *Manipulated Media* CTs are a favorite of anyone who hasn't seen their own ideology spelled out in banner headlines or heard it echo back from the six o'clock news. Nowadays given a wide forum in the free-for-all of the Internet, their odd irony is that it's only ever through the media that we're told how spun, suppressed, and censored the media is.

They Know Everything CTs

This posits that important figures behind closed doors instigate or are aware of impending disasters, but allow or encourage them to precipitate some broader, beneficial (to them) outcome. The Iraq war (started by the U.S. to guarantee its oil supply) and the September 11 attacks (sanctioned by the CIA to kick start an American pipeline project in Afghanistan) are only the latest fodder for such speculation. Oliver Stone's film *JFK* may represent its supreme example. The problem with *They Know Everything CTs* is that these kinds of elaborately murderous schemes are hardly the most effective or predictable means of steering the tides of history. It has been pointed out, for example, that if Franklin D. Roosevelt knew the Japanese were about to attack Pearl Harbor but let them proceed because he wanted a pretext for U.S. entry into World War II, why wouldn't he have prevented the attack at the last minute? Wouldn't an intercepted "surprise" have produced the same result as a successful one? Similarly, was atomizing several thousand New Yorkers an obvious, practical step to the commercial exploitation of Central Asian gas reserves? And why would the U.S. military shoot down TWA 800 over Long Island,

> *A lot of [conspiracy theories']*
> *attractiveness, logicians will*
> *say, is their dexterity at skirting*
> *the basic rules of deduction and*
> *inference.*

with so many potential witnesses? And would assassinating John F. Kennedy on a sunny afternoon safely ensure his successor's dragging the U.S. arms industry into a profitable Vietnam War? If They—whoever *They* are—really Know Everything, would They gamble so big on such catastrophic rolls of the dice? And how good are They at conspiring if Their cover gets blown so easily and so widely?

The blunt truth is that conspiracy theories very seldom make a solid case. Either they play on pre-existing prejudices (how corrupt you already take the government / the media / big business to be), or contradict each other (if the Iraq war is all about Halliburton contracts, then it can't be about Judeo-Christian millennial fanatics within the Bush administration; if the Mafia killed JFK, then the Freemasons are off the hook), or defy rational dispute (so the more the supposed conspiracy is denied, the more obviously there is one). CTs do not admit the glum, unresolved reality that public and private officials of good will may make single mistakes that spin vast webs of unintended consequences, nor do they allow that the likelihood of a few cynical individuals covertly trumping the infinite variables of human and organizational interaction, and never getting caught at it, is pretty slim. For all their curiously gratifying implications ("We didn't lose; they cheated," sums up Daniel Pipes), they permit us to forfeit our rights as engaged, aware citizens by insisting on a permanently skewed, nothing-is-as-it-seems order. If conspirators are running the world, then why bother to read, vote, think, discuss, act, progress? Today, more than ever, we should be demanding straight answers to our questions. Whether or not we think of them as "conspiracy theories," glib brushoffs about Hidden Connections, about a Manipulated Media, and about how They Know Everything, are no longer good enough.

America's Addiction to Belief

By Brian Trent
The Humanist, July 2010

Henceforth, people will be looking at the universe with the eyes of oxen.
　—*Katib Chelebi, seventeenth-century geographer*

"Barack Obama won't show us his birth certificate," insists Steve, a Connecticut resident and small business owner, while shoveling his walk during one of this year's snowstorms. "He's a Muslim terrorist. And you know what really bothers me? He is doing exactly what Hitler did."

Steve, forty-five, has plenty of other opinions relating to the American president, culture, and society. He can rattle off the prized talking points of this country's culture of belief without missing a beat: The moon landing was a hoax; the world is ending in 2012; 9/11 was an inside job; creationism is valid science.

A hard-working fellow and family man in a post-industrial factory town of a blue state, Steve does not come across as fanatical. Yet his adherence to raw belief—a position unassailable by factual counter-data—is more than an inherently dangerous American mindset. It is a deadly challenge to the aim of humanism.

The "belief" mindset is pretty common in the news these days. That much of it seems directed at the current presidential administration is almost irrelevant, though we should linger here just a moment to reflect that it's now getting legal attention: the U.S. Army is set to court-martial a soldier who refused deployment to Afghanistan because the soldier—Lt. Colonel Terry Lakin—shares with Steve the belief that President Obama is not a U.S. citizen. Neither Lakin nor Steve nor thousands of other "birthers" can put forth any evidence, documentation, or data that withstands the test of scrutiny. They just, well, believe it.

Ironically enough, their blind allegiance is precisely like the more extreme elements of their political rivals. While "birthers" are largely a Republican phenomenon, the "9/11 Truth Movement" stems chiefly from the liberal wing of American politics—as fervent in their belief that the United States' own government used controlled demolition to destroy the Twin Towers as the birthers are that Obama has perpetrated a global hoax to keep his birth certificate under wraps.

Clearly the appeal of blind faith has been part of human history since the earliest days of Babylonia. In the United States, however, we have taken this tendency to disturbing new heights. Emboldened by the sharp rise of rabid partisanship (a legacy of the post–Karl Rovian era) and the ubiquitous presence of mass media,

Americans have come to be belief's poster children. Reactionary, emotional, and almost blissfully willing to ignore facts if they contradict a cemented position.

"A conservative can wake up in the morning and never have his or her views challenged. And the same is true for liberals," said none other than MSNBC's Joe Scarborough in a *Newsweek* interview last summer. "It's just stunning to me how difficult it is to have a political conversation with adults. It's very disturbing to me as someone fired upon by the left and right pretty regularly… Where is the rational middle?"

The overriding irony is that in the United States, the culture of belief is certainly not a partisan issue. When it comes to the above-mentioned rallying points for this particular culture, people are oddly united across political divisions, faiths, and ideologies. So too is blind belief the *de facto* culture of the blogosphere and mass media.

It is a culture that thrives on the false principle that "all opinions are equal," even those without a shred of factual data, documentation, or reasoned methodology. It is a culture where 20 percent of the American people believe NASA faked the Apollo moon landings, and where *half* the population believes the world was made in six days.

> **Clearly the appeal of blind faith has been part of human history since the earliest days of Babylonia.**

When the scholar Katib Chelebi spoke the words that opened this piece, it was in response to a tidal shift in the culture of seventeenth-century Turkey. Chelebi was a cartographer, historian, traveler, philosopher, and writer. He had been exposed to the works of the ancient Greeks and appreciated their methodical approach to investigation. Yet the rationalist mindset of Turkish schools was descending into dogmatism. It appealed to emotions and impulsiveness. It catered to the basement of the human mind which today's neurologists would call the r-complex. Chelebi keenly perceived this devolution and saw the road ahead, which diverged in the proverbial woods; Chelebi was aghast at the path his people were choosing.

There is a certain irony in the case of the United States; a nation founded on Enlightenment principles of rationality, and now so eagerly becoming a culture of raw, unquestioning belief. When we hear about an alleged culture war, we tend to think of it in political terms like gay marriage or abortion. The truth goes deeper. Like Chelebi's era, our real battle is for a critical thinking. It is about our fundamental approach to the universe, and is nothing less than a line in the sand between the logical and delusional.

Consider the subject of gravity. No one doubts it. Jump off your roof and you can clearly demonstrate its reality. Great thinkers have contemplated the nature of this mysterious force, and it was Albert Einstein (elaborating on Newton) who created the geometric model we accept today.

Yet our theory of gravity is not a belief system. Einstein didn't preach from a mountain or circulate pamphlets to justify his position. More importantly, the world didn't instantly drop to its knees and chant the merits of curved space. His theory was examined and cross-examined. It was tested and retested, and accumulated such mounds of evidence that it is now accepted.

Are there alternative theories to gravity? Well, we could easily invent one: the force of gravity is in fact a cabal of ghosts pressing down on our heads. Of course, such a statement is a hypothesis, not a theory. It only becomes an accepted theory if we can test it, retest it, and provide evidence and documentation for it. It must stand up to scrutiny. Otherwise it's simply a fairy tale. To put a finer point on it, it is irrational.

This irrationality is the new American zeitgeist. Even a cursory glance at the political blogosphere and media outlets demonstrates this over and over. One example, taken not only from Steve but from a good deal of pundits and politicians is that Barack Obama is a Muslim.

In June 2009 President Obama visited Cairo and made overtures of communication to the local Muslim population. Predictably, this act relit the battle-cries from political opponents who had spent much time during the presidential election stating that Obama was in fact a secret Muslim.

That essentially is the argument in four words: *Obama* is a *Muslim*. The implication we're left with is that it's somehow wrong to be Muslim in America because (and here we tap another rampant falsity) America is a Christian nation. It encourages a kind of juvenile math: Muslim leader in charge of Christian country equals bad.

Of course, the United States was founded on a secular Constitution that saw fit to avoid religious language entirely and even took pains to include items like Article 6 (declaring that no religious test is required for public officials) and the establishment clause of the very first amendment to it: *Congress shall make no law respecting an establishment of religion.* It established a secular government that permits religious liberty, not a religious government mandating religious favoritism or fundamentalism.

As to the claim that Obama is a Muslim, it was General Colin Powell who offered the most eloquent response when he appeared on *Meet the Press* on October 19, 2008:

> I'm also troubled by, not what Senator McCain says, but what members of the party say. And it is permitted to be said such things as, "Well, you know that Mr. Obama is a Muslim." Well, the correct answer is, he is not a Muslim, he's a Christian. He's always been a Christian. But the really right answer is, what if he is? Is there something wrong with being a Muslim in this country? The answer's no, that's not America. Is there something wrong with some seven-year-old Muslim-American kid believing that he or she could be president? Yet, I have heard senior members of my own party drop the suggestion, "He's a Muslim and he might be associated with terrorists." This is not the way we should be doing it in America.

9/11 Truthers and the Creationists of Tomorrow

On the other side of the political fence, the 9/11 Truth Movement is a classic example of blind belief. Basing itself largely on cleverly edited "documentaries," that are as Machiavellian in design as anything in living memory, this collection of loosely affiliated groups—who suspect that the 9/11 attacks were part of a covert U.S. government operation—ignore hard data in favor of a raw, undocumented belief system.

I was in a café not long ago when a gentleman stated his belief that the World Trade Center towers had been brought down by controlled demolition. When faced with my open skepticism, his reaction was to ask me several questions: How could I believe the official story? How could I support George W. Bush? And did I really think that there wasn't a connection between the bin Ladens and the Bush family?

The three questions were irrelevant. Worse, they were intellectually dishonest. My acceptance of the "official story" was not predicated on belief but on data. By contrast, my friendly neighborhood conspiracy theorist was spouting the talking points from the film *Loose Change*, which has been re-edited and re-released three times and discredited each time. The question of whether or not I supported Bush was also not relevant to the discussion at hand, and neither were any ties—demonstrable or not—between the two political families.

Predictably, countering such a believer leads to vehement *ad hominem* attacks, as well as charges that the skeptic is either part of the conspiracy itself or is not being open-minded. Yet true skepticism is precisely about being open-minded—yet not so open that you become a vacuum. The advocacy here is not to dismiss any claims out of hand; rather, it is to place the burden of proof on the people making the claim. The more emotional their outcry to this condition, the more suspect their claim becomes.

Professional debunker and author James Randi, in his book *Flim Flam!*, wrote: "It is careless of a man to fail to sufficiently research a subject on which he claims to be an authority… and *it is irresponsible and callous for him to continue to misrepresent matters about which he has been informed to the contrary* (emphasis mine)." When a claim is invalidated, only a cultish mindset would continue to cling to it. My café correspondent was behaving like a cultist.

The metaphor is apt. In *When Prophecy Fails*, Leon Festinger, Henry Riecken, and Stanley Schachter documented the mentality of a doomsday cult in the 1950s. This cult believed that the world would end at midnight on December 21. Midnight arrived and the world remained surprisingly intact. The cultists openly wondered if their watches were wrong. After a few hours of horrified silence, some began to weep. Then a most remarkable thing happened: The cult's leader announced she was suddenly receiving new telepathic messages from God. The apocalypse, she claimed the message said, had been postponed! Over the following days and months, the doomsday cult jubilantly renewed their crusade to convert more people into their thrall.

This was not an isolated incident. Nor is it relegated only to the 1950s. People have been predicting the end of the world for millennia. Recent years saw national paranoia over Y2K, the 5/5/2000 apocalypse, and now the 2012 scare. No matter how many times the world refuses to end, there is never a shortage of people who believe (and often hope) it will. When 2012 passes and the world is still turning, I suspect this crowd will dig out Isaac Newton's quote about believing the world will end in 2060.

The reality is that the world we live in is irrelevant to belief. For example, I don't believe that there are fish in the sea. Rather, I have seen the evidence for fish in the sea and accept that evidence. I have seen documentaries on fish and have visited aquariums, have gone fishing, caught fish, fried fish, and eaten fish. It's not an issue of belief.

I also don't believe that humankind landed on the moon. I have seen the evidence for a moon landing and accept that evidence. (I have similarly watched the "evidence" presented by those who think the lunar visit was a hoax dissolve away at the first light of serious scrutiny.) By the same token, I don't believe in a Hollow Earth, chupacabras, or that the Holocaust was invented by Zionists, because the evidence for all three is less than compelling. It's not about emotion. It's not about disliking a claim. It's about what the proponents can show.

It would be comforting if we could trace this only to the Internet, which by virtue of its anonymity provides easy venue for irrational "trolling" as it's called. Mark Twain's warning that a lie can travel halfway around the world before the truth gets its shoes on is readily proven in the echo chamber of cyberspace: Saddam Hussein had connections to the 9/11 hijackers, Nostradamus predicted the fall of America in the twenty-first century, the Gulf of Mexico oil spill is a liberal plot, the swine flu is God's punishment against [whomever], to name a few.

In 79 CE Mount Vesuvius erupted and buried the towns of Pompeii and Herculaneum under a sea of hot ash. Predictably, many people alive at that time blamed the calamity on Zeus. Since geological science hadn't been born, assigning divine character to natural catastrophe was the best explanation going.

Today we will live in an age of rational methodology. Our laws are ideally derived from cogent debate (and are why we say "without passion or prejudice" in our legal proceedings), and we use the scientific method when dealing with worldly phenomena. A culture of belief rejects this in favor of a Neolithic worldview. The rational mechanisms behind hurricanes, plane crashes, and flu epidemics are eschewed by this crowd in favor of evil spirits, alien conspiracies, and prophecy.

That evolution and creationism are still butting heads 150 years after Darwin published *On the Origin of Species* is probably the best testament to this slide from rational culture. In 2009 half the U.S. population accepted creationism; ours is one of the only developed nations on earth where the subject is even a debate anymore.

Evolution is taught in schools not because there is a global secular conspiracy, but because it's backed up by factual data. By comparison, modern creationism (dressed up—and down—as intelligent design or as the preservation of academic freedom) lacks any credible documentation or data and fails even the most basic of rational tests. Perhaps most astonishingly, it has yet to articulate what its theory actually is. At day's end it is a position of faith; in other words, it belongs in Sunday school and not biology classrooms.

Lacking any scientific theory, the current creationist position is that students should be exposed to alternatives to evolution. Of course, there are lots of alternative explanations to evolution. There is the Nordic tale of how all of humanity sprouted from the maggots of a frost giant. There's the Chinese egg of chaos, out of which the earth hatched. The Greeks gave us their "five races of man" fable, which described how various ages of humanity were carved by the gods from gold, silver, bronze, and iron (of which we belong to this latter category.) The Sumerians believed that the arts and sciences were handed to humankind by a fish-headed god named Oannes.

Many creationists are quick to laugh at these "alternative" explanations, while blissfully ignoring the fact that all of these tales, from Genesis to the Greeks, from Amaterasu to Adam, have the exact same amount of evidence to support them: zero. Only evolution, like gravity, has data going for it—and a lot of data at that.

In a 2006 debate at the Cato Institute between science writer and *Skeptic* magazine editor Michael Shermer and intelligent design proponent Jonathan Wells, the latter was asked point-blank what his alternative to the evidence for natural selection was. "I don't think I'm obligated to propose an alternate theory," Wells publicly stated. "I don't pretend to have an alternate theory that explains the history of life."

At least Wells was honest. No theory, no rationale, no methodology. Just a thin God-of-the-gaps argument rooted in the school of belief.

Another prominent creationist, the Discovery Institute's Michael Behe, also admitted under cross-examination during the *Kitzmiller v. Dover* trial that his touted redefinition of science (to allow creationism in schools) would also permit astrology to be considered scientific theory.

Astrology is a belief system. Astronomy, by contrast, is not; it concerns itself with factual data. If I go to my local Barnes and Noble and buy a dozen astronomy books, they'll all give the same factoids about Mars, for instance. Their information is derived from decades of serious study of the Red Planet, including robotic landers and flybys.

Now for an astrological point of contrast: I recently decided to conduct an experiment which Carl Sagan did thirty years ago. I went to the store and picked up several different horoscopes. If astrology were a rational process, then there should be rough agreement among the many horoscopes regarding what a Scorpio should expect from his or her day. There isn't. Astrology, like creationism, is irrational.

But what about religion in all this? Isn't an attack on belief, one could ask, really an attack on organized faith?

Yes and no. There are many rational people who are highly religious; the two positions need not be in strict opposition. Only when religious sensibilities derail rational decision-making does it become the problem we're outlining here. Believing that long ago God ordered a father to sacrifice his son is one thing. Believing that God is commanding you right now to kill your son warrants a phone call to the police.

The Problem of the Lizard Brain

The human mind is a three-in-one deal. It's a kind of evolutionary layer cake, with newer developments growing over earlier foundations. The most recent layer is the neocortex, which is responsible for our higher brain functions. The arts and sciences owe to it. It makes rational thought possible.

Beneath it, and a few million years older, is the limbic system. Popularly called the mammalian brain, it promotes warm-blooded socialization and emotions.

Lurking deeper down is the most ancient brain, the lizard brain. The most primitive patterns are found in this prehistoric basement. Survival emotions like fear and anger reside there.

Clearly all three levels are essential to the human experience. Yet they are not all equally rational. A culture of belief stokes the fires of the lowest part, thriving on the exploitation of fear and anger. When Titus Livius said, "We fear things in proportion to our ignorance of them," he was painting an accurate guideline for any civilization.

I'll single out the issue of same-sex marriage, which recently has seen a flurry of legislation across the United States. The majority of arguments opposing it are not coming from a rational basis, but rather an emotional and fearful one. The common cry that same-sex marriage will be "the end of civilization" is a curious claim to make, and becomes stranger as civilization continues on where it has been legalized. It reminds us of the "Obama is a Muslim" protestation. As arguments such statements are illogical. They cater to the lower floors of human consciousness.

It isn't that rationality must preclude emotion. A society of cold intellectuals is not what we need; what's needed is a culture that places emphasis on reasoned debate. Perhaps the best illustration comes from Plato. Imagine, he suggested, that you have horses tethered to a chariot, and a charioteer holding the reins. Both the man and the beast are necessary to get anywhere. It is the guiding hand of a clear-thinking charioteer which needs to be in charge.

The pages of history are filled with irrational decisions. Often these decisions have world-altering results. When the Great Library of Alexandria was destroyed by fundamentalists, the classical age of scientific and artistic inquiry was obliterated. One thousand years of a dark age followed, during which (to consult Mark Twain again) a "nation of men was turned into a nation of worms."

For us today, the situation is far more dire. Belief-stricken populations and their leaders can cause unthinkable devastation to modern society. Technology has tipped the scales, and the antics of a collective adolescence threaten the global sandbox. In ancient Alexandria, an irrational policy abetted the fall of civilization. But while those book burnings required at least 451 degrees, tomorrow's censorship will be done with a search-and-replace command. Chelebi's disdain is now amplified by giant orders of magnitude. A global power, he reminds us, can become a global "sick man" in the blink of a historical eye.

If we can't address today's problems with a clear-thinking and intellectual honesty, how do we face the challenges of tomorrow? True humanism relies on a tango of free inquiry and scientific rationality. Such things are not possible in the face of emotional belief systems—indeed, an entire culture of belief.

And so we return to Steve, unwilling to engage in discussion, unable to entertain facts, and unreachable through a fortress of belief.

Let's hope that kicking this addiction to unquestioned belief becomes one of the great stories of American progress.

Brian Trent is a genre spanning writer of both fiction and nonfiction whose work has appeared in Clarkesworld, Electric Velocipede, Strange Horizons, The Humanist, Boston Literary Magazine, *and* Writer's Digest, *among other publications. He is the author of two historical novels,* Lady Philosopher *and* Never Grow Old, *and he is a public advocate for science, education, and humanism. His website is BrianTrent.com.*

Internet Conspiracies

Where the Absence of Evidence
Is Confirmation of the Claim

By Brian K. Pinaire
Skeptic, December 2005

Several years ago I was teaching a writing course at Lehigh University that relied extensively on student-led class discussions. As was often the case the conversation quickly drifted away from the assigned topic and developed into a debate about Kennedy assassination conspiracies. Eventually talk of government conspiracy and coverup led students to question the reality of Neil Armstrong's walk on the moon. The pedagogy for this course urged a passive role for instructors, and thus I sat back and watched in amazement as several students set about explaining—to me and their skeptical peers—how the "moon walk" had, in fact, never occurred. The entire spectacle was apparently a ruse, it was argued, an episode of Cold War propaganda transmitted via television into the brains of submissive citizens. I scanned the room and saw lots of nodding heads. The ringleaders continued: "Don't you guys know? The whole event was filmed in Hollywood. It was all engineered by the C.I.A." And so on.

Finally, I had to get involved. "How many of you believe that?" I asked. To my amazement, 14 students out of a class of 22 said they believed some version of this account. At that point I was torn: At the university level, we encourage our students to "think critically," to question everything, and to refuse to accept the world at face value. And, in a way, I guess that's what these students were doing. But wait, Neil Armstrong never landed on the moon? Huh?

As I pressed the students on the specifics of the conspiracy ("How has this been kept quiet for so long?" "Isn't it possible that these suspicions are little more than urban legends themselves?"), the source that was repeatedly offered as the purveyor of such information was the Internet. I was asked if I wanted the addresses of the websites that "proved" this version of events? Had I read (fill-in-the-blanks) blog dedicated to uncovering the scandal? How could I, the one who was encouraging them to look below the surface, accept the version of events proffered by "the Man?" I wasn't quite sure what to say.

To be sure, such distrust of authority and resistance to received accounts can be traced back to the American Revolution. And, additionally, for a generation raised on the *X-Files,* a tendency to accept conspiracy theories as facts is, perhaps, to be expected. But what seems to distinguish today's students from their predecessors is the ease with which they can search out information that confirms (or creates) their suspicions. Whereas earlier generations of young people might have exchanged leaflets or attended secret meetings in apartments, backyards, basements, and barns, today's students gather in cyberspace where they conspire to bring truth to power.

This phenomenon presents several problems. Put simply, most websites and web logs lack the sorts of quality controls and external validation that are essential components of the traditional research process. The practice of peer review for professional researchers, while by no means free of its own faults, at least has a structure in place for checking the veracity of one's claims, the propriety of one's methods, and the plausibility of one's conclusions. A typical blog, by contrast, seems to offer little more than what one person with a keyboard thinks is true about the world at a given moment. Are most students—or people in general—capable of evaluating the reliability of their sources on the net? What makes one website "truer" than another?

> *Whereas earlier generations of young people might have exchanged leaflets or attended secret meetings in apartments, backyards, basements, and barns, today's students gather in cyberspace where they conspire to bring truth to power.*

The information may be of great value, but as students google their way through their chosen topics, many check their critical eyes at the door, which is ironic because the search for the "real truth" is generally what makes this medium attractive in the first place.

But the reliance on the Internet for such purposes is ironic in another way as well. Not only does the screen (of the computer) now represent the conduit of facts, whereas before the screen (of the television) was the willing purveyor of propaganda, but the concept of "falsifiability" is turned on its head. In the course of research, we look for ways to disprove theories; we wonder, that is, how we might go about showing that a particular claim is invalid. Could we, in other words, demonstrate that a proposition is false? If not, how can we take it as true? And yet for conspiracy theories, it is precisely this lack of evidence that purports to support claims of the advocate.

Let us return to my students' belief that Neil Armstrong never walked on the moon. According to this logic, the conspiracy theory cannot be proven—the evidence has been hidden, corrupted, or destroyed! Witnesses, insiders, and accomplices have been killed and all records that might blow the lid off the hoax have been destroyed. This leads us to the grand irony: Conspiracy theories seem to work within the confines of an altered epistemology, wherein less proof garners greater belief; where, paradoxically, the absence of evidence is taken as confirmation of the correctness of the claim, meaning that logically there is no way that such a proposition could be disproven. The more evidence presented to bolster the "official" version of events, the more suspicion mounts; the more the government reveals, the more it is assumed that it has something to hide. How do I know this? I read it on the Internet.

Confessions of a Non-Serial Killer

Conspiracy Theories Are All Fun and Games Until You Become the Subject of One

By Michael O'Hare
The Washington Monthly, May 2009

Sometime in the early 1980s, when I lived in Cambridge, Massachusetts, I received a postcard with a name and return address I didn't recognize, bearing a cryptic image on the back. Every few weeks after that I received another card. There was one with holes punched in it, one with a symbol that resembled crosshairs, one with a picture of a man in sunglasses and a hooded sweatshirt, and one with a string of binary digits. The return addresses and postmarks kept changing. Assuming a friend from college was trying to get me to play some sort of puzzle game—a recreation for which I have no patience—I threw them in a drawer, a little guilty that he was going to all this trouble.

Then I received an article reciting details of the unsolved "Zodiac murders" that had unfolded in Northern California more than a decade earlier. In an episode that has since been recounted by countless journalists and Hollywood filmmakers, the killer had ambushed and slain five people. (The murderer has never been identified for certain, although numerous people have claimed to pinpoint the culprit—including a San Francisco woman who held a press conference in April declaring her father was the Zodiac killer.) He then sent letters to Bay Area newspapers threatening to kill many more unless they published a series of cryptic symbols, an act that created widespread panic. Included in the article I received were descriptions of the symbols, which sounded just like the ones on the postcards in my drawer. "Holy cow!" I said. "I'm getting mail from a mass murderer!" I called the local FBI branch, and a nice young woman with an FBI badge came to my office, picked up the collection of mail, said thank you, and left.

A week later, another agent came by with everything in a plastic envelope, gave it to me, and said, "Don't worry, he's harmless."

"He's what? What do you mean, harmless?"

"Don't you know about this guy?"

"I don't know what you're talking about. Do you mean the murderer?"

The agent then explained that the mail was from an amateur sleuth in California named Gareth Penn, who had been trying for some time to interest the police in the

"But this Mr. Penn says you committed them!"

"Well, I guess you have to interview him. Do you think I did it?"

"But you must know something about it."

"No, I mustn't. Are you out of your mind?"

On another occasion, a morning radio host in Los Angeles invited me to be interviewed on his show about some city planning issue. When I called in, he asked two or three clueless questions about housing, and then blurted out that he had Penn on another microphone. Apparently, he thought he was a junior Geraldo Rivera doing an ambush interview, which, naturally, would segue into a debate about whether I had killed six people. I got an apology from the station manager for that.

It was around this time that I had the idea to sue Penn. Not only had he become more vocal about his accusations, but I had also heard he had married into some money, and thus might help pay for my kids' college. I met with a well-regarded personal-injury lawyer in Boston and told him the story, giving him my cache of early Penn memorabilia. He said, "I would love to try this case. It's absolutely perfect. But I won't take it."

"Why?"

"Well, do your kids still hug you when you come home from work? Does your wife still sleep with you?"

"Yes, of course."

"Do your students still pay attention in class?"

"Still? Well, as much as ever, I guess."

"Right. So you've suffered no damages. You will win the lawsuit and get an award of one dollar, and Penn will get publicity he's obviously dying for. Forget it."

I'm a little sore at the lawyer for having discarded my file a few years later in an office cleanup, but as Penn keeps sending me the odd mysterious letter or postcard, I've accumulated another whole folder of truly bizarre correspondence for my biographer (or Penn's) to enjoy. And the lawyer's advice turned out to be sound. Indeed, the constant of this story is that, as far as I can tell, not a single person who matters in my life—not law enforcement, not friends and family, not students, not colleagues—ever gave Penn's views a minute's credence, so I've never regretted not lifting a finger to refute them or defend myself. Recently I asked my wife and daughters about how they have taken this whole thing. Daughter number one, the earnest save-the-world schoolteacher, was outraged that anyone could say such awful untrue things and not suffer any consequences. She still worries that people she doesn't know might suspect me of the crimes. Daughter number two, the free-spirited writer, loves weird, off-center stuff and browses the Internet occasionally to see what Penn is up to now. My wife first thought it was silly, then was a little afraid when Penn's fans appeared willing to take the law into their own hands, but now looks back on the whole ordeal as just an irritating distraction. I've never apologized to them—but what would I apologize to them *for*? My initials?

My contact with Penn has died down to three or four letters a year that he sends me at my office, where I drop them unopened in the folder with the others. But the Zodiac case continues to interest journalists, and Penn's enterprise sometimes gets a little play. Seven years after I moved to Berkeley in 1991 to teach at the University of California, *America's Most Wanted* was planning a program on the Zodiac murders, which was to include an interview with Penn. I was invited to be interviewed on camera as well. That seemed like one of the worst ideas ever. A local lawyer I knew through my kids' school was nice enough to send the show a letter, pointing out a recent case that had socked a newspaper with hefty damages for retailing libel by saying "Jones said X, Y, Z about Smith" and not checking to see if Jones was playing with a full deck. Penn didn't appear on the program, and later wrote my lawyer to complain. I did have to explain the entire saga to my students the week before the show was scheduled to run, to be sure they wouldn't hear about it for the first time on TV. I had the full attention of my class at least one day that semester. Of course, I had made a point of explaining the story to my deans on day one—when I worked in state government I learned not to let your boss be surprised by anything, if you can help it. (One of the deans, it turned out, had been a real cryptographer, and offered to trash Penn's efforts in that line if I ever needed him to.)

Over the years, I've gotten the occasional whiff of how hard Penn was working on his project and the kind of evidence he had collected. For instance, I spent a summer in San Francisco—in 1969, I think—working at Arthur D. Little, Inc., on a study of expanding the San Diego airport. This emerged from Penn's analysis as having been a ski condominium development in Lake Tahoe (a project I had had nothing to do with); how it connects to the crimes I have no idea. Later, he predicted that Webster's body would be found at a specific location in the Boston suburbs, and, I believe, cruelly misled her poor parents for some months (she was later found many miles away). At another point, he thought I had buried her on property I owned in Vermont. Once when I was there, tending the garden, I looked up and saw a small plane flying low overhead. An aerial photo of the house later appeared in my mailbox back in Brookline, without comment. (I think it was sent by Penn; most of the mail I believe I'm getting from him is in unmarked envelopes, or signed by various people named Mike.) I understand Penn also predicted that I would commit suicide in a particular way on a particular date, but I was not informed in time to comply and am now many years overdue.

The surreal quality of Penn's dialogue with the facts is captured by the matter of the phone number. At one time in Cambridge I had a phone number with the last four digits 6266. From this Penn, using some sort of gematria, extracted enormous meaning. But what does a number assigned by the phone company say about the person it was given to? Many of the other details Penn has used to launch his voyages of conjecture are equally beyond my control, like my birthday and my mother's name. There was also some fuss made about the fact that I was on the freshman rifle team in college. (At least two of the Zodiac murders were committed with a handgun at point-blank range, so rifle marksmanship doesn't seem germane, but go figure.)

By contrast, things I have intentionally crafted have been mostly ignored by the Penn-Zodiac crowd. Although I write for a living, only my dissertation (tables and tables of numbers!) and two other works have attracted their interest. One of them was a paper that used a hypothetical carjacking to illustrate something about persuasion; the other was a satirical op-ed I wrote for the *San Francisco Chronicle* that used Canadian wolf relocation to make fun of xenophobia. I thought it was a pretty minor effort, but it echoed through the recesses of the Internet for years. If only I could get fellow scholars to pay half as much attention to my serious work.

I wish I could say I've learned a lot from this disagreeable experience, but about all I've gleaned is how hard the subconscious mind tries to make sense of irrational circumstances. "Is this what amnesia is like?" I found myself idly thinking during the early days of Penn's obsession. "I know I didn't kill any of those people. But maybe I met them and was rude or unkind to them in some way? Or maybe this has to do with not grading my students' work carefully enough, or not having enough footnotes in my thesis…"

I have a recurrent mental image of Penn (whom, to my knowledge, I've never met). He's seated cross-legged on the floor surrounded by an enormous collection of Lego pieces, each one a fact either about me or about the Zodiac/Webster crimes. Hour after hour, day after day, he assembles an amazing structure, but the pieces from the two batches don't fit together properly, so he relabels something that looks useful, or whittles a new piece from scratch into the shape he needs. Everyone should have a hobby, I guess, and the world has survived a wide variety of philosophies about the relationship between belief and evidence. But all in all, I wish he had gone looking for a race-car driver with the initials PDQ.

Michael O'Hare teaches public policy analysis at the University of California at Berkeley, specializing in environmental and arts policy with forays into public management.

2

The Twin Towers and the Truthers: 9/11 Conspiracy Theories

(AFP/Getty Images)

A hijacked commercial plane crashes into the World Trade Center on September 11, 2001, in New York.

The 9/11 Conspiracy:
The Theories and the Evidence

By Paul McCaffrey

Conspiracy theories often emerge as a way of explaining momentous and traumatic events—of making sense of the insensible. In the twentieth century in the United States, for example, the Japanese bombing of Pearl Harbor and the assassination of President John F. Kennedy, two of our great national tragedies, are the focus of such speculation up to the present day. Given these precedents, it is hardly surprising that the 9/11 terrorist attacks would generate widespread conspiracy theorizing. Moreover, if the past is any indication, it is safe to conclude that 9/11 conspiracy theories will be with us for some time to come, and that future generations of "9/11 Truthers" will continue to look beyond the conventional narrative to understand what really happened that day.

One of U.S. history's great turning points, the 9/11 attacks ushered in a new era in American life and global affairs, marking the end of a comparatively peaceful and prosperous era and the birth of a more violent and unstable world. Not only were nearly three thousand innocent people murdered, but symbols of American power and influence were destroyed. That morning, according to official reports, nineteen terrorists affiliated with Osama bin Laden's al Qaeda network hijacked four commercial airliners, flying two into the Twin Towers of New York's World Trade Center in Lower Manhattan and one into the Pentagon complex outside Washington, DC. The fourth plane, presumably en route to a target in the nation's capital, crashed in rural Shanksville, Pennsylvania, after passengers fought back and attempted to take control of the aircraft. As the fires raged that day, the government investigations and their conclusions were a long way off, and in the confusion that reigned, the seeds of 9/11 conspiracy theories were already taking root.

The various 9/11 theories can be broken down into three basic categories: the conventional "al Qaeda did it" scenario; the "al Qaeda was allowed to do it" variation; and the "al Qaeda didn't do it, someone else did" narrative. The first form is the more or less official explanation determined by the administration of President George W. Bush and the 9/11 Commission: al Qaeda operatives, taking advantage of soft spots in airport security, and having learned to fly in US flight schools, seized control of the planes in order to crash them into emblematic targets and inflict the maximum amount of casualties. This theory assumes that the American government could not have prevented the attacks—that there was no advance warning—or that due to some combination of bureaucratic inertia, institutional incompetence, and a lack of imagination, US security agencies failed to "connect the dots" and unravel the plot.

Another branch of 9/11 theories alleges that elites, whether government operatives or business interests, had knowledge of the plot but decided not to prevent it,
reasoning that a successful attack would better serve their policy agenda. One of
the more common incarnations of this variety of speculation is that elements in the
Bush administration, fixated on toppling Iraqi leader Saddam Hussein, did not stop
the hijackers because the ensuing tragedy would provide them with the necessary
casus belli for invading Iraq.

There are those who take the plotting one step further, suggesting that rather
than merely allowing the attacks to happen, powerful government conspirators orchestrated them. In this third form of 9/11 theory, the coordinated assault potentially constituted a "false flag" operation, a covert strike by American forces on the
American people in the hopes of stirring public opinion in favor of war. Other vari-
ants of this category look outside the United States for the culprits, contending
that a foreign government—China or Iraq, perhaps—carried out the attacks. One
hypothesis that is especially prevalent in the Middle East is that the Israeli intelligence agency, the Mossad, is responsible. Proponents of the Mossad scenario also
refer to bogus reports in Arab newspapers that some four thousand Jewish workers
at the World Trade Center had been instructed to stay home on 9/11.

The spectrum of 9/11 conspiracies is vast, but the evidence marshaled in support of any particular conspiracy scenario is rather narrow. The evidence catalogued
in the seminal 9/11 Truther documentary film *Loose Change* (released in various
versions between 2005 and 2009) focuses on a number of supposed anomalies in
mainstream accounts of the attacks. In turn, the magazine *Popular Mechanics* published a comprehensive critical assessment of that evidence in a 2005 article that
was expanded the following year into a book, *Debunking 9/11 Myths: Why Conspiracy Theories Can't Stand Up to the Facts*. Of central import in this debate is how
and why the Twin Towers fell. According to some conspiracists, a commercial airplane loaded with jet fuel, even after a high-speed collision, should not have caused
either tower to collapse. Given that steel melts at temperatures in excess of 2750
degrees Fahrenheit, and jet fuel burns at only 1500 degrees or so, they reason, the
ensuing fires should not have undermined the structural integrity of the buildings.
Moreover, when the towers did collapse, these conspiracists point to small explosions of dust and debris that can be seen shooting out from the windows of lower
floors as the upper floors start to collapse. They identify these discharges as coming
from squibs, or small explosives often used to detonate larger ones; these are seen as
evidence of controlled demolition, possibly using thermite, set off from within the
towers. Further bolstering their case, they claim, is evidence of melted steel found
in the ruins of the Twin Towers, suggesting temperatures did exceed 2750 degrees,
presumably due to explosives or some other incendiary.

Skeptics discount these arguments in several ways. On one hand, they point out,
while at least 2750 degrees is required to melt steel, only 1000 degrees is needed
to seriously compromise its strength. The excessive heat would have weakened the
steel "bones" of the buildings which, combined with the damage from each plane's
impact, could have caused the ensuing collapse. As for melted steel in the rubble,

the evidence was not clear cut. What looked like melted steel to the untrained eye could have been aluminum or some other metal. The squibs observed by conspiracists, they conclude, do not indicate explosive charges, but simply the pressure of the collapsing upper floors expelling air and other material from the lower floors.

Beyond the destruction of the Twin Towers, 9/11 Truthers base much of their case on the collapse of World Trade Center Building 7 (WTC 7). WTC 7 was not hit by a plane and the fires that started as a result of residual damage from the neighboring Twin Towers, they posit, should not have been strong enough to bring it down. In addition, they refer to a television interview with the building's leaseholder, Larry Silverstein, who said that he ordered firefighters to "pull it." This they interpret as a declaration that Silverstein had the structure toppled by controlled demolition. But what would be the purpose of destroying WTC 7? As it turns out, the building had some illustrious tenants. The Secret Service, the Central Intelligence Agency (CIA), the Department of Defense, the Securities and Exchange Commission (SEC), and a host of other notable entities all had offices in WTC 7. Contained in those offices, Truthers surmise, was evidence of the 9/11 plot. So in addition to demolishing the Twin Towers, the conspirators were also covering their tracks.

More credulous observers state that the fires in WTC 7 were powerful enough to render the building structurally unsound and that Silverstein's "pull it" order was misinterpreted by conspiracists: He did not mean pull the building down, but pull out the firefighting personnel battling the flames inside it. Furthermore, if the destruction of WTC 7 was the product of a conspiracy, they conclude, it makes little sense for one of those involved to admit as much in an interview.

According to the conventional 9/11 narrative, the third plane, American Airlines Flight 77, struck the façade of the Pentagon military complex. Truthers aren't so sure. They allege that the Pentagon was either bombed or hit by a missile, claiming that the ensuing destruction was not consistent with an airplane crash. Frequently, they quote the words of CNN correspondent Jamie McIntyre, who observed, "there's no evidence of a plane having crashed anywhere near the Pentagon." Of course, conspiracy debunkers claim, McIntyre went on to state that the plane didn't crash anywhere *near* the Pentagon because it crashed directly *into* the Pentagon.

Another major focus of 9/11 conspiracy theorizing is United Airlines Flight 93. This is the plane thought to have been crashed by al Qaeda terrorists in a Pennsylvania field after its passengers launched a desperate fight to take over the aircraft. Truthers raise a number of questions about Flight 93. Some allege, based on misleading initial reports that confused Flight 93 with Flight 1989, that the plane landed safely in Cleveland, Ohio, on September 11. Others claim that it was shot down by the US military. Again, critics offer a host of arguments to undermine such suspicions. Flight 93's "black box," for example, which recorded the last minutes of the doomed flight, was retrieved from the wreckage. Played back, it revealed the sounds of a violent struggle along the lines envisioned by the conventional 9/11 narrative. The crash site, too, skeptics contend, offers nothing to contradict the official scenario.

Beyond the manner of the Twin Towers' collapse, the destruction of WTC 7, the nature of the hole in the Pentagon, and what did or didn't happen to Flight 93, Truthers often focus on several other points of interest and underlying assumptions. Among these are that North American Air Defenses (NORAD) was capable of intercepting one or more of the planes before they reached their intended targets. Another supposes that more than a few people had advanced knowledge of the attacks and sought to profit from them. In the days preceding 9/11, for example, many investors started betting that airline stocks were going to tumble, leading some observers to conclude that word of the impending catastrophe had leaked out.

As with other aspects of 9/11 conspiracy theories, the skeptics have answers to these speculations. Given the number of planes in the sky at the time, intercepting any of the hijacked flights would have been a much more complicated affair than conspiracists imply. Meanwhile, the 9/11 Commission and other investigators concluded that the suspicious trading in airline stocks was not very suspicious after all, but was in keeping with past patterns of activity.

So just how prevalent are 9/11 conspiracy theories? According to public opinion polls, belief in 9/11 conspiracies peaked in the mid-2000s. Prior to the Republican National Convention in 2004, a Zogby poll of New York City residents found that 49 percent believed the US government knew the attacks were coming but failed to act. More recent polls indicate that perhaps around 15 percent of American citizens continue to doubt the official explanations.

As the years have gone by, the composition of the 9/11 Truth movement has evolved. During the George W. Bush administration, 9/11 conspiracy theorizing in the United States was largely a left-wing phenomenon, serving, some would say, as an outlet for the discontent and distrust many on the Left felt toward the president and his post–9/11 agenda. Indications are that today's Truth movement is a decidedly right-wing and libertarian affair.

In the end, perhaps the one thing on which the most cynical Truther and the most inside-the-box thinker on the 9/11 Commission can agree is that the attacks were indeed the result of a conspiracy. Even the most conventional explanation of 9/11 amounts to a conspiracy theory, elaborating a complex plot stretching across several continents and involving dozens of operatives. Thus, one of the underlying lessons of 9/11 is that some conspiracies are real.

Viewing 9/11 from a Grassy Knoll

You won't believe what the conspiracy theorists are claiming—or will you?

By Will Sullivan
U.S. News & World Report, September 11, 2006

New York can be a tough town, especially when you're handing out fliers at ground zero claiming that the 9/11 attacks were a massive government conspiracy. "I'd like to take a f---ing box cutter and cut her," one passerby yelled after Carol Brown offered him a flier. Brown shrugged: "It happens sometimes."

If nothing else, the members of 9/11 Truth, some of whom go to ground zero every Saturday, are persistent. Even as conspiracy theories thrived abroad, they mostly fell on deaf ears in the first years after the attacks. But as the fifth anniversary nears, 9/11 Truth and its outlandish claims have become an online phenomenon—and are proving startlingly persuasive. In a July 2006 Scripps Howard poll, 16 percent of respondents said it was "very likely" that federal officials either assisted in the 9/11 attacks or allowed them to happen to justify war in the Middle East, while a further 20 percent said it was "somewhat likely."

By that measure, roughly a third of Americans suspect the seemingly unthinkable—government complicity in the deaths of some 3,000 citizens. The "somewhat likely" category is too vague to give much insight, though, says Mark Fenster, a law professor at the University of Florida and an expert on conspiracy theory movements. But he has noticed a large increase in the popularity of 9/11 Truth in the past year, which he attributes to rising disaffection with the Bush administration and the Iraq war.

Web Powered

Websites promoting theories about government involvement in the attacks get thousands of hits a day. But nothing has been more successful at spreading the movement than *Loose Change: 2nd Edition,* an 82-minute film that can be downloaded or watched free online. Made for around $6,000 by 22-year-old Dylan Avery and two friends, the movie is a superficially persuasive rundown of the major points of the conspiracy movement. "It's got a movie pace," says 26-year-old Jason Bermas, the film's researcher. "You don't feel like it's some kook in the backwoods telling you all this." The film has made Avery, who was twice rejected from film school, the toast of the 9/11 Truth movement and won him a girlfriend, who saw *Loose Change* and contacted him.

There are some divergent strands among the conspiracy theorists, but for most of them, the story has two major tenets: The World Trade Center towers and nearby Building 7, though struck by planes, were brought down by controlled demolitions, and the Pentagon was struck by a missile, not a plane.

As for who's responsible, most 9/11 Truthers point to the White House. They are particularly fond of implicating the Project for the New American Century, the conservative think tank that included Dick Cheney and Donald Rumsfeld and once posited that its goals of a beefed-up military would take a long time without an event "like a new Pearl Harbor." But the list of those branded conspirators ranges from Larry Silverstein, the leaseholder of the World Trade towers, to the members of the 9/11 commission to the mainstream media.

For evidence, they mainly point to grainy photographs, dubious sources, and quotes taken out of context. But the movement got a dose of credibility from Steven Jones, a physics professor at Brigham Young University, who contends after studying the attacks that the towers were brought down by explosive charges. Mormon, conservative, and bookish, he has become the cochair of Scholars for 9/11 Truth and an unlikely star in a movement eager for anyone with a science background and without a history of promoting conspiracy theories.

The members of the official 9/11 commission have kept their distance after deciding jointly that responding to the frequent E-mails from conspiracy theorists would only give them undeserved credibility. "I have a tremendous amount of confidence that the basic thrust of our story . . . will hold up to historians," says Jamie Gorelick, a commission member. That's not to say the conspiracy theorists go unchallenged. The National Institute of Standards and Technology, which last October issued the definitive 43-volume technical study of the towers' collapse, last week released a 14-point rebuttal of the controlled demolition theory. A blog and movie called *Screw Loose Change* both specialize in snarky commentary about *Loose Change*'s flimsy evidence. On a recent Saturday at ground zero, bickering between the 9/11 Truthers and their critics, who have also taken to showing up weekly, grew so heated that they were broken up by a police officer.

> *If nothing else, the members of 9/11 Truth, some of whom go to ground zero every Saturday, are persistent.*

Scrutiny

The most exhaustive debunking is found in a March 2005 article in *Popular Mechanics,* extended and released as a book this summer, which meticulously strikes down the movement's central scientific claims. James Meigs, the magazine's editor-in-chief, says none of the so-called evidence stood up to scrutiny, but that he can understand why people have been swayed by 9/11 Truth's endless footnotes and citations. "It has the appearance of being scholarly," he says. "But when you dig down, you see that it's not." Conspiracy theorists have an answer to that, too. They assert that Benjamin Chertoff, a researcher on the project, is a cousin of homeland security chief Michael Chertoff. He's not, though he may be distantly related. "No one in my family has ever met anyone related to Michael Chertoff," he says.

Belief in 9/11 conspiracies has flourished for years overseas, particularly in the Muslim world. In Pakistan, 41 percent of Muslims in a June 2006 Pew poll agreed that Arabs did not carry out the 9/11 attacks, compared with 15 percent who said they did. Many, like Muneer Ahmed Baloch, a Pakistani security expert and columnist, cite the long-debunked claim that 4,000 Jews did not show up for work at the towers on September 11. Egyptian singer Shaaban Abdel Rehim had a 2003 hit blaming September 11 on Israel and America. The accompanying video shows a caricatured Ariel Sharon pushing a button that causes a plane to crash into the towers.

Currently, Avery and his crew are hard at work on *Loose Change: The Final Cut,* a longer version they hope to bring to the Sundance Film Festival and then to a theater near you. On September 11, they and many other Truthers will be at ground zero spreading the word. Their presence will almost certainly outrage some who have come to mourn. But they are also hoping for reactions like those of Ron Tisdale, who began staring at 9/11 Truth's posters a few minutes after the box-cutter threat. After only a few minutes, the 52-year-old from Ohio was convinced. "It's really enlightened me," he says. "What's the world coming to?"

The Anatomy of Lunacy

By Andrew Roberts
National Review, June 6, 2011

A *review of* Among the Truthers: A Journey Through America's Growing Conspiracist Underground, *by Jonathan Kay.*

How can a nation founded on a Constitution that, in its logic and rationality, is "the crown jewel of the Enlightenment" have so fallen prey to conspiracy theorists that today no fewer than 36 percent of Americans believe that it is either "somewhat likely" or "very likely" that "federal officials either participated in the attacks on the World Trade Center and the Pentagon or took no action to stop them"? How can it be that one-sixth of Americans think it "somewhat likely" that "the collapse of the twin towers in New York was aided by explosives secretly planted in the two buildings"?

If you yourself believe either of those things, stop reading now, and please don't bother sending me your green-ink scrawling from the Planet Zog, as I get quite enough of them already. (As I was reading this book on a flight from Milwaukee to La Guardia, the lady next to me told me that JFK had been assassinated by forces loyal to Karl Rove and the Bush family. When I pointed out that Mr. Rove could only have been about 13 at the time, she replied: "That's old enough to fire a rifle in Texas!")

In attempting to understand why conspiracy theories are thriving in modern America, the (Canadian) *National Post* journalist Jonathan Kay immersed himself in the Truther movement, the people who believe 9/11 was an inside job, and also investigated various other groups, such as those who believe that vaccines cause autism, Israel controls America, George W. Bush is a follower of Nazi ideology, and FEMA is preparing to imprison political dissidents prior to imposing a totalitarian New World Order. Kay has hit these nutjobs' websites, attended their rallies, interviewed their leaders, gone on their marches, and delved deep into their sadly twisted minds.

As well as being superbly written, utterly absorbing, and occasionally very funny, this is an important book, as it investigates why we currently have what the author calls "a countercultural rift in the fabric of consensual American reality, a gaping cognitive gap into which has leaped a wide range of political paranoiacs previously consigned to the lunatic fringe—Larouchites, UFO nuts, libertarian survivalists, Holocaust deniers, and a thousand other groups besides." As my mother used to say: "There are more out than in."

Kay notes how some periods in history have created more conspiracies than others, specifying France after the Revolution, America's Great Plains after the late 19th century depression, Germany after the Great War, and the entire Western world after JFK's death, Vietnam, Watergate, and the rise of the 1960s counterculture. He argues that "these have been the moments when shrieking prophets and conspiracy theorists have found their moments." The trauma of 9/11 was clearly another such moment, and, in Kay's view, has created "a state of intellectual agitation that isn't a temporary phenomenon" but instead "has far-reaching social, political, and psychological consequences that have yet to be fully absorbed or understood."

Conspiracy theories provide what has always been demanded in a secular age, "a cosmic explanation for evil," and this also has taken place in today's postmodernist intellectual environment in which, as Kay puts it, "thanks to the rise of identity politics, it is imagined that words—and even facts—have no meaning independent of the emotional effect they produce upon their audience. Everyone feels entitled to their own private reality."

Kay also notes "the intellectual balkanization created by the World Wide Web": "For the first time in history, ordinary people can now spread their opinions, no matter how hateful or eccentric, without them first gaining the approval of editors, publishers, broadcasters, or paying consumers." Far from ushering in a world of blissful realism, freedom, and mutual comprehension, the Internet has unleashed the private fanaticism of millions of crackpots into cyberspace, where it flies around, mutating and cross-pollinating, with-

> *The proportion of Americans who say that they "basically trust their government" has fallen from 75 percent in 1958 to a mere 22 percent today.*

out any real policing or rational input from society. If there has ever been a case for old-fashioned elitism, the phobias, fanaticism, fetishism, and fascism found on the Web made it.

When an anarchist site like WikiLeaks, run by the preternaturally weird Julian Assange, publishes huge tranches of secret documents it claims undermine America's "authoritarian conspiracy" against "a more just society," fuel is heaped onto the flames of global paranoia and anti-Americanism. As it was, remarkably little in the way of any conspiracy was actually uncovered by WikiLeaks, and the U.S. seems to have been remarkably honest and open in its dealings with foreign governments, and far less twofaced than most other global hegemons in history. Yet the proportion of Americans who say that they "basically trust their government" has fallen from 75 percent in 1958 to a mere 22 percent today.

Kay rightly blames some of the excesses of the Seventies for this, such as the secret bombing of Cambodia, the My Lai cover-up, CIA assassinations, and of course Watergate, but he is probably going too far in blaming "the unsatisfying Warren Commission Report on the JFK assassination," which could hardly satisfy people who continue to insist that Kennedy was killed by anyone other than a lone, highly experienced gunman. Kay is on surer ground when he points out that every journalist's desperation to be the next Woodward or Bernstein has meant that the media have become obsessed with conspiracies and thus "interested partisans manipulating public perceptions." The way that Hollywood continually peddles movies in which any white, middle-aged male working for a government agency—especially the White House, Pentagon, or CIA—is automatically assumed to be a slimy, vicious traitor must also have had its effect on public psychology over the past four decades.

Kay is genuinely concerned that conspiracists have "spun out of rationality's ever-weakening gravitational pull, and into mutually impenetrable Manichean fantasy universes of their own construction." This is dangerous for American democracy, especially as it seems to be moving into the mainstream. In analyzing the minds of the Truthers, Kay finds "a nihilistic distrust in government, total alienation from conventional politics, a need to reduce the world's complexities to good-versus-evil fables, the melding of secular politics with apocalyptic End-Is-Nigh religiosity, and a rejection of the basic tools of discourse." These people are poisoning the well of democratic debate in modern America, and need to be countered. Instead, when Mahmoud Ahmadinejad—a committed Truther and Holocaust-denier—visited Yale last September, the senior research fellow who organized the event, Hillary Mann Leverett, claimed that his smooth performance proved that he was "not a crazy, irrational leader."

Yet if this hard-hitting, perceptive, and highly readable book proves anything, it is that impressive speaking ability and smooth charm are often to be found among crazy people. It is what they say that matters, rather than the way they say it. And what Ahmadinejad actually says about 9/11—that it was staged by the U.S. government "to reverse the declining American economy and . . . save the Zionist regime"—shows that he is the very model of a crazy, irrational leader.

Kay divides conspiracy theorists into eight distinctive categories—The Midlife Crisis, The Failed Historian, The Damaged Survivor, The Cosmic Voyager, The Clinical Conspiracist, The Crank, The Evangelical Doomsayer, and The Firebrand—and illustrates each with a case study. He points out how little serious academic research has been done into the psychology of conspiracy theorizing, despite its being a classic "symptom of a mind in flight from reality," and how Truthers are almost always men.

A young construction worker from Brooklyn called Luke Rudkowski must have won the record for multiple conspiracy beliefs, when in April 2007 he asked Zbigniew Brzezinski in a public meeting: "How do the American people know that 9/11 wasn't staged, wasn't engineered by you, David Rockefeller, the Trilateral Commission, the Committee on Foreign Relations, and the Bilderberg Group, sir?" (I love the deferential little appellation "sir" at the end of this accusation of mass murder.) But the British Truther and former MI5 agent David Shayler easily wins the prize for the most far-fetched theory; he believes that "no planes were involved in 9/11." (In fact, he says, they were giant holograms.) But then he has also stated that he is "the Messiah" and has "the secret of eternal life."

The only thing that sane people can do is to repeat, slowly and comprehensively and often, that no, Jesus wasn't the first Freemason, that *The Protocols of the Elders of Zion* was a czarist forgery, that Jews weren't told to absent themselves from work in the Twin Towers on 9/11, that William Shakespeare wrote the works of the playwright called William Shakespeare, that there wasn't a plot to kill New Orleans's black population during Hurricane Katrina, that the Queen of England is not an international drug dealer, that AIDS wasn't invented by the CIA to cull global population, that aircraft vapor trails don't contain chemicals designed to alter human behavior, that the government is not inserting microchips into our bloodstream, that Mohamed Atta does not have a body double, and so on and so interminably on. But then perhaps I've written all this just because I'm secretly in the pay of the Vatican, MI5, and the Mossad.

Andrew Roberts is the author of The Storm of War: A New History of the Second World War *(HarperCollins).*

9/11: The Roots of Paranoia

By Christopher Hayes
The Nation, December 8, 2006

According to a July poll conducted by Scripps News Service, one-third of Americans think the government either carried out the 9/11 attacks or intentionally allowed them to happen in order to provide a pretext for war in the Middle East. This is at once alarming and unsurprising. Alarming, because if tens of millions of Americans really believe their government was complicit in the murder of 3,000 of their fellow citizens, they seem remarkably sanguine about this fact. By and large, life continues as before, even though tens of millions of people apparently believe they are being governed by mass murderers. Unsurprising, because the government these Americans suspect of complicity in 9/11 has acquired a justified reputation for deception: weapons of mass destruction, secret prisons, illegal wiretapping. What else are they hiding?

This pattern of deception has not only fed diffuse public cynicism but has provided an opening for alternate theories of 9/11 to flourish. As these theories—propounded by the so-called 9/11 Truth Movement—seep toward the edges of the mainstream, they have raised the specter of the return (if it ever left) of what Richard Hofstadter famously described as "the paranoid style in American politics." But the real danger posed by the Truth Movement isn't paranoia. Rather, the danger is that it will discredit and deform the salutary skepticism Americans increasingly show toward their leaders.

The Truth Movement's recent growth can be largely attributed to the Internet-distributed documentary *Loose Change*. A low-budget film produced by two 20-somethings that purports to debunk the official story of 9/11, it's been viewed over the Internet millions of times. Complementing *Loose Change* are the more highbrow offerings of a handful of writers and scholars, many of whom are associated with Scholars for 9/11 Truth. Two of these academics, retired theologian David Ray Griffin and retired Brigham Young University physics professor Steven Jones, have written books and articles that serve as the movement's canon. Videos of their lectures circulate among the burgeoning portions of the Internet devoted to the cause of the "truthers." A variety of groups have chapters across the country and organize conferences that draw hundreds. In the last election cycle, the website www.911truth.org even produced a questionnaire with pointed inquiries for candidates, just like the US Chamber of Commerce or the Sierra Club. The Truth Movement's relationship to the truth may be tenuous, but that it is a movement is no longer in doubt.

Truth activists often maintain they are simply "raising questions," and as such tend to focus with dogged persistence on physical minutiae: the lampposts near the Pentagon that should have been knocked down by Flight 77, the altitude in Pennsylvania at which cellphones on Flight 93 should have stopped working, the temperature at which jet fuel burns and at which steel melts. They then use these perceived inconsistencies to argue that the central events of 9/11—the plane hitting the Pentagon, the towers collapsing—were not what they appeared to be. So: The eyewitness accounts of those who heard explosions in the World Trade Center, combined with the facts that jet fuel burns at 1,500 degrees Fahrenheit and steel melts at 2,500, shows that the towers were brought down by controlled explosions from inside the buildings, not by the planes crashing into them.

If the official story is wrong, then what did happen? As you might expect, there's quite a bit of dissension on this point. Like any movement, the Truth Movement is beset by internecine fights between different factions: those who subscribe to what are termed LIHOP theories (that the government "let it happen on purpose") and the more radical MIHOP ("made it happen on purpose") contingent. Even within these groups, there are divisions: Some believe the WTC was detonated with explosives after the planes hit and some don't even think there were any planes.

To the extent that there is a unified theory of the nature of the conspiracy, it is based, in part, on the precedent of the Reichstag fire in Germany in the 1930s. The idea is that just as the Nazis staged a fire in the Reichstag in order to frighten the populace and consolidate power, the Bush Administration, military contractors, oil barons and the CIA staged 9/11 so as to provide cause and latitude to pursue its imperial ambitions unfettered by dissent and criticism. But the example of the Reichstag fire itself is instructive. While during and after the war many observers, including officials of the US government, suspected the fire was a Nazi plot, the consensus among historians is that it was, in fact, the product of a lone zealous anarchist. That fact changes little about the Nazi regime, or its use of the fire for its own ends. It's true the Nazis were the chief beneficiaries of the fire, but that doesn't mean they started it, and the same goes for the Bush Administration and 9/11.

The Reichstag example also holds a lesson for those who would dismiss the very notion of a conspiracy as necessarily absurd. It was perfectly reasonable to suspect the Nazis of setting the fire, so long as the evidence suggested that might have been the case. The problem isn't with conspiracy theories as such; the problem is continuing to assert the existence of a conspiracy even after the evidence shows it to be virtually impossible.

In March 2005 *Popular Mechanics* assembled a team of engineers, physicists, flight experts and the like to critically examine some of the Truth Movement's most common claims. They found them almost entirely without merit. To pick just one example, steel might not melt at 1,500 degrees, the temperature at which jet fuel burns, but it does begin to lose a lot of its strength, enough to cause the support beams to fail.

And yet no amount of debunking seems to work. The Internet empowers people with esoteric interests to spend all kinds of time pursuing their hobbies, and if the Truth Movement was the political equivalent of *Lord of the Rings* fan fiction or furries, there wouldn't be much reason to pay attention. But the public opinion trend lines are moving in the truthers' direction, even after the official 9/11 Commission report was supposed to settle the matter once and for all.

Of course, the commission report was something of a whitewash—Bush would only be interviewed in the presence of Dick Cheney, the commission was denied access to other key witnesses and just this year we learned of a meeting convened by George Tenet the summer before the attacks to warn Condoleezza Rice about Al Qaeda's plotting, a meeting that was nowhere mentioned in the report.

So it's hard to blame people for thinking we're not getting the whole story. For six years, the government has prevaricated and the press has largely failed to point out this simple truth. Critics like *The New Yorker*'s Nicholas Lemann might lament the resurgence of the "paranoid style," but the seeds of paranoia have taken root partly because of the complete lack of appropriate skepticism by the establishment press, a complementary impulse to the paranoid style that might be called the credulous style. In the credulous style all political actors are acting with good intentions and in good faith. Mistakes are made, but never because of ulterior motives or undue influence from the various locii of corporate power. When people in power advocate strenuously for a position it is because they believe in it. When their advocacy leads to policies that create

> *Like any movement, the Truth Movement is beset by internecine fights between different factions.*

misery, it is due not to any evil intentions or greed or corruption, but rather simple human error. Ahmad Chalabi summed up this worldview perfectly. Faced with the utter absence of the WMD he and his cohorts had long touted in Iraq, he replied, "We are heroes in error."

For a long time the credulous style has dominated the establishment, but its hold intensified after 9/11. When the government speaks, particularly about the Enemy, it must be presumed to be telling the truth. From the reporting about Iraq's alleged WMD to the current spate of stories about how "dangerous" Iran is, time and again the press has reacted to official pronouncements about threats with a near total absence of skepticism. Each time the government announces the indictment of domestic terrorists allegedly plotting our demise, the press devotes itself to the story with obsessive relish, only to later note, on page A22 or in a casual aside, that the whole thing was bunk. In August 2003, to cite just one example, the New York dailies breathlessly reported what one US official called an "incredible triumph in the war against terrorism," the arrest of Hemant Lakhani, a supposed terrorist mastermind caught red-handed attempting to acquire a surface-to-air missile. Only later did the government admit that the "plot" consisted of an FBI informant begging Lakhani to find him a missile, while a Russian intelligence officer called up Lakhani and offered to sell him one.

Yet after nearly a dozen such instances, the establishment media continue to earnestly report each new alleged threat or indictment, secure in the belief that their proximity to policy-makers gets it closer to the truth. But proximity can obscure more than clarify. It's hard to imagine that the guy sitting next to you at the White House correspondents' dinner is plotting to, say, send the country into a disastrous and illegal war, or is spying on Americans in blatant defiance of federal statutes. Bob Woodward, the journalist with the most access to the Bush Administration, was just about the last one to realize that the White House is disingenuous and cynical, that it has manipulated the machinery of state for its narrow political ends.

Meanwhile, those who realized this was the White House's MO from the beginning have been labeled conspiracy theorists. During the 2004 campaign Howard Dean made the charge that the White House was manipulating the terror threat level and recycling old intelligence. The Bush campaign responded by dismissing Dean as a "bizarre conspiracy theorist." A year later, after Homeland Security Secretary Tom Ridge retired, he admitted that Dean's charge was, indeed, the truth. The same accusation of conspiracy-mongering was routinely leveled at anyone who suggested that the war in Iraq was and is motivated by a desire for the United States to control the world's second-largest oil reserves.

For the Administration, "conspiracy" is a tremendously useful term, and can be applied even in the most seemingly bizarre conditions to declare an inquiry or criticism out of bounds. Responding to a question from NBC's Brian Williams as to whether he ever discusses official business with his father, Bush said such a suggestion was a "kind of conspiracy theory at its most rampant." The credulous style can brook no acknowledgment of unarticulated motives to our political actors, or consultations to which the public is not privy.

The public has been presented with two worldviews, one credulous, one paranoid, and both unsatisfactory. The more the former breaks apart, the greater the appeal of the latter. Conspiracy theories that claim to explain 9/11 are wrongheaded and a terrible waste of time, but the skeptical instinct is, on balance, salutary. It is right to suspect that the operations of government, the power elite and the military-industrial complex are often not what they seem; and proper to raise questions when the answers provided have been unconvincing. Given the untruths to which American citizens have been subjected these past six years, is it any surprise that a majority of them think the government's lying about what happened before and on 9/11?

Still, the persistent appeal of paranoid theories reflects a cynicism that the credulous media have failed to address, because they posit a world of good intentions and face value pronouncements, one in which the suggestion that a government would mislead or abuse its citizens for its own gains or the gains of its benefactors is on its face absurd. The danger is that the more this government's cynicism and deception are laid bare, the more people—on the left in particular and among the public in general—will be drawn down the rabbit hole of delusion of the 9/11 Truth Movement.

To avoid such a fate, the public must come to trust that the gatekeepers of public discourse share their skepticism about the agenda its government is pursuing. The antidote, ultimately, to the Truth Movement is a press that refuses to allow the government to continue to lie.

The American Empire and 9/11

By David Ray Griffin
Tikkun, March 5, 2007

Editor's Note: Because we at Tikkun are aware of extensive arguments that have appeared elsewhere against the perspective presented by the author of this piece, we debated long and hard about whether to present David Ray Griffin's argument here. We decided it was still important, given that if his view is true, the position he articulates would provide adequate grounds for impeachment of the president, grounds far more substantive than those that formed the basis of the impeachment by a Republican dominated Congress of President Bill Clinton. Space prevents us from providing the author's footnotes, and required us to shorten the piece (though it is already longer than most that we publish). A fuller version along with the author's footnotes, and a critique by Rabbi Michael Lerner of the political assumptions underlying the 9/11 conspiracy theorists, can be found on our website at www.tikkun.org. You are invited to give your responses to this piece at our website.

The American Empire

In his 2002 book *American Empire*, Andrew Bacevich pointed out that it had long been a "cherished American tradition [that] the United States is not and cannot be an empire." The words "American empire" were "fighting words," so that uttering them was an almost sure sign that the speaker was a left-wing critic of America's foreign policy. As Bacevich also pointed out, however, this had all recently changed, so that even right-wing commentators were freely acknowledging the existence of the American empire. As columnist Charles Krauthammer put it in 2002: "People are coming out of the closet on the word 'empire.'"

Given this consensus about the *reality* of the American empire, the only remaining issue concerned its *nature*. This empire was generally portrayed as benign. Robert Kagan spoke of "The Benevolent Empire." Dinesh D'Souza, after writing that "America has become an empire," added happily that it is "the most magnanimous imperial power ever."

Commentators from the Left, however, presented a radically different view. A 2003 book by Noam Chomsky was subtitled *America's Quest for Global Dominance*. Richard Falk wrote of the Bush administration's "global domination project," which posed the threat of "global fascism." Chalmers Johnson, once a conservative who believed in an American foreign policy aimed at promoting freedom and democracy, described the United States as "a military juggernaut intent on world domination." Bacevich, although still a conservative, had come to accept the Left's assessment of this empire. He ridiculed the claim that "the promotion of peace, democracy, and human rights and the punishment of evil-doers—not the pursuit of self-interest—[has] defined the essence of American diplomacy." Pointing out that the aim of the U.S. military has been "to achieve something approaching omnipotence," Bacevich mocked the idea that such power in America's hands "is by definition benign."

The historical evidence clearly supports this critical view of the American empire. Part of this evidence is the fact that U.S. political and military leaders have arranged "false-flag operations" as pretexts for war. We did this to begin the wars with Mexico, the Philippines, and Vietnam.

Also important is Operation Northwoods, a plan submitted by the Joint Chiefs of Staff to President Kennedy containing "pretexts which would provide justification for U.S. military intervention in Cuba." Some of the ideas, such as a proposal to "blow up a U.S. ship in Guantanamo Bay and blame Cuba," would have required killing Americans.

This history shows that U.S. military and political leaders have not been averse to using the same tricks as the leaders of other countries with imperial ambitions, such as Japan, which in 1931 manufactured the Mukden incident as a justification for taking control of Manchuria, and the Nazis, who in 1939 had German troops dressed as Poles stage attacks on German posts at the Polish border, allowing Hitler to present his attack on Poland the next day as a "defensive necessity." In each case, evidence was planted to implicate the people these governments wanted to attack.

9/11: A False-Flag Operation?

Given this background information, I might have immediately concluded that the 9/11 attacks were false-flag attacks orchestrated by the Bush administration to expand the U.S. empire under the guise of the "war on terror." But when I first heard this allegation, about a year after 9/11, I did not think even the Bush administration would do such a heinous thing. I checked out some proffered websites but found the evidence unconvincing.

A few months later, however, another colleague suggested that I look at a website containing the massive 9/11 timeline created by Paul Thompson. I found that it contained an enormous number of reports, all from mainstream sources, that contradicted the official account. This discovery started a process that led me to publish *The New Pearl Harbor*, which summarized much of the evidence that had been discovered by previous researchers—evidence, I concluded, that provided a "strong *prima facie* case for official complicity." The evidence can be couched in terms of the following six questions.

I. How Could Hijacked Airliners Have Struck the WTC and the Pentagon?

If standard operating procedures of the FAA and the U.S. military had been carried out on 9/11, American Airlines Flight 11 and United Airlines Flight 175 would have been intercepted before they reached Manhattan, and Flight 77 would have been intercepted long before it could have reached the Pentagon. Such interceptions are routine, and are carried out about 100 times a year. A month after 9/11, the *Calgary Herald* reported that in the year 2000, the North American Aerospace Defense Command (NORAD) had scrambled fighters 129 times. Just a few days after 9/11, Major Mike Snyder, a NORAD spokesperson, told the *Boston Globe* that, "[NORAD's] fighters routinely intercept aircraft." Why did such interceptions not occur on 9/11? We have never been given a plausible explanation. Indeed, we have received three mutually inconsistent stories.

In the first few days, military officials said that no fighter jets were dispatched until after the 9/11 strike on the Pentagon at 9:38 AM, even though signs that Flight 11 was in trouble had been observed at 8:15 that same morning. That would mean that although interceptions usually occur within 15 minutes, in this case over 80 minutes elapsed before any fighters were even airborne. This suggested that a "stand-down" order had been issued.

Within a few days, a second story was put out, according to which NORAD *had* ordered fighters aloft, but they did not arrive in time, because FAA notification had unaccountably come very late. Critics showed, however, that even if the FAA notifications had come as late as NORAD's timeline indicated, there was sufficient time for interceptions. This second story did not, therefore, remove the suspicion that a stand-down order had been given.

The 9/11 Commission Report, issued in 2004, gave a third account, according to which, contrary to NORAD's timeline of September 18, 2001, the FAA did not notify NORAD about Flights 175, 77, and 93 until after they had crashed.

In August 2006, Michael Bronner, who was an associate producer for the film *United 93*, published an essay, "9/11 Live: The NORAD Tapes," which popularized the 9/11 Commission's description of events and emphasized tapes from 9/11 supplied by NORAD, on which it is based. This new story was further publicized by the simultaneous publication of *Without Precedent* by Thomas Kean and Lee Hamilton, the chair and vice chair, respectively, of the 9/11 Commission. This book caused a minor sensation by suggesting that the account given by the military between 2001 and 2004—which only partly absolved itself from responsibility for failing to prevent the attacks—had been a lie. The new story puts all the blame on the FAA, except for a little confusion on the military's part, thereby lessening the grounds for suspicion that the military had been given a stand-down order. This new story, in spite of its proposal that the military told a lie, has been widely accepted.

However, as I show in my most recent book, *Debunking 9/11 Debunking*, this new story, besides contradicting many well documented reports, is inherently implausible, claiming that military leaders lied in a way that made them look worse than does the truth. This new story does not, accordingly, remove grounds for suspicion that a stand-down order had been issued.

II. Why Did the Twin Towers and Building 7 of the World Trade Center Collapse?

The Bush administration has also failed to provide a credible explanation for the destruction of the World Trade Center buildings. According to the official explanation, the Twin Towers (WTC 1 and 2) collapsed due to the impact of the airplanes and the heat of the ensuing fires. But this explanation faces several formidable problems.

First, building 7 of the WTC also collapsed, and in roughly the same way. This similarity implies that all three buildings collapsed from the same causes. However, unlike buildings 1 and 2, WTC 7 was not hit by an airplane.

Second, the fires in all of these buildings were not as big, hot, or long lasting as previous fires in steel-frame high-rises, which did *not* induce collapse. For example, in 1991, a fire in Philadelphia burned for eighteen hours; in 2004, a fire in Caracas burned for seventeen hours. But neither fire produced even a partial collapse. The WTC's north and south towers burned only 102 and 56 minutes, respectively, before they collapsed. According to some witnesses and all the photographic evidence, moreover, WTC 7 had fires on only a few floors.

Third, complete collapses of steel-frame high-rise buildings have never been brought about by fire plus externally caused structural damage. Such collapses have only been caused by explosives used in controlled demolitions.

Fourth, the collapse of these three buildings manifested many standard features of the kind of controlled demolition known as implosion, such as: sudden onset; straight-down collapse; collapse at virtually free-fall speed (indicating that the lower floors were offering no resistance); total collapse (indicating that the massive steel columns in the core of each building had been broken into many pieces); the production of molten metal; and the occurrence of multiple explosions. Although none of these six features can be explained by the official story, let us focus on only the last two.

Many people have been led to believe, by misleading TV documentaries, the Twin Towers collapsed because their steel frames melted. But steel does not begin to melt until it reaches 2800°F, and open fires based on hydrocarbons such as kerosene—which is what jet fuel is—cannot get much hotter than 1700°F, even with an ideal mixture of fuel and oxygen, which seldom occurs in building fires. Nevertheless, reports revealed that when some of the steel beams were lifted from the rubble, they were dripping molten metal. That would not have been surprising if the buildings' steel columns had been sliced by the use of high-temperature explosives, such as thermite, thermate, or RDX, which are regularly used to cut steel.

Dozens of people, including journalists, police officers, WTC employees, emergency medical workers, and firefighters reported hearing explosions in the Twin Towers. Some of them explicitly stated that the collapses appeared to be instances of controlled demolition. A fire captain said, "I hear an explosion and I look up. It is as if the building is being imploded, from the top floor down, one after another, *boom, boom, boom.*" A paramedic noted, "[I]t was [like a] professional demolition where they set the charges on certain floors and then you hear 'Pop, pop, pop, pop, pop.'" Another firefighter said, "It seemed like on television [when] they blow up these buildings. It seemed like it was going all the way around like a belt, all these explosions."

Steven Jones, a physicist and former professor at Brigham Young University, has asserted that to believe the official account of the events of 9/11 is to believe that some of the basic laws of physics were violated.

It is not surprising that when a controlled demolition expert in Holland was shown videos of the collapse of WTC 7, without being told what the building was, he said, "They have simply blown away columns . . . A team of experts did this . . . This is controlled demolition." Concurring with this view, two emeritus professors of structural analysis and construction at Zurich's prestigious ETH Institute of Technology say that WTC 7 was "with the highest probability brought down by explosives."

The 9/11 Commission Report failed to respond to such challenges. The Commission, in fact, simply assumed the truth of the official story. All evidence pointing to government complicity was either distorted or completely ignored. Indeed, after FEMA, the first agency given the task of explaining the collapse of the WTC, said that its best explanation for the collapse of WTC 7 had "only a low probability of occurrence," the 9/11 Commission simply failed to mention this collapse in its 571-page report.

The Commission's approach was not surprising given the fact that its executive director was Philip Zelikow, who was virtually a member of the Bush administration: He had worked with Condoleezza Rice in the National Security Council during the first Bush presidency; during the Clinton years, Zelikow and Rice co-authored a book; Rice then, as National Security Advisor for the second President Bush, asked Zelikow help make the transition to the new National Security Council, after which he was appointed to the President's Foreign Intelligence Advisory Board; Rice later commissioned Zelikow to be the primary author of the 2002 National Security Strategy of the United States of America, which used 9/11 to justify a new doctrine of preemptive-preventive warfare. The idea that the 9/11 Commission was independent and impartial is, therefore, ludicrous.

The other most important investigation of 9/11, the supposedly definitive report on the destruction of the World Trade Center, suffered from the same problem. It was carried out by the National Institute for Standards and Technology (NIST), which is an agency of the U.S. Commerce Department and hence of the Bush administration. NIST's explanation of the collapse of the Twin Towers—at the time of this writing, it still had not published a report on WTC 7—itself collapses when scrutinized from a scientific point of view, as I show in *Debunking 9/11 Debunking*.

III. Could the Official Account of the Plane Crash on the Pentagon Possibly Be True?

According to the official report, the Pentagon was struck by American Airlines Flight 77 under the control of Al-Qaeda hijacker Hani Hanjour. This account is challenged by many facts.

First, it was alleged that Flight 77, after making a U-turn in the Midwest, flew back to Washington undetected for forty minutes, even though it was then known that hijacked airliners were being used as weapons, and despite the fact that the U.S. military has the best radar systems in the world.

Second, in order to hit Wedge 1 of the Pentagon, the aircraft had to execute an amazing downward spiral, and yet Hanjour was known as a terrible pilot who could barely fly a single-engine airplane. Russ Wittenberg, a retired pilot who flew large commercial airliners for thirty-five years after serving in Vietnam as a fighter pilot, has said that it would have been impossible for Flight 77 to have "descended 7,000 feet in two minutes, all the while performing a steep 270-degree banked turn before crashing into the Pentagon's first floor wall without touching the lawn." It

> *These problematic issues, besides conflicting with the official account, collectively indicate that the strike on the Pentagon was orchestrated by forces within our own government.*

would, he added, have been "totally impossible for an amateur who couldn't even fly a Cessna to maneuver the jetliner in such a highly professional manner."

Third, terrorists brilliant enough to outfox the U.S. military's defense system would not have struck Wedge 1. This part of the building had been reinforced, so the strike caused less damage than would have a strike anywhere else; it was still being renovated, so relatively few people were there; and the secretary of defense and all the top brass, whom terrorists would presumably have wanted to kill, were on the opposite side of the Pentagon.

Fourth, there is considerable evidence that the aircraft that struck the Pentagon was not even a Boeing 757. Unlike the strikes on the Twin Towers, the Pentagon strike did not create a detectable seismic signal. Also, according to photographs and eyewitnesses, the kind of damage and debris that would have been produced by the impact of a Boeing 757 was not evident in the aftermath of the strike on the Pentagon.

Karen Kwiatkowski, one of the eyewitnesses who was then an Air Force Lieutenant Colonel employed at the Pentagon, writes of "a strange lack of visible debris on the Pentagon lawn, where I stood only moments after the impact." Another eyewitness was CNN's Jamie McIntyre, who said during a live report from the Pentagon on 9/11, "The only pieces left that you can see are small enough that you pick up in your hand."

With regard to the damage, retired pilot Ralph Omholt, discussing the photographic evidence, writes: "There is no hole big enough to swallow a 757 . . . There is no viable evidence of burning jet fuel . . . The expected 'crash' damage doesn't exist . . . Even the Pentagon lawn was undamaged! The geometry of the day certifies the 'official' account as a blatant lie."

A fifth reason to be dubious of the official story is that, as with the attack on the World Trade Center, evidence was quickly destroyed. Shortly after the strike, officials picked up debris in front of the impact site and carried it off. Shortly thereafter the entire lawn was covered with dirt and gravel, so that any remaining forensic evidence was literally covered up.

FBI agents, moreover, immediately confiscated videos from security cameras on nearby buildings. After long refusing to release any of the footage, the Justice Department in May 2006 finally released film purporting to show a Boeing 757 striking the Pentagon. But it did not. Even Bill O'Reilly of Fox News had to say,

"I can't see a plane there." If there were footage that validated the official story, would we not have seen them as often as we have seen the strikes on the World Trade Center?

These problematic issues, besides conflicting with the official account, collectively indicate that the strike on the Pentagon was orchestrated by forces within our own government.

In the light of these challenges to the official account, we can reflect on President Bush's advice not to tolerate "outrageous conspiracy theories about the attacks of 11 September." This is excellent advice. But it deflects attention from the fact that the truly outrageous conspiracy theory is the official theory, according to which a group of Muslim terrorists conspired to defeat not only the most sophisticated defense system in history, but also some basic laws of physics. The problems in the official account, however, do not end there.

IV. Why Did the President and His Secret Service Agents Remain at the School After the Attacks?

Upon hearing that a plane had struck one of the Twin Towers, President Bush reportedly believed that it was an accident. It was not terribly strange, therefore, that he decided to go ahead with the photo-op at the school in Sarasota. Word of the second strike, however, should have indicated to his Secret Service agents—assuming that these strikes were unexpected—that the country was undergoing an unprecedented terrorist attack. And yet he was allowed to remain at the school for another half hour.

This behavior was very strange. The president's location had been highly publicized. If the attacks were indeed unexpected, the Secret Service, having no idea how many planes had been hijacked, would have suspected that the president himself was one of the targets. After all, what could be more satisfying to foreign terrorists aiming to attack high-value targets than to kill the president? Surely the Secret Service would have suspected a hijacked airliner might have been bearing down on the school at that very minute, ready to crash into it, killing Bush and everyone else there—including the Secret Service agents themselves. It is, in any case, standard procedure for the Secret Service to rush the president to a safe location whenever there is any sign that he may be in danger. And yet these agents, after allowing the president to remain in the classroom another ten minutes, permitted him to deliver his regularly scheduled TV address, thereby announcing to the world that he was still at the Sarasota school.

This behavior would be explainable only if the head of the Secret Service detail knew that the targets did not include Bush. And how could this have been known unless the attacks were being carried out by people within our own government? The 9/11 Commission, far from asking these questions, said only: "The Secret Service told us they . . . did not think it imperative for [the president] to run out the door." A serious inquiry into this matter, therefore, remains to be made.

V. Why Did the 9/11 Commission Lie about Vice President Cheney's Activities?

One sign of the complicity of Vice President Cheney is the fact that the 9/11 Commission evidently felt a need to lie about the time of two of his activities on the day of the attacks: his entry into the Presidential Emergency Operations Center (PEOC) under the White House and authorization to shoot down any hijacked airliners.

It had been widely reported that Vice President Cheney had gone down to the PEOC shortly after the second strike on the WTC, hence about 9:15 a.m. The most compelling witness was Secretary of Transportation Norman Mineta, who testified to the 9/11 Commission that when he entered the PEOC at 9:20, Cheney was already there. *The 9/11 Commission Report,* however, claimed that Cheney did not enter the PEOC until "shortly before 10:00, perhaps at 9:58." Mineta's testimony was simply omitted from the final report of the Zelikow-led 9/11 Commission. Why would the Commission go to such lengths—telling an obvious lie and omitting publicly available evidence—to conceal the true time of Cheney's entry into the PEOC?

One possible reason would involve the testimony of Mineta, who explained that, "during the time that the airplane was coming in to the Pentagon, there was a young man who would come in and say to the Vice President, 'the plane is 50 miles out, the plane is 30 miles out.'" And when it got down to "the plane is 10 miles out," the young man also said to the Vice President, "Do the orders still stand?" And the Vice President . . . said, "Of course the orders still stand. Have you heard anything to the contrary?"

Mineta reported that this conversation occurred at about 9:25 or 9:26 a.m. Former Secretary of Defense Donald Rumsfeld's spokesman, in explaining why the Pentagon was not evacuated before it was struck, claimed that "[t]he Pentagon was simply not aware that this aircraft was coming our way." The 9/11 Commission supported this claim, alleging that there was no warning about an unidentified aircraft heading toward Washington until 9:36 a.m. and hence only "one or two minutes" before the Pentagon was struck at 9:38 a.m. Mineta's account, however, says that Cheney knew about an approaching aircraft more than ten minutes earlier. There would have been over twelve minutes for the Pentagon to be evacuated; 125 lives could have been saved.

Mineta's account also implies that Cheney had issued stand-down orders. Mineta himself did not make this allegation, saying instead that he assumed "the orders" were to have the plane shot down. But that interpretation does not fit what actually happened—the aircraft was *not* shot down. It would also make the story unintelligible: the young man's question whether the orders still stood would not make sense unless they were orders to do something unexpected—*not* to shoot the aircraft down. By omitting Mineta's testimony and stating that Cheney did not enter the PEOC until almost 10:00 a.m., the 9/11 Commission implied that Cheney could not have given a stand-down order to allow an aircraft to strike the Pentagon.

The full brazenness of the Commission's lie is illustrated by the fact that it contradicts Cheney's own account, which can still be read on the White House Website. Speaking on NBC's "Meet the Press" five days after 9/11, Cheney said:

"[A]fter I talked to the president . . . I went down into . . . the Presidential Emergency Operations Center . . . [W]hen I arrived there within a short order, we had word the Pentagon's been hit." So he got there, as Mineta said, some time *before* the Pentagon was struck, not twenty minutes afterwards.

The lie about Cheney's entry into the PEOC was also important to the controversy over whether the U.S. military shot down Flight 93. The 9/11 Commission, simply ignoring a vast amount of evidence that the plane had been shot down, supported the official claim that it was not by contending that Cheney, not having arrived at the PEOC until almost 10:00, did not issue the shoot down order until after 10:10—which would have been seven or more minutes *after* Flight 93 had crashed (at 10:03). But in addition to the evidence that Cheney had been in the PEOC since about 9:15, we also have evidence—including statements from Richard Clarke, who was a National Security Council advisor at the time, and Colonel Robert Marr, the head of NORAD's northeast sector (NEADS)—that Cheney's shoot-down order was issued *well before* 10:00 a.m.

The 9/11 Commission's obvious lies about Cheney's activities give reason to suspect that, under the leadership of Philip Zelikow, it was trying to conceal Cheney's responsibility for the Pentagon strike and the downing of Flight 93.

VI. Did the Bush Administration Have Motives for Orchestrating the 9/11 Attacks?

When prosecuting attorneys seek to prove the culpability of a defendant, they have to show "means, motive, and opportunity." It is clear that the Bush administration had the means and the opportunity to orchestrate the events of 9/11. Of the several motives high officials in the administration would have had, I will mention three:

1) *Afghanistan*: Zbigniew Brzezinski's 1997 book, *The Grand Chessboard*, said that establishing military bases in Central Asia would be crucial for maintaining "American primacy," partly because of the huge oil reserves around the Caspian Sea. But American democracy, he added, "is inimical to imperial mobilization," which requires "economic self-denial (that is, defense spending) and . . . human sacrifice (casualties even among professional soldiers)." Explaining that the public had "supported America's engagement in World War II largely because of the shock effect of the Japanese attack on Pearl Harbor," Brzezinski suggested that Americans would support the needed military operations in Central Asia only "in the circumstance of a truly massive and widely perceived direct external threat."

Support for these operations was generated by the 9/11 attacks plus the claim by the Bush-Cheney administration that these attacks had been planned in Afghanistan by Osama bin Laden. But the administration refused to provide any proof for this claim, and even the FBI admits that it is not based on any "hard evidence."

A more specific motivation was provided by the "pipeline war." The Bush administration supported UNOCAL's plan to build an oil-and-gas pipeline through Afghanistan, but the Taliban, being unable to provide sufficient security, had become regarded as an obstacle. In a July 2001 meeting in Berlin, representatives of the administration, trying to get the Taliban to share power with other factions, reportedly said, "Either you accept our offer of a carpet of gold, or we bury you under a carpet of bombs." When the Taliban refused, the Americans reportedly said that "military action against Afghanistan would go ahead . . . before the snows started falling in Afghanistan, by the middle of October at the latest." The attack began on October 7.

2) *Iraq*: Key members of the Bush-Cheney administration had in the late 1990s been active members of the Project for the New American Century (PNAC), which advocated attacking Iraq to remove Saddam Hussein, establish a strong military presence, and control the oil. PNAC's *Rebuilding America's Defenses*, released late in 2000, reiterated this goal. Immediately upon taking office, both Paul O'Neill and Richard Clarke have revealed, the Bush administration was obsessed with going after Saddam. The only question was "finding a way to do it," as O'Neill put it. "The terrorist attacks of September 11," said Bob Woodward, "gave the U.S. a new window to go after Hussein." Although no Iraqis were among the alleged hijackers, the Bush administration was able to use 9/11 as a pretext to attack Iraq. Given the state of fear created in the American psyche by 9/11, the administration needed only to fabricate evidence that Saddam was acquiring nuclear weapons while also suggesting that he *had* been involved in 9/11.

3) *Increased Military Spending*: PNAC wanted to increase America's military superiority sufficiently to establish a global *Pax Americana*. After saying that this *Pax Americana* "must have a secure foundation on unquestioned U.S. military preeminence" and that such preeminence will require a technological transformation of the US military, PNAC added that this process of transformation will "likely be a long one, absent some catastrophic and catalyzing event—like a new Pearl Harbor." When 9/11 came, it was treated as "the Pearl Harbor of the 21st century" and described by several members of the Bush administration as providing "opportunities."

The Preeminent Importance of 9/11

The above evidence, plus the fact that all the "evidence" that seems to implicate the alleged hijackers, such as cell phone calls, airport photos, and discovered luggage and passports, appears to have been fabricated, leads to the conclusion that 9/11 was a false-flag operation orchestrated by the Bush administration for primarily imperial reasons.

If this conclusion is correct, then exposing the falsity of the official account of 9/11 should be high on the agenda of everyone committed to reversing the present policies of the U.S. government, for at least three reasons.

First, 9/11 has provided the pretext for most of the destructive policies of the Bush administration since that day. When any objection is raised to these policies—from illegal invasions, to torture, to illegal spying, to weaponizing space, to talk of a nuclear first strike—the answer is always the same: "The critics fail to understand that the world changed on 9/11." Until the truth about 9/11 is exposed, it will remain a blank check for virtually anything desired by this administration.

Second, 9/11 as an inside job goes far beyond any "high crimes and misdemeanors" previously cited as cause for impeaching a president. The attacks constitute treason, as defined by Article 3 of the U.S. Constitution. If we fail to expose and prosecute this treason, there is little hope for the survival of the democratic forms we still have.

Third, the project of creating an American empire of truly global scope has been a long and bipartisan project. The replacement of the Bush administration by Democratic leadership for some reason other than 9/11 would likely result in a reversion to the subtler, more sophisticated, and hence more effective form of imperialism that the United States previously exercised.

What needs to be publicly recognized is that this project of global domination is propelled by a fanaticism based on a deeply perverted value system. Those who read books and magazines about U.S. imperialism know that there has long been abundant evidence for this assessment. But the public revelation of the truth about 9/11 could have an educational value extending far beyond the circles of those who read policy-oriented books and magazines. If Americans came to see that the attacks of 9/11 were, in the minds of those who planned them, *justified* by the goal of creating an all-encompassing empire, this realization could lead to widespread revulsion against the goal itself and the values implicit in it—values that are diametrically opposed to basic values embedded in all the world's religions and ethical systems.

David Ray Griffin is professor emeritus of philosophy of religion and theology at Claremont School of Theology. He has published thirty-two books, including The American Empire *and* The Commonwealth of God.

Professors of Paranoia?

By John Gravois
Chronicle of Higher Education, June 23, 2006

Nearly five years have gone by since it happened. The trial of Zacarias Moussaoui is over. Construction of the Freedom Tower just began. Oliver Stone's movie about the attacks is due out in theaters soon. And colleges are offering degrees in homeland-security management. The post-9/11 era is barreling along.

And yet a whole subculture is still stuck at that first morning. They are playing and replaying the footage of the disaster, looking for clues that it was an "inside job." They feel sure the post-9/11 era is built on a lie.

In recent months, interest in September 11-conspiracy theories has surged. Since January, traffic to the major conspiracy Web sites has increased steadily. The number of blogs that mention "9/11" and "conspiracy" each day has climbed from a handful to over a hundred.

Why now?

Oddly enough, the answer lies with a soft-spoken physicist from Brigham Young University named Steven E. Jones, a devout Mormon and, until recently, a faithful supporter of George W. Bush.

Last November Mr. Jones posted a paper online advancing the hypothesis that the airplanes Americans saw crashing into the twin towers were not sufficient to cause their collapse, and that the towers had to have been brought down in a controlled demolition. Now he is the best hope of a movement that seeks to convince the rest of America that elements of the government are guilty of mass murder on their own soil.

His paper—written by an actual professor who works at an actual research university—has made him a celebrity in the conspiracy universe. He is now co-chairman of a group called the Scholars for 9/11 Truth, which includes about 50 professors—more in the humanities than in the sciences—from institutions like Clemson University, the University of Minnesota, and the University of Wisconsin.

But even as Mr. Jones's title and academic credentials give hope to the conspiracy theorists, his role in the movement may undermine those same credentials. What happens when science tries to function in a fringe crusade?

It was a gorgeous early June day in Chicago. Jetliners taking off from O'Hare were throwing clean, quick shadows on the ground. And a tall, biblically hairy man was weaving his way through the crowded first floor of the airport Embassy Suites hotel wearing a black T-shirt with Steven Jones's picture on it.

On this Friday afternoon, 500 conspiracy theorists descended on the Embassy Suites for a conference called "9/11: Revealing the Truth—Reclaiming Our Future." It was the most substantial gathering of the "9/11 truth movement," as the conspiracy theorists call themselves, to date. And for Mr. Jones, it was a coming out of sorts.

The 57-year-old professor, who has a long history of research in the controversial field of cold fusion, had not ventured outside Utah since he first posted his paper about the collapses seven months before. He was by now a huge figure in the movement—he was slated to deliver a keynote address that night—but he had not actually met many people involved, not even his co-chairman of Scholars for 9/11 Truth. On the airport shuttle ride to the hotel, he was almost sheepish. "This is one of the more unusual conferences I've been to," he said. "I don't know quite what to expect."

He probably did not know to expect that two journalists from Finnish TV would accost him at the hotel before he made it to the front desk. Or that the conference would draw so heavily on references to *The Matrix*.

That night, the first keynote address was delivered by Alex Jones (no relation to Steven), a radio personality from Austin, Tex., who has developed a cult following by railing against the New World Order. He is a bellicose, boyish-looking man with a voice that makes him sound like a cross between a preacher and an announcer at a cage wrestling match.

"It energizes my soul at its very core to be here with so many like-minded people," he began, "defending the very soul of humanity against the parasitic controllers of this world government, who are orchestrating terror attacks as a pretext to sell us into even greater slavery."

"If they think they're gonna get away with declaring war on humanity," he thundered, "they've got another think coming!"

The audience was a mix of rangy, long-haired men with pale complexions, suntanned guys with broad arms and mustaches, women with teased bangs, serious-looking youngsters wearing backpacks and didactic T-shirts, and elderly people with dreadlocks. But everyone seemed to get behind what Alex Jones had just said. In fact, they went absolutely wild with cheers.

Alex Jones then plunged into a history of what he called "government-sponsored terror." In this category, he included the Reichstag fire of 1933, the sinking of the USS *Maine*, the Gulf of Tonkin incident, and a shadowy, never-executed 1962 plan called Operation Northwoods, in which the Joint Chiefs of Staff approved false terror attacks on American soil to provoke war with Cuba.

Then he got to matters closer at hand. He mentioned the Project for the New American Century, the think tank of prominent neoconservatives that wrote a report in 2000 called "Rebuilding America's Defenses," which includes a line that many 9/11 Truthers, as they call themselves, know by heart: "The process of transformation, even if it brings revolutionary change, is likely to be a long one, absent some catastrophic and catalyzing event—like a new Pearl Harbor."

To Alex Jones and to those in the audience, this was as good as finding the plans for September 11 in the neoconservatives' desk drawers.

"These people are psychopathic predators," Alex Jones rumbled. "They've got to be met head on!" The audience cheered like it was ready to tar and feather someone.

When Alex Jones finished, it was Steven Jones's turn to speak. The audience gave the professor a standing ovation before he had even said a word.

He stepped up to the podium in a tweed jacket. He had a kind face, a round nose, and hair somewhere between corn-silk blond and pale gray. He began to speak. His voice was reedy and slightly nasal. Someone yelled: "Louder!"

One of the most common intuitive problems people have with conspiracy theories is that they require positing such complicated webs of secret actions. If the twin towers fell in a carefully orchestrated demolition shortly after being hit by planes, who set the charges? Who did the planning? And how could hundreds, if not thousands of people complicit in the murder of their own countrymen keep quiet? Usually, Occam's razor intervenes.

Another common problem with conspiracy theories is that they tend to impute cartoonish motives to "them"—the elites who operate in the shadows. The end result often feels like a heavily plotted movie whose characters do not ring true

Then there are other cognitive Do Not Enter signs: When history ceases to resemble a train of conflicts and ambiguities and becomes instead a series of disinformation campaigns, you sense that a basic self-correcting mechanism of thought has been disabled. A bridge is out, and paranoia yawns below.

Steven Jones's contribution to the September 11 conspiracy movement is that he avoids these problems—or at least holds them at bay—by just talking about physics.

Like many others in the movement, Mr. Jones sees a number of "red flags" in the way the buildings fell. Why did the towers collapse at speeds close to the rate of free fall? Why did they fall straight down, instead of toppling over? Why did World Trade Center 7, a 47-story high-rise that was never hit by a plane, suddenly collapse in the same fashion—fast and straight down—on the evening of September 11?

A rather hefty report by the National Institute of Standards and Technology explains how high-temperature fires started by jet fuel caused the buildings' outer columns to bow in, leading to the buildings' collapse. But the conspiracy theorists complain that the report stops short of showing computer models of the collapses.

Mr. Jones's hypothesis is that the buildings were taken down with preplanted thermite—a mixture of iron oxide and aluminum powder that burns hot enough to vaporize steel when it is ignited. Mr. Jones says that this hypothesis offers the most elegant explanation for the manner in which the buildings collapsed. He says it best explains various anecdotal accounts that molten metal remained pooled in the debris piles of the buildings for weeks. And he says it offers the only satisfying explanation for a weird sight captured in video footage of the south tower just before its collapse.

Near a corner of the south tower, at around 9:50 a.m., a cascade of a yellow-hot substance started spewing out of the building. The National Institute of Standards and Technology says in its report that the substance was most likely molten aluminum from the airplane fuselage. But Mr. Jones points out that aluminum near its melting point is a pale-silver color, not yellow. By his reckoning, then, that spew is a thermite reaction in plain sight.

Mr. Jones is petitioning Congress to release the raw data that went into the National Institute of Standards and Technology report. "If they just give us the data," he says, "we'll take it from there."

Soon after Mr. Jones posted his paper online, the physics department at Brigham Young moved to distance itself from his work. The department released a statement saying that it was "not convinced that his analyses and hypotheses have been submitted to relevant scientific venues that would ensure rigorous technical peer review." (Mr. Jones's paper has been peer-reviewed by two physicists and two other scholars for publication in a book called *9/11 and American Empire: Intellectuals Speak Out*, from Olive Branch Press.)

The Brigham Young college of engineering issued an even stronger statement on its Web site. "The structural engineering faculty," it read, "do not support the hypotheses of Professor Jones." However, his supporters complain, none of Mr. Jones's critics at Brigham Young have dealt with his points directly.

While there are a handful of Web sites that seek to debunk the claims of Mr. Jones and others in the movement, most mainstream scientists, in fact, have not seen fit to engage them.

"There's nothing to debunk," says Zdenek P. Bazant, a professor of civil and environmental engineering at Northwestern University and the author of the first peer-reviewed paper on the World Trade Center collapses.

"It's a non-issue," says Sivaraj Shyam-Sunder, a lead investigator for the National Institute of Standards and Technology's study of the collapses.

Ross B. Corotis, a professor of civil engineering at the University of Colorado at Boulder and a member of the editorial board at the journal *Structural Safety*, says that most engineers are pretty settled on what happened at the World Trade Center. "There's not really disagreement as to what happened for 99 percent of the details," he says.

Thomas W. Eagar is one scientist who has paid some attention to the demolition hypothesis—albeit grudgingly. A materials engineer at the Massachusetts Institute of Technology, Mr. Eagar wrote one of the early papers on the buildings' collapses, which later became the basis for a documentary on PBS. That marked him for scrutiny and attack from conspiracy theorists. For a time, he says, he was receiving one or two angry e-mail messages each week, many accusing him of being a government shill. When Mr. Jones's paper came out, the nasty messages increased to one or two per day.

So Mr. Eagar has become reluctantly familiar with Mr. Jones's hypothesis, and he is not impressed. For example, he says, the cascade of yellow-hot particles coming out of the south tower could be any number of things: a butane can igniting, sparks from an electrical arc, molten aluminum and water forming a hydrogen reaction—or, perhaps most likely, a spontaneous, completely accidental thermite reaction.

Occasionally, he says, given enough mingled surface area, molten aluminum and rust can react violently, à la thermite. Given that there probably was plenty of molten aluminum from the plane wreckage in that building, Mr. Eagar says, it is entirely possible that this is what happened.

Others have brought up this notion as well, so Mr. Jones has carried out experiments in his lab trying to get small quantities of molten aluminum to react with rust. He has not witnessed the reaction and so rules it out. But Mr. Eagar says this is just a red herring: Accidental thermite reactions are a well-known phenomenon, he says. It just takes a lot of exposed surface area for the reaction to start.

Still, Mr. Eagar does not care to respond formally to Mr. Jones or the conspiracy movement. "I don't see any point in engaging them," he says.

Hence, in the world of mainstream science, Mr. Jones's hypothesis is more or less dead on the vine. But in the world of 9/11 Truth, it has seeded a whole garden of theories.

"Steven Jones! Who'd like Steven Jones!" hollered a man outside the main convention room as people exited Mr. Jones's speech. "Dripping metal! Steven Jones!"

He was selling DVD's of a speech Mr. Jones gave a few months earlier in Utah.

Another man walked by on the conference floor and pointed to a picture of the yellow-hot spew from the south tower. "There's your smoking gun," he said, to another conferencegoer.

The evening ended just after midnight, with the 9/11 Truthers chanting en masse in the conference hall, "We're mad as hell, and we're not gonna take it anymore."

"We have all kinds of weird conferences," said the concierge the next morning. "I mean, not to say this is weird. Last year we had one that was all tall people."

"For a while there, people who wanted to dismiss us could say, 'Well, it's just a bunch of crazies on the Internet,'" says David Ray Griffin, a well-known theologian and philosopher and a prominent member of Scholars for 9/11 Truth. "The very existence of the organization has added credibility," he said.

By many accounts, scholarly contributions to the movement began with Mr. Griffin, who retired from the Claremont School of Theology in 2004. About a year and a half after September 11, Mr. Griffin began reading books and Web sites arguing that the U.S. government was complicit in the attacks. Eventually, they won him over.

That left him feeling a peculiar sense of obligation, he says. The official story had all the voices of authority on its side, and the case for government complicity in the attacks had no real standing. "It was not reaching a really wide audience," he says.

So Mr. Griffin wrote his own book, trading on his authority as an academic. He called it *The New Pearl Harbor*. It was mostly just a synthesis of all the material he had read, tidied up by a philosopher's rhetorical skills.

When it was finished, he aggressively pursued blurbs for the book jacket—and eventually scored one from Howard Zinn, the radical professor emeritus of political science at Boston University. Mr. Zinn said the book was "the most persuasive argument I have seen for further investigation on the Bush administration's relationship to that historic and troubling event."

It went on to become one of the most successful books on the purported conspiracy.

"There's a big chasm between those who are even willing to entertain the hypothesis enough to look at the evidence and those who aren't," Mr. Griffin says. "The only way to overcome that is by appeal to authority."

"You can't just appeal in terms of straight argument," he says.

> *"The degree of perfidy involved here is so great, that in the time of Aeschylus, Sophocles, and Euripides, frenzied mobs would have dragged these men out of their beds in the middle of the night and ripped them to shreds!"—James H. Fetzer*

"You've got to do something to break through, to get people to look at the evidence."

Now that the movement has progressed, and more voices of authority have joined, Mr. Griffin is more convinced than ever.

"I think now it's just irrefutable," he says. People who don't question the official story, he says, are "just whistling in the dark."

James H. Fetzer, the co-chairman of Scholars for 9/11 Truth, retired last month from his post as a distinguished McKnight university professor of philosophy at the University of Minnesota at Duluth. He wanted to focus more on the movement. "Whether there's another critical-thinking course being taught at the University of Minnesota is relatively trivial," he says, "compared to this."

Mr. Fetzer, a voluble, impassioned man who often speaks in long paragraphs, is no stranger to conspiracy theory. Before September 11, he had a side career investigating the assassination of President John F. Kennedy. But the issues surrounding the Scholars for 9/11 Truth are far more acute, he thinks. In Mr. Fetzer's mind, the country is in a state of dire emergency.

Hence, it does not much bother Mr. Fetzer that outside scientists have largely refrained from tackling the group's arguments. "I don't think it's a problem," he says, "because we have so much competence and expertise among ourselves."

911myths.com, a Web site run by a software developer in England, is one of the few venues that offers a running scrutiny of the various claims and arguments coming out of the 9/11 Truth movement. Mr. Fetzer has heard of 911myths.com, but he has never visited the site.

"I have been dealing with disinformation and phony stories about the death of JFK for all these years. There's a huge amount of phoniness out there," he says. "You have to be very selective in how you approach these things."

"I can assure you the things I'm telling you about 9/11 have objective scientific status," he says. 911myths.com, he says, "is going to be built on either fabricated evidence, or disregard of the real evidence, or violations of the principles of scientific reasoning."

"They cannot be right," he says.

On the second afternoon of the conference, Mr. Fetzer gave a speech in one of the hotel salons to a standing-room-only crowd. It began like an introductory lecture in moral philosophy he might have given at the University of Minnesota. He discussed different theories for the origins of right and wrong—moral egoism, utilitarianism, deontological moral rights. Then he came to the emergency.

"The threat we face," he said, is "imminent and ominous." He recommended arming the citizenry.

During the question-and-answer session, an audience member asked whether there might be a way to capture a TV station, to get the word out about September 11. Mr. Fetzer upped the ante on the idea.

"Let me tell you, for years, I've been waiting for there to be a military coup to depose these traitors," he said from the podium.

"Yeah!" shouted some men in the audience.

"There actually was one weekend," Mr. Fetzer went on, "where I said to myself, my God, it's going to happen this weekend, and I'm going to wake up and they will have taken these guys off in chains."

His voice was building. "Listen to me," he said. "The degree of perfidy involved here is so great, that in the time of Aeschylus, Sophocles, and Euripides, frenzied mobs would have dragged these men out of their beds in the middle of the night and ripped them to shreds!"

"Yeah!" cried a chorus of voices in the audience. "Yeah!"

Amid the cheers and applause that swept the room, there was Steven Jones, sitting quietly in a chair against the wall. He had one leg crossed over the other, and he was looking around at the cheering audience with a vaguely uncomfortable smile on his face, holding his foot in his hands.

500 Conspiracy Buffs Meet to Seek the Truth of 9/11

By Alan Feuer
New York Times, June 5, 2006

In the ballroom foyer of the Embassy Suites Hotel, the two-day International Education and Strategy Conference for 9/11 Truth was off to a rollicking start.

In Salon Four, there was a presentation under way on the attack in Oklahoma City, while in the room next door, the splintered factions of the movement were asked—for sake of unity—to seek a common goal.

In the foyer, there were stick-pins for sale ("More gin, less Rummy"), and in the lecture halls discussions of the melting point of steel. "It's all documented," people said. Or: "The mass media is mass deception." Or, as strangers from the Internet shook hands: "Great to meet you. Love the work."

Such was the coming-out for the movement known as "9/11 Truth," a society of skeptics and scientists who believe the government was complicit in the terrorist attacks. In colleges and chat rooms on the Internet, this band of disbelievers has been trying for years to prove that 9/11 was an inside job.

Whatever one thinks of the claim that the state would plan, then execute, a scheme to murder thousands of its own, there was something to the fact that more than 500 people—from Italy to Northern California—gathered for the weekend at a major chain hotel near the runways of O'Hare International. It was, in tone, half trade show, half political convention. There were talks on the Reichstag fire and the sinking of the Battleship *Maine* as precedents for 9/11. There were speeches by the lawyer for James Earl Ray, who claimed that a military conspiracy killed the Rev. Dr. Martin Luther King, and by a former operative for the British secret service, MI5.

"We feel at this point we've done a lot of solid research, but the American public still is not informed," said Michael Berger, press director for 911Truth.org, which sponsored the event. "We had to come up with a disciplined approach to get it out."

Mr. Berger, 40, is typical of 9/11 Truthers—a group that, in its rank and file, includes professors, chain-saw operators, mothers, engineers, activists, used-book sellers, pizza deliverymen, college students, a former fringe candidate for United States Senate and a long-haired fellow named hummux (pronounced who-mook) who, on and off, lived in a cave for 15 years.

The former owner of a recycling plant outside St. Louis, Mr. Berger joined the movement when he grew skeptical of why the 9/11 Commission had failed, to his

Beginning in February 2010, I obtained a convenience sample of 60 members of the Facebook group for the chapter. Total membership of the group fluctuates regularly. On July 31, 2010, when this portion of the study was finalized, membership was 508. Members were not sampled in any systematic fashion and these 60 people represent names that appeared at the top of a randomized membership menu when it was requested from Facebook. Of these, 58 useful Facebook profiles were obtained.

The high commitment (HC) believers are members of WAC who took part in a series of 9/11-related demonstrations in New York City held in 2009. The first of these was the 9/11 memorial demonstration held to commemorate the September 11 attacks. The second demonstration held on September 27, 2009 was organized to draw attention to a petition the group supported calling for a new investigation into the 9/11 attacks. The petition is referred to as NYCCAN.[7]

Both of these demonstrations were recorded at the time, and many photos and videos of the event were posted on individual Facebook accounts and on YouTube. WAC videos of the memorial demonstration were taken in a way that made counting attendance very difficult. My estimate of the clearest videos, which are no longer available on YouTube, was that slightly more than 100 people attended. The NYCCAN demonstration was filmed by a member of James Randi Educational Foundation Forum and is still posted on YouTube.[8] While it is difficult to distinguish protestors from pedestrians, I have counted the demonstration several times and arrived at approximately the same number as I obtained for the 9/11 memorial demonstration—slightly more than 100.

In addition, Facebook accounts of participants have featured photographs from the two events with the names of other participants labeled. By comparing the labeled names found on different Facebook accounts, I was able to recover a total of 53 names for people who attended the two events. Fifty-two (52) of these names appeared in photos of both demonstrations. Only one person appeared in a photo of the NYCCAN demonstration but not a photo of the 9/11 memorial demonstration, leading me to believe that participation was almost identical. I was then able to gather publicly available background information about the participants from their Facebook accounts.

Results

The overwhelming majority of both groups were male. Seventy-nine percent of the LC (n = 45) and 75% of HC (n = 40) were male. Age could be identified for 49 of the LC and 28 of the HC believers. The mean age of participants was 27.4 years and 28.0 years, respectively. The median age was not substantially different.

Employment information for 21 members of the LC group was obtained. Six members of the LC group identified themselves as students. Three are currently still in high school. At least one appears to be a part-time student. Two members described themselves as self-employed. Only 3 of the surveyed members reported clearly professional occupations, identifying themselves as teacher, pharmacist and lab manager. The remaining members (12) appeared to be marginally employed, reporting such jobs as drivers, clerks, phone bank operators, or simply, "have 5 part-time jobs."

Employment was rarely reported for members of the HC group, although they did claim a substantial level of education. Two HC members reported graduate degrees and several stated having graduated from top-ranked schools. Results from the HC point to a significant level of computer sophistication. One member identified himself as the owner of a computer store. Three others reported education and employment in computer-related fields. This may explain the large number of high quality videos the group is able to place on the Internet.

Four members of the LC group stated their religion as Muslim. It's not clear if this reflects a larger pattern of belief in 9/11 conspiracies or WAC membership, or is the result of the influence of a prominent member of the group who also claims to be Muslim. Identified religious affiliation of the HC group was almost completely Christian. The only identified Muslim in the HC group is also a member of the LC group. In fact, the degree of Christian affiliation claimed by the HC group was substantial. Seven of the HC group either endorsed a Christian-themed Facebook group or identified themselves as Christians. Three others are members of the Constitution Party, which has as its platform to "restore American jurisprudence to its Biblical foundations."[9] One member of the HC group has run for public office with the Constitution Party.

While Facebook does not require members to post political information, many members of the LC group did so. In my sample, I was able to recover information about the political affiliation of 7 members. The labels used by members include "Constitutionalist," "Christian Constitutional Party," and "member of the Tea Party." One member who identified himself as a "libertarian Mormon" had pictures of himself using firearms posted in his profile. No surveyed member identified with a mainstream political party or a moderate political philosophy, such as liberal or conservative. The HC group was much more likely to identify a political direction or affiliation. By far the strongest affiliation was with the Libertarian Ron Paul. Twenty-two (22) members of the HC group belonged to Facebook groups that support Ron Paul, including a substantial number who had photographs of themselves with Ron Paul posted in their Facebook account. Two additional members described themselves as "paleo-conservative." Two (2) identified themselves as "tea party members" and 1 as a "birther." As noted above, 3 HC group members belong to the Constitution Party which, in addition to its position on separation of Church and State, opposes gun control and public health insurance, and advocates an isolationist foreign policy. Almost every HC group member belonged to groups that support 2 members of WAC who are Libertarian Party candidates in New York.

The Facebook profiles of many HC group members identified many other political causes and affiliations. These included pro-gun groups, the John Birch Society, or pro-life groups. Only one member of the HC group described herself as "liberal," making her the only person in the total 111 surveyed members to do so.

One unexpected result of this study was the attrition rate of members. The complete study covered almost an entire year. During this time, some members dropped out of each group. While verifying information, I discovered that several members whose profiles I had surveyed earlier in the year had removed their Facebook profiles. In the LC group, I was able to confirm that one professionally employed member and another who worked in a high profile company had removed their membership, not just from WAC, but completely from Facebook. The HC group showed much stronger stability. Two members of the HC group have also become impossible to reach through Facebook, although I believe they are still active in WAC. An additional member, who was recently married, has become much more actively involved in the political campaign of Ron Paul and subsequently less involved in WAC/9/11 conspiracy activities.

Interpretation

This paper reports on a study of members in a group that advocates 9/11 conspiracy. It examined members who demonstrated different levels of commitment to the belief. A low commitment group was marginally involved in promoting the idea, having only joined a Facebook group. A high commitment group, on the other hand, was composed of members involved in a public demonstration of this belief. Despite the differences in their level of commitment to the idea, both groups were very similar in composition.

Both groups were overwhelmingly young males. The low commitment group contained many marginally employed members. Members with better jobs seemed to be drifting away. The highly committed group contained more well-educated members and, in this group, drifting away seemed connected to growing family commitments. It is not clear from this analysis if education levels reflect characteristics of believers in 9/11 conspiracies or differences between followers and their leadership. Both groups were largely affiliated with a formalized organization that has a name (We Are Change) and leadership positions with titles. The deeper involvement of a more educated group may be a result of qualification and preparation for leadership roles.

More significant results pertained to political affiliations. Earlier research on 9/11 conspiracies described the belief as appealing to supporters of the Democratic Party. In addition, discussions I have seen on such venues as the James Randi Educational Foundation Forum describe 9/11 conspiracy as a non-partisan issue with no specific appeal to either the left or right. This was not confirmed by my samples. The individuals surveyed here were overwhelmingly involved in right-wing politics, particularly with Ron Paul, the Constitution Party and the Libertarian Party.

What has happened to Democrats and other left-wing proponents of 9/11 conspiracies? Several contacts who read earlier drafts of this manuscript suggested they are still around but belong to other 9/11 conspiracy groups, such as Architects and Engineers for 9/11 Truth[10] and thus were not counted in my study. While this is possible, another explanation seems more likely. Democratic and left-wing supporters have generally lost interest or even forgotten their commitment to 9/11 conspiracies now that Barack Obama is in the White House. Many prominent

Hollywood personalities were among the most vocal of the original voices challenging government explanations for the events of September 11. For example, Barbra Streisand and particularly her husband Josh Brolin[11], as well as Sean Penn[12] and Michael Moore[13] are all on record as doubting official explanations for the 9/11 attacks originating from the Bush Administration. Despite their vocal opposition, I have been unable to find any statements made by them about 9/11 since the 2008 Presidential election.

There are other reasons to believe the left has become inconsequential to 9/11 conspiracy groups. We Are Change appears to be the only 9/11 conspiracy organization able to mount significant public demonstrations. Increasingly individuals interested in speaking on this topic must align themselves with WAC to attract an audience. Outside of Hollywood, only a few prominent left-wing figures that have built reputations around the concept of a 9/11 conspiracy seem unwilling to give it up. They can now be found speaking at WAC sponsored events. Sander Hicks,[14] Cynthia McKinney,[15] and Cindy Sheehan[16] are among the prominent left-wing supporters of a 9/11 conspiracy who remain vocal. The last two spoke at the 9/11 memorial organized by WAC in 2010. Sander Hick's recent attempt to inaugurate a new political party based around 9/11 conspiracy claims was attended by prominent members of We Are Change, and the party's website states the event was co-hosted by the group.[17]

Much of the confusion found among observers of the 9/11 conspiracy movement about the political affiliation of its members may stem from the fact that movement members have an orientation that falls outside the traditional two party political structure of the United States. None of those surveyed in this study, either in the high or the low commitment group, reported affiliation with either of the major parties. Many reported seeing little difference between the two because both were seen as clearly involved in the secretive New World Order and subsequently the government conspiracy that destroyed the World Trade Center buildings. As such, it may be difficult for some to accurately label the situation. Those involved with 9/11 conspiracy beliefs, however, identify with labels and personalities that clearly affiliate them as right-wing.

The patterns found in this data do not support the contention that affiliation with the Democratic Party predicts belief in 9/11 conspiracy theories. While it is understandable that Democrats could have supported a conspiracy theory that placed a Republican president at the center, with the election of a Democratic president, a 9/11 conspiracy has disappeared as an important issue for all but the most committed. Even relatively low commitment to 9/11 conspiracy theories is associated with affiliations to groups and individuals with extreme right-wing political beliefs. Greater commitment found a correspondingly larger affiliation to these ideas with no meaningful exception to this pattern. It would appear that patterns of belief in 9/11 conspiracies have changed dramatically with the changing political landscape of America, and now belief is localized almost exclusively among right-wing supporters of parties and personalities outside traditional bipartisan politics.

Notes

1. Most Americans Reject 9/11 Conspiracy Theories. Available at: http://www.angus-reid.com/polls/38598/most_americans_reject_9_11_conspiracy_theories/

2. A summary of polls about 9/11 conspiracy beliefs can be found on Wikipedia. September 11 Attacks Opinion Polls, Available at: http://en.wlkipedia.org/wiki/September_11_attacks_opinion_polls

3. Stempel, C., T. Hargrove, and G. H. Stempel III. 2007. "Media Use, Social Structure and Belief in 9/11 Conspiracy Theories." *Journalism and Mass Communication Quarterly* 84: 353–372.

4. Ibid, p. 1.

5. The 15% of Americans willing to endorse belief in a 9/11 conspiracy is similar to the number stating that President Obama was not born in the United States, although the latter may be even higher: "'Birther' Poll Shows That More Than a Quarter of Americans Think Obama Was Not Born in The U.S." Huffington Post August 8, 2010. Available at: http://www.huffin-gtonpost.com/2010/08/05/birther-poll-shows-that-m_n_670435.html. In addition, it is difficult to tell how many of these respondents are a part of the general confusion concerning the facts of the 9/11 attacks. For example, see: Misconceptions on 9/11 Persist in U.S., Canada. Available at: http://www.angus-reid.com/polls/35980/misconceptions_on_9_11_persis t_in_us_canada/

6. Jacobson, M. 2006. "The Ground Zero Grassy Knoll." New York, March 19. Available at: http://nymag.com/news/features/16464/ See also: Mole, P. 2006. "9/11 Truth Movement in Perspective." Skeptic. Available at: http://www.skeptic.com/eskeptic/06-09-11/

7. NYCCAN Vote for Accountability. Available at: http://www.nyccan.org/

8. NYCCAN March Sep 27, 2009—The smallest protest in NYC, ever. Available at: http://www.youtube.com/watch?v=AwjKDmA7Gi4

9. Constitution Party Platform. Available at: http://www.constitutionparty.com/party_platform.php#Preamble

10. Architects and Engineers for 9/11 Truth. Available at: http://www.ae911truth.org/

11. James Brolin follows David Lynch to publicly doubt 9/11. Available at: http://www.youtube.com/watch?v=ZthwZF284pc

12. The full range of Sean Penn's beliefs about 9/11 is not clear. He has spoken many times concerning 9/11 and his beliefs in the Bush Administration's involvement, as well as the war in Iraq, for example: "Sean Penn Speaks Out for Impeachment." Tribe January 18, 2007. Available at: http://911truth.tribe.net/thread/c972a66a-69d6-41cf-895e-4152201519 d9 However, it appears that since the election of President Obama in 2008, he has become been conspicuously silent on the issue.

13. Confronting Michael Moore and Amy Goodman with 9/11 Truth P2, Available at: http://www.youtube.com/watch?v=l1gk7iqNksg For a description of the

interview see Aaron Dykes, Michael Moore: 9/11 Could Be Inside Job. http://www.prisonplanet.com/articles/june2007/190607Moore.htm.

14. What's The Truth Party—Sander Hicks. Available at: http://www.sanderhicks.com/truthparty.html

15. In this video, Cynthia McKinney can be seen honoring We Are Change founder Luke Rudkowski. Cynthia McKinney-We are Change meeting. Available at: http://www.youtube.com/watch?v=RI67qPKvStE She also appeared as a speaker at 9/11 memorial organized by We Are Change in 2010.

16. A long list of posts and videos regarding Cindy Sheehan's connections with 9/11 conspiracy claims can be found in the category list "Cindy Sheehan" available at: http://screwloosechange.blogspot.com/search/label/Cindy%20Sheehan

17. For a description of the founding of the Truth Party see: http://www.sanderhicks.com/TGschedule.html

3
Shots in Dallas:
The JFK Assassination

US President John F. Kennedy, his wife Jacqueline, and Texas Governor John Connally shortly before Kennedy's assassination in Dallas.

American Enigma: Lee Harvey Oswald and the JFK Assassination

By Paul McCaffrey

On Friday, November 22, 1963, at approximately 12:30 p.m. (CST), the crack of a rifle rang out across Dealey Plaza in downtown Dallas, Texas. In an instant, the festive mood that reigned among the crowd of onlookers that sunny early afternoon gave way to horror, panic, and disbelief. "My God, they're shooting at the president!" a witness yelled. Riding in a convertible limousine, President John Fitzgerald Kennedy slumped in his seat, shot through the upper back. A moment later, another bullet struck, hitting him in the head. As confusion and fear enveloped the plaza, the president's motorcade sped off to Parkland Hospital, where a team of surgeons tried in vain to save his life. Roman Catholic priests administered last rites, and at 1 p.m. (CST), the president, only forty-six years old, was pronounced dead.

After Kennedy was struck down, suspicion fell on twenty-four-year-old Lee Harvey Oswald, a warehouse worker at the Texas School Book Depository, which overlooked Dealey Plaza and the route of the president's motorcade. Several witnesses claimed to have seen a rifle pointing out of a window of the depository both before and after the shots were fired. Police entered the depository not long after the incident and scoured the building. An officer encountered Oswald in the second-floor cafeteria. On the sixth floor, police found a sniper's nest improvised out of cardboard book cartons. They also located several spent shell casings and a 1940 6.5-millimeter Mannlicher-Carcano bolt-action rifle, which they later determined had been purchased through a mail-order catalog by Oswald under the alias A. Hidell. Earlier that day, Oswald had arrived at work with an awkward paper-wrapped bundle that he claimed contained curtain rods he planned to install in his apartment. The paper wrapping was found near the sniper's nest.

In the minutes after the assassination, before the depository was sealed off by police, Oswald allegedly left the building, possibly running into NBC News reporter Robert MacNeil on his way out. As police interviewed Oswald's coworkers, his absence was noted and he became a wanted man. Across town, at approximately 1:15 p.m., two witnesses observed Oswald shooting down Dallas policeman J. D. Tippit. Dallas officers converged on a movie theater where Oswald had fled after killing Tippit, and following a brief struggle, arrested him.

As the evidence against him piled up, Oswald was charged with the murder of both Officer Tippit and President Kennedy. Still, after two days of interrogation, he admitted nothing. Then, on November 24, 1963, at around 11:21 a.m., as Oswald was being transferred from the Dallas Police Station to the county jail, Jack Ruby, a local nightclub owner, worked his way through the throng of security and press and gunned down Oswald at point-blank range. Television cameras covering Oswald's transfer broadcast the shooting live on television. Rushed to Parkland Hospital, Oswald died soon after his arrival.

In order to determine who was responsible for the president's death and to deal with the onslaught of hearsay and rumor that ensued following the events in Dallas, President Lyndon Baines Johnson, Kennedy's vice president and successor, established the Warren Commission within days of the assassination, on November 29, 1963. Headed by Supreme Court Chief Justice Earl Warren, the commission spent months investigating the crimes, interviewing a number of witnesses and hearing testimony from ballistic experts and other specialists. In September 1964, the commission issued its final report, declaring that Oswald, acting alone, was responsible for the assassination of President Kennedy. Jack Ruby, the commission further concluded, had killed Oswald on his own initiative and without outside help.

The Warren Commission Report was subjected to extensive criticism upon its release, and time has not increased its credibility in the eyes of the public. Citing its failure to investigate a number of captivating leads, the author Norman Mailer wrote that "as inquiry, the Warren Commission's work resembles a dead whale decomposing on a beach." Nevertheless, Mailer himself agreed that the Oswald-lone-gunman theory was the most plausible. In the late 1970s, the US House of Representatives established the Select Committee on Assassinations. One of its tasks was to reinvestigate Kennedy's death. Though it lauded much of the Warren Commission's work, the committee concluded that the assassination was "probably" the result of a conspiracy and that there was evidence to suggest there was a second shooter in Dealey Plaza. A poll conducted in 2003 found that fully seven in ten Americans suspected Kennedy's death was the product of a conspiracy.

The potential culprits to the conspiracy are legion. The veil of suspicion has fallen on the Mafia, Fidel Castro, anti-Castro Cubans, the Soviets, Central Intelligence Agency (CIA) operatives, and political extremists on either the Right or the Left—even Lyndon Johnson has been a suspect. Over the years people have even confessed to shooting Kennedy in Dealey Plaza, among them E. Howard Hunt, one of the Watergate burglars, and Charles Voyde Harrelson, a convicted killer and the father of actor Woody Harrelson. The veracity of their claims, however, is difficult if not impossible to confirm. Those closest to Kennedy were not afraid to draw their own conclusions. Johnson, for example, though he set up the Warren Commission, disagreed with its findings, suspecting that Castro was responsible for Kennedy's murder.

Whatever their final conclusions, those seeking to understand Kennedy's assassination must grapple with one central question: Who was Lee Harvey Oswald, and what motivated him to shoot the president? One of the great enigmas of the twentieth century, Oswald has taken on the amorphous and subjective contours of a national Rorschach test, with Americans are inclined to see in him what they want to see. Indeed, some JFK conspiracists see two of him, suspecting that Oswald in fact had a "double."

Born on October 18, 1939, in New Orleans, Louisiana, Oswald endured a chaotic childhood. His father passed away shortly before his birth, and his mother had difficulty caring for him and his older and half brothers. The family moved frequently, residing in Louisiana, Texas, and New York. While still a toddler, Oswald spent over a year at a New Orleans orphanage, his mother having declared herself unable to provide for her children. After moving to New York City in the early 1950s, Oswald attended school sporadically and often passed his days wandering the Bronx Zoo alone. Picked up by a truant officer, Oswald landed in a juvenile detention center for a time, where psychiatrists noted a variety of psychological problems. But before Oswald received any treatment, his mother opted to take him back to New Orleans. After dropping out of high school, Oswald joined the US Marine Corps at seventeen, despite a pronounced interest in Marxism.

Oswald's service record as a marine appears undistinguished. He received two courts martial, one for assaulting a noncommissioned officer, the other for accidentally shooting himself with an unregistered pistol. Trained as a radar operator, Oswald received a security clearance and was stationed in Japan for part of his enlistment. On September 11, 1959, he applied for and received an early and honorable hardship discharge from active duty, after claiming he was the only source of support for his indigent mother.

Rather than care for his mother, however, Oswald boarded a boat to Europe. After making his way to Moscow, he attempted to renounce his American citizenship and defect. Though given a job and an apartment by the Soviets in Minsk, Oswald grew disenchanted with his new life. He married a Russian woman named Marina in April 1961 but sought to return to the United States soon after. In June 1962, with Marina and their newborn daughter, Oswald arrived in New York. Before long, they reunited with his family in Texas.

Oswald had difficulty readjusting to life in the United States. Unable to hold down a steady job and prone to beating Marina, he often lived apart from his wife and child. On April 10, 1963, Oswald allegedly attempted to assassinate Edwin Walker, a former US Army general who had become a leading right-wing political figure. Sitting at a desk in the study of his Dallas home, Walker narrowly escaped death when the bullet fired at him struck a slat on a windowpane, altering its course just enough to miss him. According to Marina, Oswald came home that night and confessed his crime, and she kept the information to herself. The police never questioned Oswald in connection with the attempted murder.

Settling for a time in New Orleans, Oswald gained some notoriety as a local agitator, canvassing on behalf of a pro-Castro organization, the Fair Play for Cuba Committee (FPCC), albeit without official consent from the FPCC. Once he was arrested for disturbing the peace. In late September 1963, Oswald traveled to Mexico City, where he went to the Cuban and Soviet embassies in hopes of obtaining visas to visit both countries. His requests were denied, and he returned to Texas in early October.

Back in Dallas, Oswald received a lead on a job from Ruth Paine, the woman with whom his wife and daughter were residing. On October 15, 1963, he started working at the Texas School Book Depository. Five days later, his second daughter was born. Still, Oswald did not live with his family but stayed at a rooming house under an alias during the week and at the Paine household on weekends. He paid his last visit to his family on November 21, 1963. His wife refused to talk with him, angry that he had rented his room under a false name. The morning of November 22, Oswald left $170 on Marina's bureau and placed his wedding ring in a cup. Then, carrying his "curtain rods," he walked to the house of a coworker and the two drove to the Texas School Book Depository.

If the Warren Commission is to be believed, Oswald was little more than an unhinged loner. Isolated and troubled, a failure at just about everything, he nevertheless possessed an inflated and grandiose sense of his own destiny. Believing himself a man of historical consequence, he lacked both the talent and the will to realize that vision. Rather than settle for the ordinary and anonymous life that his limited capabilities and resources could provide, he chose to pick up a rifle and make his name.

While the portraits of Oswald as a sordid and solitary figure—a lone assassin—are compelling and believable, for someone so rootless, he had a number of colorful and intriguing connections. Oswald had associations with right-wing groups, alleged CIA operatives, and the Mafia, not to mention the communists, the Soviets, and the KGB. Given the sheer volume of these alleged contacts, it is hard to discount them all as purely incidental. Yet it is much more difficult to try to unravel them and come up with a plausible theory that stands up under scrutiny. Over the years, many have tried. Countless books and films espousing various scenarios have been produced, but no one theory has achieved preeminence. Indeed, as Oliver Stone depicted in his film *JFK*, Jim Garrison, a New Orleans district attorney, even convinced a grand jury to indict New Orleans businessman Clay Shaw for conspiring with Oswald and others to murder the president. But when the case went to trial, the jury needed only an hour to come back with a verdict of not guilty.

Whatever the degree of Oswald's culpability, whether he was a lone gunman or part of a larger plot, JFK conspiracy theories have become ingrained in the American psyche. Terms associated with the case—"grassy knoll," "magic bullet," "Zapruder film"—have entered the popular lexicon. In a way, the myriad of conspiracy theories in this case is understandable. The horror of those days in Dallas has raised too many unanswered questions and left a great number of loose ends, straining the faith Americans have in their government and in one another.

Still, whoever killed Kennedy, perhaps the most disturbing scenario is the most likely one: that Lee Harvey Oswald, acting alone, gunned down the leader of the free world. The lesson is frightening: Someone as vital, inspiring, and significant as Kennedy could be murdered, not by some complicated plot involving the Mafia, the KGB, or the CIA, but by a random, maladjusted sociopath with the means and the opportunity.

Oswald Shoots JFK:
But Who Is the Real Target?

By William Rubinstein
History Today, October 1999

William Rubinstein reviews the research of "amateur historians" on the Kennedy assassination—and suggests a new motive for Lee Harvey Oswald's actions.

The assassination of John F. Kennedy in Dallas, Texas, on November 22nd, 1963, was one of the watershed events of the twentieth century. Everyone who remembers it also knows where they were when they heard the news. If (as is often suggested) it led to America's disastrous involvement in Vietnam, it was also one of the most momentous. Yet it is one of contemporary history's most enduring mysteries. Although the apparent assassin was arrested within ninety minutes of the killing, the assassination has often been termed the greatest unsolved crime in American history. A Presidential commission of inquiry headed by America's Chief Justice Earl Warren concluded in 1964 that Lee Harvey Oswald, the alleged assassin, acted alone, and that Jack Ruby, who killed Oswald two days after the assassination, also acted alone, but many hundreds of books and articles have been written to prove that Kennedy was assassinated as a result of a far-reaching conspiracy. Not one of these critics of the Warren Report is a professional historian, yet their efforts probably constitute the largest body of work by amateur historians on any single subject. Astonishingly, to the best of my knowledge, no academic historian has ever investigated Kennedy's assassination and the theories surrounding it.

Although Lee Harvey Oswald (1939–63), was only twenty-four at the time of the killing, his life had already been so strange as to seem out of a novel. Oswald's father died young, and his itinerant mother had lived in several American cities. As a teenager in New York he encountered left-wing political propaganda and became an avowed Marxist. Oswald was a keen reader, a loner, and a classic autodidact. He saw, however, no contradiction in joining the US Marines at only sixteen while at the same time learning Russian with the intention of emigrating to the Soviet Union. This he did in late 1959, being given a dishonorable discharge from the Marine Reserves as a result. Oswald lived in Russia from 1959 until June 1962, marrying a Russian girl, Marina Pruskova, in 1960. He re-emigrated to America in 1962, moved to the Dallas–Fort Worth area, and had a series of low-paying dead-end jobs. During the week he lived apart from his wife, who roomed with a Quaker couple in suburban Dallas while Oswald lived in a cheap boarding house in Dallas itself.

In 1963 Oswald did several other unusual things. In March, using the name A. J. Hidell, he purchased a mail-order rifle and revolver. (The rifle was used, according to the Warren Report, to kill the President, and the pistol to kill police officer J. D. Tippit forty-five minutes after the assassination in another part of Dallas.) Shortly after purchasing the Italian-made rifle he used it in an unsuccessful attempt to kill Edwin Walker, an extreme rightwing ex-general who lived in Dallas. Oswald proclaimed himself to Marina as 'a hunter of fascists'.

In mid-1963 he went to New Orleans, where he founded a pro-Castro organisation, the 'Fair Play for Cuba Committee,' of which he was the only member. He also visited Mexico City with the aim of obtaining a Cuban visa from the Soviet embassy, but was rebuffed.

He returned to Dallas in early October completely demoralized, and began a poorly-paid warehouse job at the Texas School Book Depository Building in central Dallas. According to the Warren Report, at 12:30 pm on November 22nd, 1963, Oswald fired three shots from an upstairs window in that building at President Kennedy, riding by in an open limousine, seriously wounding both him and Texas Governor John Connally (riding in the same car) with the second shot and killing Kennedy with the third.

Oswald then fled from the Depository, returned to his boarding house and, at about 1:14 pm, shot and killed Dallas police officer J. D. Tippit, who had stopped Oswald as he was walking down the street. At 1:51 pm Oswald was arrested in a nearby movie theatre and charged with killing Tippit; he was later charged with the assassination of the President.

As he was being transferred to a normal jail, two days later, on the morning of Sunday, November 24th, Oswald was shot and killed in the basement of the Dallas police headquarters by Jack Ruby (1911–67), a local nightclub owner. From a dysfunctional immigrant background, Ruby was a ne'er-do-well fringe businessman, pro-Kennedy but essentially apolitical, who killed Oswald, so he claimed, to spare Kennedy's widow Jacqueline the ordeal of having to testify at Oswald's trial. Ruby, who had swallowed many anti-depressant pills the previous day, was also in chronic financial difficulties. According to the Warren Report, Oswald and Ruby had never met.

Within days of the assassination, the new President, Lyndon Johnson, appointed a panel to investigate the killing. Headed by Chief Justice Earl Warren (and hence known as the 'Warren Commission') it included the future president (then congressman) Gerald Ford, former CIA director Allen Dulles, and John J. McCloy, formerly High Commissioner in the American zone of occupied Germany. It was given virtual carte blanche powers by the President, and by a vote in Congress, to investigate the assassination as thoroughly as possible, with the full co-operation of the FBI and other Federal agencies. It was also declared to be the only government body to investigate the assassination, thus preempting an investigation by Dallas or the state of Texas.

The Warren Commission was provided with a full-time staff of twenty-eight who actually did the work of investigation. Most were lawyers with Ivy League backgrounds, young and very bright. Most of the lawyers were in private practice; only a small minority worked for the US government. In practice, since all of the Warren Commission's members had full-time jobs, the Warren Report was prepared by its staff, especially, it would seem, by three younger lawyers: Arlen Specter, David Belin, and Wesley Liebeler. In particular, many of the key conclusions appear to have been Specter's, then a thirty-three year old graduate of Yale Law School (and today a prominent Republican Senator from Pennsylvania).

The Commission did a remarkable job and produced a twenty-seven volume report, containing around ten million words, by September 24th, 1964, only ten months after it had been appointed. On its behalf the FBI conducted 25,000 interviews, the Secret Service another 1,550. The Commission itself took testimony from 552 witnesses, of whom ninety-four appeared before it. The conclusions reached by the Warren Commission are well-known: Oswald assassinated President Kennedy, acting alone. There was no conspiracy of any kind. Oswald was in turn killed by Ruby, also acting alone; Oswald and Ruby had never met. Oswald fired three bullets: the first missed; the second, dubbed by critics the 'magic bullet', hit Kennedy in the upper back, seriously wounding him, and then also hit John Connally, who sat in the same limousine two feet in front of the President, nearly killing him. The third and final bullet killed Kennedy by striking him in the right side of his head and blowing out a portion of his brain. All of the shots were fired within eight seconds or so from the Depository Building, and no one else was involved.

Having discharged its functions, the Warren Commission disbanded. Even before it reported, however, there were already theories of conspiracies and within a few years the first books to criticise its findings appeared. There was much about the format of the Warren Commission to arouse suspicion and engender criticism. It was composed exclusively of Washington insiders. With the notable exception of Earl Warren, all of its members could be considered politically right-of-centre. None had any real expertise of such technical matters as ballistics or forensics. The involvement of former CIA director Allen Dulles as a Commission member, and the central role of the long-serving FBI director J. Edgar Hoover and his Agency in gathering information, was deeply suspicious to many. The Warren Commission was, moreover, not a trial: the dead Oswald had no defence lawyer, and the Commission did not have to prove his guilt beyond a reasonable doubt to a jury. Its task was merely to arrive at a conclusion, using such evidence as it liked to support its findings.

The fact that Kennedy's assassination seemed to signal a precipitous and disastrous change in America's Vietnam policy also seemed to many Warren critics to be more than coincidental. As both William Manchester and Gerald Posner have perceptively noted, to many it seemed inconceivable that so important an event as Kennedy's assassination could have been accomplished by a maladjusted loner with a mail-order rifle: surely so momentous an event required an equally far-reaching conspiracy? In part as a result, in the 1970s there was a fully-fledged subculture of Warren 'critics' (as they are known), numbering hundreds. So great was the public outcry that in 1975 Congress held a second investigation. This had been given impetus by the notorious investigation conducted by New Orleans district attorney Jim Garrison in the late 1960s which claimed that three New

Orleans–based anti-Castro right-wingers were behind the assassination. This claim (which is certainly nonsensical) received world-wide fame decades later as the basis for Oliver Stone's 1991 film *JFK*. Literally hundreds of books and articles have appeared by Warren critics since the early efforts of Edward Jay Epstein, Mark Lane, Josiah Thompson and Harold Weisberg. One of the most influential and bizarre was David S. Lifton's *Best Evidence: Disguise and Deception in the Assassination of John F. Kennedy* (1981), which claimed that Kennedy's corpse underwent a pre-autopsy operation to make it seem as if the bullets came from the back rather than from the front as he claimed was actually the case—arguing that the fatal shots were not fired from the Depository Building at all, but from the 'grassy knoll' from which escape would have been easier. The author holds a doctorate in engineering from the University of California, and the work, over 900 pages long, contains over thirty pages of footnoted references. Lifton's work has become a stock-in-trade of the Warren critics.

The case that Oswald did not kill Kennedy, or did not act alone, is superficially fairly strong. There are some frequently reiterated points made by the Warren critics. Oswald had no motive: he never expressed hostility to Kennedy and made no political pronouncements when captured but said he was innocent: an unlikely stance if the killing had been politically motivated. Oswald's career as a US Marine yet a Marxist who lived in Russia was so suspicious that it has seemed inconceivable to many that he was not a government agent or double agent. Some eyewitnesses (although, contrary to what is frequently said, only a minority) thought that some shots came from the 'grassy knoll' in front of Kennedy's limousine. Any such shots must have come from a second assassin, and almost all 'conspiracy theories' of the assassination revolve around the existence of a second or third gunman. The time-frame for the assassination is frequently seen as too narrow for Oswald to have fired all the shots. Many critics believe that Oswald lacked the time to run down from the sixth floor of the Depository before police arrived. Some argue that Oswald could not have walked from his boarding house and killed Tippit in the estimated time of twelve to fifteen minutes. Many claims have been made that evidence was tampered with, for instance, the famous backyard photographs of Oswald holding the assassination rifle, taken by Marina Oswald on March 31st, 1963. No direct transcript was made of Oswald's statements in custody, and at no time did he have a lawyer. Similarly, it has been argued by many critics that Ruby must have killed Oswald as part of a conspiracy. Critics point out that the Warren Report asks us to believe that Ruby just happened to enter the basement (carrying a loaded revolver) of the Dallas Police Headquarters at the precise moment that Oswald was being led through the basement, and managed to kill him from the front in full view of dozens of policemen and TV cameramen.

> **Although Lee Harvey Oswald ... was only twenty-four at the time of the killing, his life had already been so strange as to seem out of a novel.**

Ruby allegedly had links with organised crime figures. He claimed to be a Kennedy supporter, but had not bothered, two days previously, to see Kennedy drive by in the Dallas motorcade.

Given these suspicions surrounding the key participants in the assassination, it is not surprising that theory after theory has been posited since 1963 about the true nature of the killing. At least five major groupings of conspirators have been proposed over the years: a right-wing conspiracy within the American government, often including the CIA, J. Edgar Hoover, and Lyndon Johnson; a conspiracy of right-wing dissidents outside the government ('rogue' CIA agents, right-wing Texas oil magnate H. L. Hunt, international extreme right wing groups); anti-Castro Cubans and their alleged supporters like Clay Shaw and David Ferrie; left-wing pro-Castro groups; and the Mafia, angry at Kennedy for launching a war against American organised crime. In some scenarios, members of these groups co-operated: for instance, the Mafia and anti-Castro Cubans (the Mafia had lost its lucrative casinos in Havana when Castro came to power in 1959). It is probably fair to say that the Mafia has emerged, in recent decades, as the leading candidate among conspiracy theorists as the group most likely to have carried out the assassination.

Reading the works produced by the Warren critics rapidly becomes a tedious business. There are such striking similarities in their approach, however much their theories differ, that the effect is like reading a detective novel from which the last ten pages have been torn out. There is circumstantial evidence in plenty, but nothing definite or clearly true beyond a reasonable doubt. In over thirty-five years of theorising on the assassination, no Warren critic has ever been able to provide cogent or convincing answers to the two most basic questions of any valid conspiracy theory: who masterminded it and what were the precise roles of Oswald and Ruby. No 'smoking gun' has ever been traced, and the sheer plethora of theories clearly shows that the critics of the official explanation cannot agree among themselves.

Nevertheless, it is undeniable that, by sheer weight of numbers, the critics have had a profound effect upon the public perception of the assassination. By the late 1980s, polls showed that as many as 80 per cent of the American public did not believe the Warren Commission, and did believe that others were involved besides Oswald. The critics held the field almost entirely to themselves until 1993, when Gerald Posner, a Wall Street lawyer and author of several previous works, published *Case Closed: Lee Harvey Oswald and the Assassination of JFK*, certainly the most important book ever written on the assassination. Posner became convinced that the Warren Report was essentially correct in everything it asserted, and went over every claim made by the Report's critics in elaborate detail, often with new evidence, refuting all of the claims made by the critics. For instance, critics have frequently claimed that over one hundred witnesses and others connected with the assassination have 'died mysteriously.' Posner examined every such alleged death and showed that not a single one was actually mysterious. (Posner also wryly noted that not a single critic of the Warren Report has ever died mysteriously.) Significantly, no Warren critic has written a detailed refutation of Posner in the six years since his book appeared.

> ## OFFICIAL EXAMINATIONS OF JFK'S ASSASSINATION
>
> The Warren Commission is not the only official body to have examined the death of John F. Kennedy. In 1975, alter Watergate, the President's Commission on Central Intelligence Agency Activities within the United States (known as the Rockefeller Commission, alter Vice-President Nelson Rockefeller) investigated the CIA's alleged illegal domestic activities and concluded that the CIA was not involved in Kennedy's killing. In 1975–76 the separate Senate Select Committee to Study Governmental Operations with Respect to Intelligence Activities (the Church Committee, alter its chairman Senator Frank Church) concluded the CIA had plotted to assassinate Fidel Castro, but had failed to provide this information to the Warren Commission. A separate subcommittee of the Warren Commission also investigated the intelligence agencies' handling of the Kennedy investigation.
>
> In 1976, the House of Representatives established a Select Committee on Assassinations (HSCA), which investigated the killings of Kennedy and Martin Luther King. Its conclusion, that Kennedy was probably killed as a result of a conspiracy, probably involving organised crime rings in America, received much publicity: but Posner queried as flawed the evidence by which HSCA arrived at this conclusion.
>
> In 1992 the President John F. Kennedy Assassination Records Collection Act was established, to secure the public release of all records relating to the assassination. A Review Board was set up of rive 'impartial private citizens' not employed by the government: uniquely, it was to include at least one professional historian recommended by the American Historical Association or the Organization of American Historians, and who could not be removed except by impeachment. The Act also expressed the 'sense of Congress' that the American Secretary of State ought to collect all relevant material from the Russian government. The Review Board was to release and collect all material relevant to the assassination by 2017. After reviewing the evidence, its initial findings were that there was no conspiracy.
>
> The Review Board is unlikely to stop the Warren critics. It can only release documents which actually exist, not those which have been destroyed. It can review documents in any agency relating to the assassination, but not material which ostensibly has no direct relevance but which might turn out to be pertinent, such as FBI material on organised crime collected several years before 1963. Nor has it the power to collect material from non-governmental sources.

Although Posner's book did not end the efforts of the Warren critics, which continue to appear in considerable numbers, *Case Closed* has probably changed the balance of public opinion on Kennedy's assassination in a significant way, so that a number of important studies of aspects of the assassination have appeared which also accept the findings of the Warren Report. For example, TV journalist Dale K. Myers' *With Malice: Lee Harvey Oswald and the Murder of Officer J.D. Tippit* (1998), a 702-page account of Tippit's murder concluded that Oswald killed Tippit precisely as the Warren Report stated.

Indeed, it is possible to show, almost by the force of logic alone, that Oswald and Ruby must have acted as the Warren Report claimed. How did Oswald come to gain access to the sixth floor of the Depository building? He was found a job there purely by chance by a neighbour of the Paines (with whom Marina Oswald lodged) who worked there. No one has ever linked any of these persons with a conspiracy. Oswald was interviewed for the job and was hired because the superintendent of the Depository thought that he was unusually respectful. Oswald began working there on October 16th, before Kennedy's trip to Texas was announced. The route of Kennedy's motorcade was not chosen until a week before the assassination, and not published until two days prior to the killing. Oswald could thus not have been planted ahead of time in the Depository Building by any conspirators.

Another key question is what inducement was offered to Oswald to kill the President. Oswald and his family were living in poverty. The Warren Commission examined Oswald's finances in detail and found that his income, between returning to America in June 1962 and the assassination, totalled only $3,666. (These findings have been ignored by all Warren critics.) He had earned no more than $225 in any of the five months prior to the killing. Would he not have demanded a huge upfront payment to kill the President? There are other basic questions as well: would the conspirators not have organised an escape route? If there was a second gunman in the Depository Building, why has no one ever claimed to see him?

The case that Ruby acted alone is even stronger. Ruby shot Oswald in an area containing seventy policemen and dozens of reporters. If Ruby was not shot dead on the spot (which was more than likely), he faced the absolute certainty of conviction for murder. No one in his right mind would agree to take part in a conspiracy to commit murder under these conditions. The first thing he would have demanded would be a guaranteed means of escape. Indeed, the first thing any conspirators would ensure would be an escape route for Ruby: otherwise, they might well merely have traded one conspirator in custody for another. Nor would any conspirators, for the absolutely crucial task of silencing Oswald, have used a middle-aged low-life nightclub owner, on anti-depressant pills, with no real knowledge of guns. Any conspiracy would certainly have used a 'professional killer' with a successful track record of murders. As with Oswald, there is no evidence of any kind that Ruby was offered any financial gain. Although there are indeed some curious loose ends in the Warren Commission's case, it does seem overwhelmingly likely that Oswald and Ruby acted alone and that there was no conspiracy.

What is the true explanation of what happened and why? Buried in the first volume of the Warren Report (p. 314) is a remarkable suggestion, which has received no publicity then or since, but which might just represent the truth of the assassination. This is the possibility that Oswald's real target was not Kennedy but John Connally. There is a surprising amount of circumstantial evidence to support this possibility. Oswald apparently held a grudge against Connally, who had (as Secretary of the Navy) signed a letter to Oswald stating that his dishonourable discharge from the Marine reserves would not be reviewed. For the 'hunter of fascists', Connally was a plausible target: a right-wing Democrat who subsequently joined the Republican Party. Significantly, when Marina Oswald heard the news of the assassination, she thought that her husband 'was shooting at Connally rather than Kennedy'. It would have been easy for Oswald to have aimed at Connally, hesitated for a fraction of a second, and shot the President, sitting two feet behind him in the moving car. This intriguing suggestion has been totally ignored by all Warren critics, since, if Connally was the target, there was plainly no conspiracy. This theory should certainly be studied more closely.

A central aim of this article has been to examine how well the amateur historians have done. Not very well, although they have performed an extremely useful function by their dogged research and in compelling the American government to open its files for public inspection. The failure of the amateurs in this case has one main cause: they are not open-mindedly searching for the objective truth, but argue from the premise that the Warren Report was wrong. Since, however, the Commission's conclusions about the identity of the assassin and of the absence of a conspiracy are almost certainly correct, it is not surprising that the critics have been unable to identify a conspiracy in a convincing way. That no academic historian has ever examined Kennedy's assassination is a reproach to the historical profession. The training of academic historians in assessing evidence could hardly have been put to better or more important use, and this is one case in which academic historians should have left the ivory tower.

William D. Rubinstein is Professor of Modern History at the University of Wales, Aberystwyth.

A Prosecutor Takes on the JFK Assassination

By Sheldon M. Stern
Skeptic, 2008

A Review of Vincent Bugliosi's Reclaiming History: The Assassination of President John F. Kennedy, *New York: Norton, 2007.*

It is all but impossible to avoid hyperbole and clichés when writing about the assassination of John F. Kennedy in Dallas, Texas, on November 22, 1963. The shooting in Dealey Plaza *really was* "the crime of the century" and those who lived through the four days of non-stop television coverage *really do* remember in extraordinary detail exactly what they were doing and feeling. Millions of Americans, and countless people around the world, regard the JFK assassination as a personal and historical turning point—which ultimately elevated the slain forty-six-year-old president, as Vincent Bugliosi observes, "into a mythical, larger-than-life figure whose hold on the nation's [and the world's] imagination resonates to this very day" (p. xi).

I was a graduate student in history on that unforgettable day, but I could never have imagined that fourteen years later I would become historian at the Kennedy Library in Boston. And, like it or not, I would have to repeatedly confront the increasingly bitter controversy about who was responsible for the JFK assassination. In the interest of full disclosure, I want readers to understand that, like countless others, I was for a time drawn to the siren songs of some conspiracy theories. However, I am now absolutely convinced, beyond a reasonable doubt, that the evidence put forward by Mr. Bugliosi is incontrovertible: Lee Harvey Oswald, acting alone, killed President Kennedy.

Reclaiming History is not really a "book" at all in the conventional sense—it is more like a comprehensive reference work—an encyclopedia of the Kennedy assassination and its aftermath.[1] "In defense of its length," Bugliosi explains, "conspiracy theorists have transformed Kennedy's murder into the most complex murder case ever. . . . The scope and breadth of issues flowing from the Kennedy assassination are so enormous that typically authors write entire books on just one aspect of the case alone, such as organized crime, or the CIA, or Castro, or Jack Ruby, or Oswald's guilt or innocence." He acknowledges that his book "keep[s] piling one argument upon another to prove his point" but notes that "the Warren Commission also made its point, and well, over forty years ago, yet today the overwhelming majority of Americans do not accept its conclusion that Oswald acted alone, a great number

---

From *Skeptic* 14, no. 4 (2008): 64–67. Copyright © 2011 by *Skeptic*. Reprinted with permission. All rights reserved.

not even believing he killed Kennedy. Hence, the overkill in this book is historically necessary" (pp. xliv–xlv).

Bugliosi's commitment to "reclaiming" the real story of the Kennedy assassination began in 1986 when London Weekend Television invited him to serve as prosecutor in a 20+ hour "trial" of Lee Harvey Oswald. He was skeptical at first, but changed his mind when he was assured that there would be no script and that most of the original key witnesses, "many of whom had refused to even talk to the media for years," had agreed to testify—and most importantly—to be subjected to cross examination. Gerry Spence, one of the nation's leading criminal defense lawyers, was chosen to represent Oswald. Bugliosi put aside his legal career and devoted about one hundred hours a week for five months to preparing the case. The jury, after deliberating for six hours in what *TIME* magazine called the closest "to a real trial as the accused killer of John F. Kennedy will probably ever get," convicted Oswald of the murder of President Kennedy.

The guilty verdict in London energized Bugliosi to undertake a comprehensive account of the historical impact of the JFK assassination—building on the research by the Warren Commission (1964) and the House Select Committee on Assassinations (1979):[2]

> I am unaware of any other major event in world history which has been shrouded in so much intentional misinformation as has the assassination of JFK. Nor am I aware of any event that has given rise to such an extraordinarily large number of far-fetched and conflicting theories. For starters, if organized crime was behind the assassination, as many believe, wouldn't that necessarily mean that all the many books claiming the CIA (or Castro or the KGB, and so on) was responsible were wrong? And vice versa? Unless one wants to believe, as Hollywood producer Oliver Stone apparently does, that they were all involved. I mean, were we to believe Mr. Stone, even bitter enemies like the KGB and the CIA got together on this one. Indeed, at one time or another in Mr. Stone's cinematic reverie, he had the following groups and individuals acting suspiciously and/or conspiratorially: the Dallas Police Department, FBI, Secret Service, Vice President Lyndon B. Johnson, CIA, KGB, Fidel Castro, anti-Castro Cuban exiles, organized crime, and the military-industrial complex. Apparently nobody wanted President Kennedy alive. But where did all these people meet to hatch this conspiracy? Madison Square Garden? (p. xxix)

Potential readers should first be aware of the massive scope of Bugliosi's investigation: Book One (969 pp), "Matters of Fact: What Happened," begins with a riveting 300+ page description of those four tragic days in November 1963—driven throughout by the logical and indisputable conclusion that Oswald was the killer. He then discusses the official investigations, the JFK autopsy, John Connally's wounds, the Zapruder film, the single-bullet conclusion, the bizarre life of Lee Harvey Oswald, Oswald's possession of the murder weapon, evidence linking him to the sniper's nest, Oswald's motive, and a summary of his guilt.

Book Two (1,464 pp), "Delusions of Conspiracy: What Did Not Happen," dissects every major conspiracy theory (after demolishing the "zanies" at the end of

Book One): Mark Lane, the mysterious and suspicious deaths, the second Oswald, David Lifton and the alteration of JFK's body, Ruby and the mob, organized crime, the CIA, the FBI, the Secret Service, the KGB, the right wing, LBJ, Cuba, Jim Garrison and the Oliver Stone film *JFK*.

Vincent Bugliosi is not a historian—he is a lawyer and an extremely skillful prosecutor. As a result, he presents his evidence as if he were talking to a jury—and he is—the jury of public opinion and history. He does not pretend to be objective and often frames his conclusions, as already cited above, in withering irony and humor. Two prominent conspiracy "researchers," for example, asked him, "What would it take to convince you of the existence of a conspiracy and cover-up in the death of JFK? What would it take to persuade you of Oswald's innocence?" Bugliosi's reply:

> *[Vincent] Bugliosi goes after the conspiracy mongers by name and relentlessly exposes their shameless lies and distortions.*

"Only evidence." And that is indeed the key to Book Two—Bugliosi's relentless demolition of the "evidence" invented and manipulated by the conspiracy industry—not a shred of which was able to stand up to scrutiny by the jury in 1986. And nothing added since, especially Oliver Stone's *JFK* (more later), is any better.

The extraordinary length of this self-proclaimed "anti-conspiracy book" and the editorial limits on the length of this review, make it impossible to discuss the entire volume in detail (p. 974). Instead, I will concentrate on three representative examples of Bugliosi's analysis and methodology: his chapter on one of the founding fathers of the conspiracy theorists, Mark Lane; his deconstruction of Oliver Stone's film *JFK*; and his account of the botched "evidence" that led to the 1979 claim by the House Select Committee on Assassinations that Kennedy "was probably assassinated as a result of a conspiracy."

One of the most refreshing things about *Reclaiming History*, which helps the reader to successfully navigate through its enormous length, is that Bugliosi goes after the conspiracy mongers by name and relentlessly exposes their shameless lies and distortions. His analysis of Mark Lane's 1966 bestseller *Rush to Judgment* exposes a systematic effort by "the Pied Piper of conspiracy theorists" to erase crucial witnesses against Oswald from the historical record. Lane never even mentions, for example, the Dallas photographer in the motorcade, or any of the other eyewitnesses, who saw the rifle protruding from the sixth-floor window, the shoe store manager who watched Oswald duck into the entryway to his store and turn his back toward the street to hide from police after he shot Officer Tippit, and the Dallas policeman who testified that Oswald said "Well, it's all over now" when he was arrested in a movie theater (pp. 1000–3).

Bugliosi also documents Lane's tawdry efforts to prevent the Warren Commission from hearing a taped interview with a woman who had witnessed the shooting of Officer Tippit and had subsequently picked Oswald out of a Dallas police lineup. Lane, acting as her attorney before the Warren Commission in 1964, distorted the woman's testimony beyond recognition. Lane finally agreed to release the tape—but only after being granted immunity from prosecution. Years later, Bugliosi confronted Lane during a debate and began reading from the tape transcript to expose the shocking difference between what the witness actually said and what Lane claimed she said. Lane cut him off, "I'll sue you if you get into this. It's defamation." Bugliosi is at his ironic and prosecutorial best in his contemptuous response:

> Such a threatened lawsuit by Lane would stake out new legal ground. Not only is truth a complete defense against defamation, and I was about to read Lane's own words, but defamation is when someone makes a false and harmful statement about you. Here, Lane would be arguing in effect that his own words defamed him, and therefore he didn't want anyone to repeat them. I don't know about you, but I think this is very funny. (p. 1009)

Bugliosi is not the first writer to expose Mark Lane's fabrications, but no one has enjoyed it more. And, believe it or not, the witness/tape recording episode is not the most egregious example in his brief against Lane. In *Rush to Judgment,* Lane claimed that Jack Ruby had literally begged Chief Justice Earl Warren to bring him to Washington for additional testimony. "Ruby made it plain," Lane declares, "that if the Commission took him from the Dallas County Jail and permitted him to testify in Washington, he could tell more there; it was impossible for him to tell the whole truth so long as he was in jail in Dallas" (p. 1004). Lane even quotes Ruby's testimony as proof of this claim:

> Ruby: "But you [Warren] are the only one that can save me. I think you can."
>
> Warren: "Yes?"
>
> Ruby: "But by delaying, you lose the chance. All I want to do is tell the truth, and that is all" (p. 1006).

Bugliosi's conclusion is devastating:

> The unmistakable implication that Lane seeks to convey is that if Ruby were questioned in Washington, he would divulge the existence of a conspiracy. *Yet the very next words* that Ruby uttered after "that is all" were "There was no conspiracy." These four words, which completely rebutted the entire thrust of Lane's contention, were carefully omitted from *Rush to Judgment.* (p. 1004)

"The students who crowded Lane's lectures in the 1960s and 1970s," Bugliosi warns correctly, "are the parents and teachers of today." In the early 1990s, as a case in point, when I spoke in a high school auditorium to several Advanced Placement U.S. history classes about the Cuban missile crisis, a teacher jumped up and demanded to know if I believed there had been a conspiracy in the JFK assassination. I replied that I was 100 percent sure that Oswald was guilty and 99.9 percent sure that there was no conspiracy.[3] The teacher angrily admonished the students to disregard anything I had said since I was obviously "part of the conspiracy."[4]

Compared to Oliver Stone's 1991 film *JFK*, even Mark Lane's work is a model of historical accuracy and the scrupulous use of evidence. Demolishing Lane required a mere twelve pages; Bugliosi's tour de force deconstruction of Oliver Stone's film fills one hundred pages. The movie, about New Orleans district attorney Jim Garrison's bizarre and unsuccessful 1967–1969 prosecution of Clay Shaw[5] for conspiracy to murder President Kennedy, grossed more than $200 million worldwide and, Bugliosi accurately contends, had an enormous impact on public opinion:

> Those who saw it who already believed in a conspiracy had their myths about the case not only confirmed, but expanded and fortified. Those who knew nothing about the case and had formed no opinion (i.e. the nation's youth) overwhelmingly bought Stone's cinematic fantasy—hook, line, and sinker. At the public tennis courts where I play when I can find time, a teen who had seen *JFK* overheard me telling a third party that there was no evidence of a conspiracy in the Kennedy assassination. "Mr. Bugliosi," he said, "I'm surprised you don't think there was a conspiracy. *They even made a movie about it*" (pp. 1353-4).[6]

"Oliver Stone's *JFK*," Bugliosi demonstrates, "at its very core, was one huge lie"—hardly a surprise since the film is based on Garrison's farcical "case" against Clay Shaw (p. 1381). The book documents, in relentless and almost numbing detail, dozens of examples of Stone's duplicity. The film transforms Jim Garrison's failure to convict Clay Shaw into a heroic struggle by an all-American hero against the inexorable power of the dark side. One would never guess that even leading conspiracy theorists denounced Garrison as "a reckless, irrational, even paranoid demagogue" who had destroyed the credibility of responsible critics of the Warren Commission (p. 1352).

Stone depicts Oswald as an extreme right-wing fanatic who pretended to be a Marxist, systematically ignoring the overwhelming evidence that Oswald was in fact a dedicated and committed Marxist. Incredibly, the film never mentions any of the vast and irrefutable physical, scientific, and forensic evidence that points directly to Oswald's guilt. Stone further manipulates the viewer by showing only witnesses who claim that the gunfire in Dealey Plaza came from the grassy knoll. One would never guess that the overwhelming majority of eyewitnesses identified the Book Depository as the source of the shots. Likewise, the film pretends that there was only one witness who saw Oswald kill Officer Tippit. In fact there were ten eyewitnesses and the cartridges found at the scene came from the revolver in Oswald's possession when he was arrested.

Stone also recklessly and cynically concocts his own "facts": a character asserts that even expert marksmen could never duplicate the impossibly brief time for the alleged three shots from the sixth floor. In fact, several have actually improved on Oswald's time. He invents a scene in which the so-called "magic bullet" is placed on a hospital stretcher by a mysterious, unidentified figure (resembling Jack Ruby) and even duplicates Mark Lane's appalling deception about Ruby telling Earl Warren that he must come to Washington where he can safely tell the truth about the conspiracy.

Bugliosi proves conclusively that "Stone couldn't find any level of deception and invention beyond which he was unwilling to go.[7] And yet, the whole thrust of the movie is that what was being depicted on the screen was the truth, and everyone *else* was lying" (p. 1431). A *JFK* high school study guide, funded by Warner Brothers and prepared by Learning Enrichment, Inc., was even distributed to thousands of teachers nationwide, urging them to tell their students "about the intensive research Oliver Stone undertook before making the film." The cover of the guide quotes Stone himself: "I hope they [the viewers of his movie] become more aware of how politics are played out *and how our kings are killed*" (p. 1435). During filming, Stone acknowledged that "I'm *shaping* history, to a degree," and he later commented in the introduction to a book written by one of the conspiracy "advisers" for *JFK*: "Who owns reality? Who owns our history? He who makes it up so that everyone believes it. That person wins" (p. 1436).

Many readers may conclude that one hundred pages debunking Oliver Stone's bogus history is preposterous overkill. Perhaps—perhaps not. In April 1992, the *American Historical Review*, the scholarly journal of the prestigious American Historical Association, published a forum on *JFK*, with a full-color cover picture of director Oliver Stone with actor Kevin Costner (playing Jim Garrison). In the forum, Marcus Raskin, co-founder of the Institute for Policy Studies and author of books on government, political theory, and national security (whose article also includes a full-page photograph of Costner as Garrison) asserts, "Contrary to what some would like to believe, [*JFK*] is surprisingly accurate. On the complex question of the Kennedy assassination itself, the film holds its own against the Warren Commission." Even more striking, Robert A. Rosenstone—professor of history in the Division of the Humanities and Social Sciences at the California Institute of Technology, founding editor of *Rethinking History: The Journal of Theory and Practice*, associate editor of *Film Historia*, and author of seven books—describes Garrison as "the heroic, embattled, incorruptible [!] investigator who wishes to make sense of Kennedy's assassination and its apparent cover-up, not just for himself but for his country and its traditions—that is, for the audience, for us." Rosenstone concludes that "even if contradictions do exist, the main line of the story is closed and completed, and the moral message is clear: the assassination was the result of a conspiracy that involved agencies and officials of the U.S. government. . . . [W]hatever its flaws, *JFK* has to be among the most important works of American history ever to appear on the screen." Rosenstone's unmistakably post-modernist assessment of Garrison and *JFK* calls to mind actor Leonard Nimoy's spoof on "The Simpsons": "The following tale of alien encounters is true . . . and by true, I mean false. It's all lies. But they're entertaining lies, and in the end isn't that the real truth? The answer . . . is no."[8]

Some months ago I agreed to serve as a content consultant for a junior high school level book on the JFK assassination. When the final manuscript arrived, I was stunned to see the author's misleading and incomplete claim that the 1979 report by the House Select Committee on Assassinations had concluded that President Kennedy was "probably assassinated as a result of a conspiracy." That statement is technically correct, but fails to mention that the committee's judgment was based on an audiotape that surfaced near the end of their deliberations—a tape ultimately shown to be completely worthless.[9] The tape in question, from a Dallas police radio transmission at the time of the assassination, appeared to prove that four or five shots had been fired in Dealey Plaza, which, Bugliosi admits, would have "virtually assured a second shooter and, therefore, a conspiracy" (p. 376). In fact, until the tape turned up, the comprehensive reexamination of the assassination by several hundred members of the HSCA staff "had only confirmed the conclusions of the Warren Commission. Even in those areas where the committee felt the Commission's investigation had been careless, inept, or scant, the HSCA's more detailed and scientific examination of the evidence had only strengthened the Commission's conclusions" (p. 376).

Bugliosi's 65-page scrutiny of the genesis, hyping, and eventual complete scientific discrediting of this audiotape is a high point of the book—and provides extraordinary insight into the fine line that distinguishes the true believers from the con-men in the JFK conspiracy industry. (Regrettably, Bugliosi relegates his virtuoso dissection of the tape story to the endnotes on the accompanying CD-ROM—highlighting the substantive importance of additional material often found in the notes, for example, on the "magic bullet.") Bugliosi recalls, with evident satisfaction, that Gerry Spence did not even mention the Dallas police tape in the 1986 London trial, presumably to deprive the prosecution of the chance to demolish it in the presence of the jury.

About twenty years ago, I heard the distinguished Harvard paleontologist Stephen Jay Gould lecture on the contentious topic of creationism. For an hour, without notes, Gould marched around the stage, delivering a witty and scholarly performance. At the end of his remarks, the three hundred people in the audience rose as one and gave him a sustained, standing ovation. Gould, evidently pleased, sat down and was followed to the rostrum by another scientist (whose name I have unfortunately forgotten). Her comment took Gould and the audience completely by surprise: "Steve," she said, "that was brilliant but irrelevant. Creationism is religion, not science, and debunking it scientifically is pointless."

Bugliosi, likewise, declares repeatedly and correctly that there is no evidence for any of the conspiracy theories. In a sense, this contention, much like Gould's, is largely irrelevant. The assassination true believers cannot and will not be persuaded either by evidence—*or by the lack of it*. About ten years ago a colleague directed me to a website that claimed JFK had been murdered by aliens. I asked: "Where is your evidence for this?" A short time later I received the following reply, "Evidence! Evidence! That's all you people talk about is evidence!" Of course, conspiracy enthusiasts are just as likely to respond by insisting that the evidence has been suppressed or destroyed. The lack of evidence, in their *Alice Through the Looking Glass* perspective, is turned upside down and inside out and actually becomes proof that there *really was* a conspiracy.[10]

Reclaiming History is a book for the future. In 2063, when all the people who remember the JFK assassination are long gone, this is the reference work that will stand the test of time.[11] Bugliosi is sometimes overly susceptible to the Camelot imagery and mythology associated with John F. Kennedy and his brief presidency; nonetheless, Clio, the ancient Greek muse of history, is permanently in his debt.

Sheldon M. Stern served as historian at the John F. Kennedy Library and Museum in Boston from 1977 through 1999. He is the author of Averting 'the Final Failure': John F. Kennedy and the Secret Cuban Missile Crisis Meetings *(2003), and* The Week the World Stood Still: Inside the Secret Cuban Missile Crisis *(2005).*

Notes

1. Bugliosi acknowledges that "if this book (including endnotes) had been printed in an average-sized font and with pages of normal length and width, at 1,535,791 words, and with a typical book length of 400 pages and 300 words per page, this work would translate into around 13 volumes" (p. xliv).
2. Bugliosi endorses the anti-conspiracy findings of Gerald Posner's *Case Closed: Lee Harvey Oswald and the Assassination of JFK* (1993). But he nonetheless accuses Posner of adopting the pro-conspiracy writers' tactic of frequently presenting "only the evidence that supports the case he's trying to build, framing this evidence in a way that misleads readers who aren't aware that there's more to the story." "I will not," Bugliosi asserts, "*knowingly* omit or distort anything" (pp. xxxviii–xxxix).
3. *Reclaiming History* has erased my remaining one tenth of a percent of doubt about a conspiracy.
4. The chairman of the history department apologized privately for this outburst. He obviously did not think that his responsibility to his students included openly challenging his colleague's remarks. This experience was repeated, in one form or another, on many occasions. In most cases, students and teachers merely smirked at each other knowingly after my reply. The worst example took place at the Kennedy Library when an eleventh-grade student asked the same conspiracy question, got the same answer, and then shouted angrily: "No one believes that s—t. You're a f———g liar." The teachers with the group said absolutely nothing.
5. The jury acquitted Shaw in less than an hour.
6. The film did have at least one positive side effect: the enactment of the 1992 JFK Assassination Records Collection Act.
7. Stone's 1995 film, *Nixon*, is no exception—he implies, *without any evidence*, that the infamous 18-minute gap on a key Watergate tape somehow links Nixon to the Kennedy assassination.
8. Marcus Raskin, "JFK and the Culture of Violence," *American Historical Review* 97 (April 1992): 487; Robert A. Rosenstone, "*JFK*: Historical Fact/Historical Film," *American Historical Review* 97 (April 1992): 507–8, 511.
9. The editor finally agreed to add that the HSCA's conspiracy conclusion was based on: "audiotape evidence that was eventually completely discredited."

10. This phenomenon is alive and well in the current 9/11 conspiracy movement. See David Dunbar and Brad Reagan, eds., *Debunking 9/11 Myths: Why Conspiracy Theories Can't Stand Up to the Facts—An In Depth Investigation by Popular Mechanics* (2006).

11. Bugliosi, inevitably, did make mistakes. Max Holland, author of a forthcoming study of the Warren Commission, has pointed out, for example, that Bugliosi overlooked important new evidence that Oswald likely had eleven seconds, rather than only eight, to fire the three shots in Dealey Plaza. (Max Holland, "New Book on Kennedy Killing Arrives at Old Conclusions," *Wall Street Journal*, June 13, 2007).

Assassination of John F. Kennedy

Conspiracy theorists agree that anyone who accepts the Warren Commission's "lone gunman" and "magic bullet" theories is living in the Land of Oz.

By Brad Steiger and Sherry Steiger
Conspiracies and Secret Societies, 2006

On November 22, 1963, at precisely 12:30 p.m. in Dealey Plaza, Dallas, Texas, John Fitzgerald Kennedy, the thirty-fifth president of the United States, was shot while riding in a motorcade. Less than half an hour later, Kennedy was pronounced dead.

In September 1964 the findings of the U.S. Commission to Report upon the Assassination of President John F. Kennedy, popularly called the Warren Commission, concluded that the shots that killed President Kennedy and wounded Texas governor John Connally were fired from the sixth-floor window at the southeast corner of the Texas School Book Depository. Three shots were fired by Lee Harvey Oswald, who was the sole assassin. Oswald also killed Dallas police patrolman J. D. Tippit approximately forty-five minutes after the assassination. No conspiracy was involved in the death of the president.

The Warren Commission, which included Earl Warren, chief justice of the United States; Senators Richard B. Russell and John Cooper; U.S. Representatives Hale Boggs and Gerald R. Ford; and Allen W. Dulles, former director of the Central Intelligence Agency, concluded that a single bullet passed through President Kennedy's body and continued on a course that allowed it to strike Governor Connally, who, with his wife, Nellie, was riding in the open car with President and Mrs. Kennedy. According to the Warren Commission, a second shot from Oswald struck the president in the head and killed him. The commission also concluded that another bullet missed the presidential automobile altogether—making a total of three rounds allegedly fired from Oswald's bolt-action rifle in a seemingly impossible blur of time.

Conspiracy theorists immediately dismissed the so-called magic bullet that the government experts stated had passed through President Kennedy and continued to plow through the back, ribs, right wrist, and left leg of Governor Connally. From the very first days of the investigation, Governor and Mrs. Connally insisted that two bullets had struck the president and that a third and separate bullet had wounded the governor.

On July 3, 1997, former president Gerald Ford, the last surviving member of the Warren Commission, admitted that he had assisted the "magic bullet" theory in the report on JFK's death by altering the commission's description of the gunshot that killed him. According to Ford, the original text said that a bullet had entered Kennedy's back at a point slightly above the shoulder and to the right of the spine. Ford changed the bullet's entrance point from Kennedy's upper back to his neck, thus making the final commission text refer to the bullet entering "the base of the back of the neck." Such a seemingly minor alteration would support the Warren Commission's single-assassin hypothesis, which was based on the "magical" path of a single bullet that was able to pass through Kennedy's neck before striking Connally's back, ribs, right wrist, and left leg.

Skeptics of the "magic bullet" theory and the Warren Commission's final report have always pointed to the famous Zapruder home movie of the assassination and insisted that Kennedy appears hit long before Connally, who continued to hold his hat in his hand, was struck by the remarkable bullet.

Gerald Ford displayed no guilt or remorse about the fraud that he had perpetrated. In fact, he told the Associated Press, "My changes were only an attempt to be more precise. I think our judgments have stood the test of time."

A poll conducted by the University of Ohio and Scripps Howard News Service in 1997 revealed that 51 percent of the American public dismissed the "magic bullet" theory. Nearly 20 percent of those polled expressed their belief that Kennedy was assassinated by agents of the federal government. Another 33 percent maintained that a conspiracy of political insiders was "somewhat likely" in the murder of JFK.

In November 1998 Nellie Connally, the last surviving passenger of the car in which President Kennedy was assassinated, stubbornly asserted the claim that she had made since November 23, 1963: the Warren Commission was wrong about their conclusion that one bullet struck both JFK and her husband. "I will fight anybody that argues with me about those three shots," she told *Newsweek*. "I do know what happened in that car." John Connally died in 1993 at age seventy-five, but he and his wife had always insisted that the first shot hit Kennedy, a second bullet wounded the governor, and a third struck Kennedy's head, killing the president.

The Warren Commission concluded that there was also a bullet that entirely missed the president's automobile. If the Connallys' account is accurate, that makes four bullets allegedly fired with great accuracy—three hits, one miss—from Oswald's bolt-action rifle.

Mrs. Connally remembered that after they heard the first shot, her husband turned to his right to look back at the president and then turned quickly to the left to get another look at Kennedy. When Connally realized that the president and he, himself, had been shot, he cried out, "My God, they are going to kill us all!"

Mrs. Connally also had a clear memory of Mrs. Kennedy screaming, "Jack! Jack! They've killed my husband. I have his brains in my hand."

While Lee Harvey Oswald continues to be the assassin of record and is named in official documents as the lone gunman responsible for the death of President Kennedy, conspiracy researchers have always disputed the allegation that Oswald acted alone and was such an incredible marksman that he could accurately hit a moving target at a considerable distance with the bolt-action rifle allegedly in his posses-sion. Conspiracy theorists insist there is physical, medical, and ballistics evidence that would force any fair-minded panel of experts to conclude that one person could not have fired so many shots so quickly with such a rifle. Although the rifle had a clip containing a number of cartridges, the bolt had to be manually pulled back to eject the spent cartridge after each shot, then slammed into place again to move a fresh cartridge into the breech. Those experienced with such rifles severely doubted that a steady bead on a target could be maintained with the accuracy shown in the assassination of JFK.

Various students of the Kennedy assassination have amassed evidence that a large number of more likely assassins than Lee Harvey Oswald existed, including Kennedy's own Secret Service bodyguards, the Mafia, the CIA, or Cuban activists.

Perhaps the most popular theory is that President Kennedy was killed by a small group of rogue CIA agents in retaliation for passing National Security Action Mem-os 55, 56, and 57, which essentially splintered the CIA into hundreds of competi-tive branches and defused the power that the Agency had enjoyed since its creation at the end of World War II. These rogue agents also enlisted the aid of dissatisfied members of military intelligence and angry Mafia mobsters who felt betrayed by Kennedy when he failed to acknowledge their role in swinging the Chicago vote during the 1960 presidential election.

Another theory that ranks high with conspiracy theorists is that the military as-sassinated Kennedy in revenge for his refusing to provide air cover for the exiled Cubans and Special Forces members in the Bay of Pigs invasion in 1961. President Kennedy also sought peace with the Soviets and an end to the cold war, and he had promised to withdraw from Vietnam, ordering the first one thousand troops home for Christmas.

And tying both conspiracies together, seeing that all the pieces of the puzzle fell into place, was the secret government, always working in the shadows behind the scenes to bring about the ultimate goal—a New World Order, a One World Government.

On February 13, 2005, radio journalist Jeff Rense posted on his Web site a photo-copy of a "United States Memorandum" that appears to be solid proof that Lee Har-vey Oswald was trained by the CIA and worked for the Office of Naval Intelligence. The photocopy is stamped "Confidential," dated March 3, 1964, and is addressed to James J. Rowley, Chief, U.S. Secret Service from John McCone, Director, Central Intelligence Agency. The memorandum, allegedly McCone's response to Rowley's request for information regarding Oswald's activities and assignments on behalf of the CIA and the FBI, states in part that "Oswald . . . was trained by this agency, under cover of the Office of Naval Intelligence, for Soviet assignments . . . In 1957 [Oswald] was active in aerial reconnaissance of mainland China and maintained a security clearance up to the 'confidential' level."

Mysterious rumors and stories about Lee Harvey Oswald continue to swirl about the man's memory. According to some who claimed to have known Oswald before that terrible day in November of 1963, he often spoke of an international league of people who had permitted Satan to possess them so they might do his bidding. The "Devilmen" of whom he spoke were, in effect, a secret world power with members in key positions within each national government.

Many investigators have pondered the strange links between Lee Harvey Oswald, a CIA trained assassin; airplane pilot David Ferrie, a possible CIA operative; and Jack Ruby, the enigmatic nightclub owner who killed Oswald. A number of witnesses who spoke to investigators concerning the events leading up to the killing of President Kennedy swear that they saw Oswald, or a man looking very much like him, speaking with Ruby in Ruby's Carousel Club in Dallas on a number of occasions before November 23. Several of those witnesses suffered mysterious fatal accidents not long after making such an identification.

Ferrie, according to some Oswald-Kennedy assassination buffs, may have been employed by the CIA as a U-2 spy plane pilot. Loss of body hair was rumored to be a hazard of flying the U-2, allegedly from radiation levels at high altitudes, and Ferrie wore a garish red wig and bemoaned the absence of his body hair. It is also known that before he became a commercial pilot, Ferrie had studied for the priesthood. He had been dismissed from Eastern Airlines because of an arrest record for homosexual activities. Later he posed as a psychiatrist, worked as a private detective, and hired out for various jobs connected with aviation until he became Oswald's instructor in the Civil Air Patrol in New Orleans.

> *Various students of the Kennedy assassination have amassed evidence that a large number of more likely assassins than Lee Harvey Oswald existed . . .*

According to certain witnesses, Ferrie talked a lot about the occult, hypnotism, and politics in the years before the assassination of JFK. Oswald seemed to be an eager listener as Ferrie talked about demonology, witchcraft, and the power of the mind. Some say that Ferrie was obsessed with the belief that God and Satan were waging battle for control of the world. One of his favorite topics was how the priests in the Spanish Inquisition had merely driven Satan and his demons underground. Ferrie claimed that the devil and his minions would appear in their own time as a demonic evil horde.

On November 22, 1963, word reached District Attorney Jim Garrison in New Orleans that the FBI had found Ferrie's library card in Oswald's wallet shortly after they apprehended the assassin in Dallas. Although this bit of intelligence would certainly suggest that the two men knew each other, strangely enough, the library card was not in Oswald's effects checked in by the Dallas police.

Shortly after the assassination, numerous individuals remembered that they had seen Oswald and Ferrie at several ritual parties in the Quarter—private affairs where circles were drawn on the floor, black candles lighted, and chickens and small animals sacrificed. Oswald and David Ferrie were undoubtedly a strange pair—a young ex-Marine who had defected to the Soviet Union, then returned to his native America with a beautiful Russian wife, and a nervous, hawk-faced, hairless man with false eyebrows and a weird red wig.

Many analysts of the official scenario of the day of death in Dallas have pointed out how Oswald behaved in a foolish, irrational manner after the murder of Kennedy. Some have remarked that he appeared to be under some sort of hypnotic control, such as that depicted in the motion picture *The Manchurian Candidate*. When such an observation is made, the investigators remind us of the friendship between Oswald and Ferrie and the latter's proficiency as a hypnotist.

Jack Ruby, the pudgy Dallas nightclub owner who shot down Oswald on live network television, scored a successful prediction of his own fate when he stated that he would die in jail. A fervent believer in astrology who relied on his daily horoscope as if it were Holy Writ, Ruby enjoyed having the showgirls in his club read aloud to him from books on the occult. It has been reported that his two favorite topics of conversation shortly before the terrible events of November 22, 1963, were demonic possession and the influences of the new hallucinogens on the human mind.

In 1970, conspiracy researchers began circulating a photocopied manuscript entitled *Nomenclature of an Assassination Cabal*, by William Torbitt. Among the document's assertions condemning those involved in the murder of JFK are the following:

- The assassination was carried out by FBI director J. Edgar Hoover's elite Division Five.

- NASA and a little-known group headed by Wernher von Braun, Defense Industrial Security Command, had a part in the assassination.

- The same cabal had unsuccessfully planned the assassination of Charles de Gaulle in 1962.

- If the lone-gunman theory failed, the cabal had deceptions in preparation that would blame the anti-Castro groups in Florida or Fidel Castro himself.

- Lyndon B. Johnson, John Connally, and Clay Shaw, a New Orleans businessman with alleged CIA connections, were involved in the plot.

More recent surveys regarding public attitude toward the Warren Commission's 1964 findings indicate that only 11 percent of Americans accept the commission's decision that there was no conspiracy involved in the events that transpired in Dealey Plaza on November 22, 1963. Among the reasons people reject the commission's findings and believe conspiracy researchers' theories are the following:

- The parade route was altered at the last minute, bringing it into Dealey Plaza, where the assassins awaited the president.

- There was limited protection that day for the president because someone had ordered the 112th Military Intelligence Group, an army unit specially trained in protection, to stand down.

- The Zapruder film of the assassination clearly shows JFK's head thrust violently backward and to the left, inconsistent with a shot allegedly fired from behind.

- Lee Harvey Oswald, the alleged assassin, was discovered by a co-worker only ninety seconds after the shooting, calmly drinking a soda on the second floor of the Texas School Book Depository. The rifle allegedly used in the assassination was found on the sixth floor, along with shell casings.

- After the assassination, several people who were in Dealey Plaza stated that they had encountered individuals identifying themselves as Secret Service agents. The Secret Service has repeatedly claimed that it had no agents on the ground in Dealey Plaza at any time that day.

- Numerous witnesses in the plaza stated that their attention was drawn to men behaving strangely behind the picket fence on the so-called grassy knoll, a sloping hill leading to a concrete wall on the north side of Elm Street. Some witnesses who had military experience stated firmly that they recognized the sound of gunshots coming from behind them while they were standing on the grassy knoll.

- Acoustical evidence proves that at least four shots were fired that day in Dealey Plaza.

- Experienced Dallas doctors reported the president's throat wound as an entry wound, meaning that he was shot from in front.

- While Dallas doctors should have performed an autopsy, Kennedy's body was flown back to Washington for a military autopsy.

- News media around the world reported Oswald's guilt, complete with extensive background data on this allegedly unknown assassin, before he was even charged with the crime.

- On May 29, 1992, two former navy medical technicians who witnessed the autopsy of President Kennedy on the night of November 22, 1963, said that the Warren Commission had been supplied with fake photographs and X-rays. Jerrol Custer, who X-rayed the body, and Floyd Riebe, who photographed the autopsy proceedings, said that they were told by the Secret Service to keep their mouths shut about what they had seen.

- President Kennedy's brain has never been found.

- Perhaps as many as 120 witnesses or individuals who had knowledge of the Kennedy assassination have died mysteriously.

Over the years, conspiracy researchers have arrived at many theories about who killed President Kennedy and why. As might be expected, there are those who believe that the whole terrible business was orchestrated by the Freemasons. They offer the following as evidence:

- The assassination took place in Dealey Plaza, site of the first Masonic temple in Dallas.

- Dallas is located just south of the thirty-third degree of latitude. The thirty-third degree is the highest degree one can achieve in Freemasonry.

- Mason Lyndon B. Johnson appointed Mason Earl Warren to investigate Kennedy's death.

- Gerald Ford, a thirty-third-degree Mason, was instrumental in suppressing evidence of a conspiracy that reached the commission.

- J. Edgar Hoover, another thirty-third degree Mason, provided carefully censored information to the commission.

- Former CIA director and Mason Allen W. Dulles was responsible for bringing the Agency's information to the panel.

Bibliography

Crenshaw, Charles A. *Trauma Room One: The JFK Medical Coverup Exposed*. New York: Paraview Press, 2001.

Lane, Mark. *Plausible Denial*. New York: Thunder's Mouth Press, 1991.

"Proof Lee Harvey Oswald, Trained by CIA, Worked for ONI." *Rense.com*. http://www.rense.com/general62/Oswald.htm.

McAdams, John. "The Kennedy Assassination." http://mcadams.posc.mu.edu/home.htm.

Prouty, Fletcher L. *JFK: The CIA, Vietnam, and the Plot to Assassinate John F. Kennedy*. Carol Stream, IL: Carol, 1996.

Shackleford, Martin, updated by Debra Conway. "A History of the Zapruder Film." http://www.jfklancer.com/History-Z.html.

Summers, Anthony. *Conspiracy*. New York: Paragon House, 1989.

Vankin, Jonathan, and John Whalen. *The 60 Greatest Conspiracies of All Time: History's Biggest Mysteries, Coverups, and Cabals*. New York: Barnes & Noble, 1996.

"William Torbitt: Biography." http://www.spartacus.schoolnet.co.uk/JFKtorbitt.htm.

New Insights into Kennedy's Assassination

Documents show that Oswald, the mob, Anti-Castro Cubans, and right-wing groups really did conspire to kill the president

By David Kaiser

Chronicle of Higher Education, March 28, 2008

Sometime in the last week of September or the first few days of October 1963, three men knocked at the door of Silvia Odio, a young, divorced Cuban woman living in Dallas. Odio was packing for a move with the help of her sister. Their parents were in prison in Cuba, where they had been arrested after participating in an unsuccessful assassination conspiracy against Fidel Castro. Odio belonged to JURE, the Revolutionary Junta in Exile, an anti-Castro organization. By the fall of 1963, JURE, with covert American assistance, was preparing for a descent upon Cuba.

Two of the three men at the door identified themselves as "Leopoldo" and "Angelo." The third man, a young, slim American introduced as "Leon," said almost nothing. The men asked for assistance in identifying possible Dallas-area donors to the Cuban cause. Odio was polite but noncommittal, and they left.

A day or two later, she received a phone call from Leopoldo. The call, she surmised, reflected some romantic interest on his part, but he also asked what she thought of "the American." When she had nothing to say, he explained that the American was a former marine and an excellent shot, a slightly crazy fellow who might do anything. He speculated that Leon might be able to shoot Castro if he could be gotten into Cuba and also reported that Leon himself had commented that Cubans should have shot President Kennedy after the Bay of Pigs.

As Odio explained to the Warren Commission, investigating the assassination of John F. Kennedy many months later, she felt they were feeling her out to see if she had useful contacts in the Cuban underground. But she had no such contacts and did not reciprocate Leopoldo's romantic interest. A little less than two months later, after the assassination of President Kennedy, she saw Lee Harvey Oswald's picture and recognized him as Leon. Within two weeks she had given the essence of her story to the Federal Bureau of Investigation, but the agency did nothing to pursue it for more than six months.

The Odio incident was immediately recognized by Warren Commission investigators and by readers of the commission's 1964 report as one of the most provocative pieces of evidence in the case. But it has taken more than 40 years, and the release of millions of pages of original documentation in the late 1990s, to finally identify who Odio's callers were and how their visit confirms that President Kennedy was assassinated by a conspiracy for which Oswald was simply the trigger man.

As it turns out, the visit links Oswald and his crime to an enormous network of mobsters, anti-Castro Cubans, and right-wing political activists. Together with other new evidence, it allows us to name several key players in the conspiracy. The men who visited Odio were almost certainly Loran Hall, Lawrence Howard, and Oswald. Hall was an American military veteran and part-time mercenary who went to Cuba in 1959, joined Castro's army as a trainer, and then spent several months in a Cuban transit prison after falling afoul of the authorities. In the same prison at the same time was one of the United States' most notorious criminals, Santo Trafficante Jr., owner of several Havana casinos and mob boss of northern Florida. During that summer, Trafficante was also visited in his cell by a Dallas club owner named Jack Ruby.

Hall had been involved in many discussions of assassination plots against Castro and had also heard a good deal of talk about assassinating President Kennedy. As he implied to Odio, he realized that in Oswald he had come across a man willing to do either job. Hall, moreover, was not the only Trafficante associate in Dallas early that fall. His visit coincided with a talk by John Martino, who was involved in gambling in both the United States and Havana, and who had been jailed from 1959 through 1962 by Castro. Once released and repatriated to the States, Martino became a link between Trafficante and anti-Castro Cubans in the Miami area. Sometime in November 1963, he was watching the television news with his family when the newscaster referred to President Kennedy's trip to Texas. "If he goes to Dallas," Martino remarked, "they are going to kill him."

The Central Intelligence Agency had nothing to do with Kennedy's assassination, but it was involved with organized-crime figures while pursuing anti-Castro activities. In late 1960, agency operatives used the private investigator Robert Maheu to recruit mobsters, particularly those who had lost their Havana casinos, to kill Castro. Their efforts continued well into 1963. Both the Eisenhower and Kennedy administrations allowed the CIA to create a large zone of illegality within which it carried out various acts of sabotage, propaganda, and conspiracy against Castro.

In all probability, Oswald's attempt to reach Cuba via Mexico City—a trip he undertook either immediately after or immediately before "Leopoldo" introduced him to Odio—was designed to give him a chance to assassinate Castro. But the Cuban consulate in Mexico City refused to grant him a visa. Oswald then returned to Dallas and, within five weeks, accepted the assignment of assassinating President Kennedy for a "significant sum" of money.

Oswald, just 24 years old in 1963, grew up with a single parent in New Orleans and joined the Marines at the age of 17. Immediately after his discharge, in 1959, he traveled to the Soviet Union and publicly defected from the United States. Three years later, he managed to return to the United States with a Russian wife, Marina, and a new baby. Within a few months, he had begun corresponding with American Communist and socialist groups, and in the spring of 1963, after moving from

Dallas to New Orleans, he formed a one-man chapter of a Communist-front organization. For four and a half decades, those activities have convinced most Americans that Oswald was a sincere leftist.

But the evidence suggests otherwise. His later activities fit into a well-documented, broader effort by the FBI and independent right-wing groups to discredit left-wing organizations in the 1950s and 1960s, especially in the South.

The organized-crime bosses whom the CIA recruited to help assassinate Castro masterminded the killing of President Kennedy. They did that because of Attorney General Robert F. Kennedy's unprecedented effort to put the American mob out of business. Robert Kennedy's other key target was Jimmy Hoffa, of the Teamsters, who had close business ties and shared a lawyer with Trafficante.

In May 1963, Hoffa received a message from two mob bosses that it was time to execute President Kennedy. Both Carlos Marcello, a New Orleans mobster, and Trafficante had already discussed or foretold the killing of the president, and Sam Giancana, a Chicago mob boss, in conversations recorded by the FBI, had frequently expressed his resentment of the Kennedys. Jack Ruby, who killed Oswald just two days after the Kennedy assassination, had links to all three men. The killing of President Kennedy, followed by the resignation less than a year later of Robert Kennedy, seriously curtailed the government's effort to clean up organized crime—just as intended.

The Kennedy assassination, then, must be understood in the context of two much larger stories. The first is the government's campaign against organized crime, which actually began in the late 1950s, after the discovery of an infamous Mafia conclave, held in Appalachin, N.Y., proved that a national crime syndicate existed. The campaign accelerated dramatically under Robert Kennedy. The second story recounts the efforts of two administrations, and various private groups as well, to bring down Castro. A great deal has been written on those two subjects in the last 30 years, much of it exaggerated and far off the mark. The truth provides ample interest.

The Eisenhower administration recruited top mobsters to assassinate Castro, and their plots continued during the Kennedy years, though the Kennedy administration thought they had stopped. On the other hand, JFK's administration clearly viewed the assassination of Castro as a possible solution to the problem of Communism in Cuba, and it encouraged the CIA to bring about that result without involving the mob.

Ironically, however, the administration's failure to support the Bay of Pigs invasion, in 1961, combined with its refusal to take military action during the Cuban missile crisis, convinced most Cuban exiles that John and Robert Kennedy had no intention of toppling Castro. The Kennedys' favoritism toward relatively leftist exiles angered conservative Cubans and their American allies still further.

The assassination of the president was not a random event. At bottom it grew out of moralistic obsessions in American life: the insistence on outlawing the satisfaction of certain human appetites for gambling, sex, and drugs that created and sustained organized crime; and the refusal to respect the rights of foreign regimes that seemed to threaten American values and interests. Those two broad problems made the assassination possible; the actions of particular men made it happen. Oswald was an extraordinarily useful assassin, and his sudden death at the hands of Ruby—despite its highly suspicious nature—made it much harder for the truth to emerge.

In the 1970s, when key events in the background of the crime became known to law-enforcement agencies, the additional murders of Giancana and crime figure Johnny Roselli kept the details secret for two more decades and shielded living conspirators from legal action. The only prosecution of the crime, by District Attorney Jim Garrison in New Orleans, was a farce, and those conspirators who can now be identified are long since dead. But the truth of the assassination, its historical impact, and the ways in which it is still with us can now be told.

This is possible as a result of the release during the 1990s of enormous documentation by the Kennedy Assassination Records Collection Act of 1992 and the very thorough and intrepid work of the Assassination Records Review Board, led by the historian Anna K. Nelson, which was appointed to put it into effect. The records include not only all of the original FBI files on the investigation of the assassination itself, but also FBI files on numerous key organized-crime figures. More astonishingly, the CIA was persuaded to release not only all of the materials it had provided to the House Select Committee on Assassinations in 1977–78, but also individual files on a large number of Cuban exiles and exile groups.

Unfortunately, a few important files were overlooked, and it has now become harder than ever to secure their release in usable form. Still, the new CIA and FBI materials allow us to tell far more of the assassination story than has ever been told before, and also to evaluate, based on the original FBI reports, many of the key incidents in Oswald's life. Also released was all of the original testimony before the Senate select committee known as the Church Committee of 1975–76, which had been convened to study government intelligence activities. That testimony included a great many important facts that did not make it into the committee's final report. The files of the House of Representatives' assassination committee—which concluded that President Kennedy had "probably" been assassinated by a conspiracy involving organized crime—have also been made available. Hundreds of books on the Kennedy assassination have appeared, but not by professional historians who have done research in the available archives.

> *A true understanding of President Kennedy's assassination requires the reconstruction of a complex network of relationships among mobsters, hit men, intelligence agents, Cuban exiles, and America's cold-war foreign policy.*

Ruby's murder of Oswald and the apparent improbability of some of the critical evidence in the case—including the single-bullet theory, which the House committee convincingly determined to be true—got research into the Kennedy assassination off to an unfortunate start. Much of the early work became an exercise in trying to show that Oswald, who was indeed guilty, had not committed the crime. On the other hand, most of those who believed that Oswald was the assassin argued vehemently, in the face of a great deal of contrary evidence, that he had acted without any help or encouragement from anyone.

The truth lies squarely between those two extremes. A true understanding of President Kennedy's assassination requires the reconstruction of a complex network of relationships among mobsters, hit men, intelligence agents, Cuban exiles, and America's cold-war foreign policy. The story touches on an extraordinary range of locales and includes a remarkable cast of characters. It also involves the paradoxical policies of John F. Kennedy himself, who sought the relaxation of the cold war but apparently could not resign himself to the continuance of the Castro regime. And there are heroes as well, such as the hundreds of FBI agents who carefully put information on paper, the investigators for the House committee, and a few CIA operatives who believed that the American people deserved to know the truth. And now, at long last, we can see how all those various paths converged, and how a conspiracy of mobsters and misfits got away with assassinating a president.

David Kaiser, a historian, is a professor at the Naval War College. His books include American Tragedy: Kennedy, Johnson, and the Origins of the Vietnam War *(Harvard University Press, 2000). This essay is adapted from his* The Road to Dallas: The Assassination of John F. Kennedy, *to be published this month by Harvard University Press, copyright 2008 by David Kaiser.*

Researchers at A&M Discredit JFK Theory

By Holly Huffman
The Bryan-College Station Eagle, May 19, 2007

Neither Cliff Spiegelman nor Dennis James ever had a particular fascination with the vast conspiracies surrounding the assassination of John F. Kennedy.

But work recently completed by the Texas A&M researchers has thrust the pair into the midst of the most recent in a long, long line of controversies associated with the issue.

James and Spiegelman analyzed bullets that reportedly hailed from the same batch of ammunition used to kill the president in 1963. They said their findings, published in a recent statistics journal, discredit the original analysis used to rule out the possibility of a second shooter.

"There is nothing we have done that suggests in any way there are additional shooters or additional bullets," James said Friday. "All we're saying is, the scientific evidence used to rule out additional bullets and additional shooters is flawed.

"In fact, the testimony given at that time is most likely overstated."

The Annals of Applied Statistics article urged officials to re-analyze the original assassination bullet fragments by using more modern methods.

The first analysis was conducted in the mid-1960s by chemist Vincent Guinn, then a professor at the University of California at Irvine. Guinn, who has since died, reviewed five bullet fragments found after the slaying and concluded that they came from just two bullets.

Guinn testified before the House Committee on Assassinations that the chemical properties of individual bullets were unique. Because the fragments had similar properties, he deduced they originated from just two bullets, both of which were fired from Lee Harvey Oswald's rifle.

But Spiegelman and James—who worked with four fellow researchers, including A&M Statistics Department Head Simon Sheather—said their recent review showed the chemical properties of bullets aren't as unique as previously thought.

Working with them was William Tobin, a retired FBI lab chief and an expert in metallurgy whose research initiated new FBI guidelines in 2003 for the proper analysis of bullets.

Conducting a modern analysis similar to the process used by Guinn, the A&M researchers said they analyzed 30 Winchester Cartridge Co. Mannilicher-Carcano bullets. Just four lots of the bullets, the same type used in the assassination, were made.

The analysis showed that many bullets from the same box had the same chemical composition—an expected finding, they said. But the researchers said they also stumbled upon a more jolting revelation: One of the bullets had the same composition as a bullet fragment from the assassination.

Spiegelman likened the analysis to crumbled M&Ms. If there are two red pieces and three yellow pieces, it doesn't necessarily mean they are from just one red M&M and one yellow M&M, he explained.

"If you have two pieces of M&Ms that don't fit together like a jigsaw, you don't know if they are pieces of the same M&M or two M&Ms," Spiegelman said.

'Justice is done'

Both 59, the researchers were teenagers when the president was killed. The two said the event had a major impact on them, just as it did on most everyone else in America. But it didn't foster in them a desire to delve into the world of conspiracy theorists.

Though their reasons differed, both researchers said they were wary when asked to participate in the project.

Spiegelman, who has worked at Texas A&M for the past two decades, was the first to be consulted about the project a few years ago. The professor was on the National Resource Council overlooking FBI procedures for the chemical analysis of bullets. An expert on the interface between chemistry and statistics, he gave a talk about chemical analysis and mentioned its use following President Kennedy's assassination.

After posting a summary of his lecture online, he said he was contacted by two assassination buffs—Stuart Wexler, a high school teacher, and Tom Pinkston, a chemist. The men had acquired bullets from the same batch used to kill the president and they wanted someone to analyze them, Spiegelman said.

At first, Spiegelman was leery, he said. The statistics professor didn't know much about the details of the assassination, he said, and he hadn't even seen the famed Oliver Stone movie, *JFK*.

But he changed his mind after meeting with the men and reading testimony given to the House committee, some of which just didn't make sense, he said.

> *"All we're saying is, the scientific evidence used to rule out additional bullets and additional shooters is flawed."—Dennis James*

Spiegelman lauded Texas A&M for letting himself and James devote so much time to the research. Spiegelman said he has been working on the project since 2004. James was brought on board the following year, and the majority of analysis was conducted in 2006, they said.

"I want to be real clear: We don't know if there is one or two shooters," Spiegelman said. "We only care . . . in the sense that justice is done. We have no stake."

A significant event

James, too, said he was hesitant. Guinn had been a well-respected scientist and friend, so the last thing James wanted to do was "kick him when he's down," said the research chemist who has been at Texas A&M for 27 years.

He did most of the analysis at A&M's Nuclear Science Center using the Neutron Activation Analysis process, which can determine the concentration of elements in a material. Guinn's original work was done at a similar facility at the University of California at Irvine.

When James started, he knew little about the assassination, he said. He quickly began reading all that he could—including Guinn's work. James designed his experiments so they would correlate with those conducted by Guinn. In all, he reviewed the 30 bullets—10 each from three different lots—after they were broken into roughly 300 pieces, he said.

Despite the exhaustive work, both Spiegelman and James said they remain out of the conspiracy loop—though many buffs now are trying to pull them into the fray. Both men have been receiving phone calls and e-mails from journalists—and conspiracy theorists—from across the country.

The pair said they expected attention, but they weren't prepared for the onslaught.

"This is one of the most significant events in our country's history. Because of that, I think it's important we have all the information we can get," James said. "Whether or not re-analyzing fragments would provide definitive information, I don't know. But we certainly won't know unless we try."

Martha, Steward

Forty years after JFK's assassination, conspiracy theorists still rely on a retired Marion schoolteacher to keep the facts straight.

By Bill Shaw
Indianapolis Monthly, November 1, 2003

If you visit Martha A. Moyer of Marion seeking an analysis of the assassination of President John F. Kennedy, be prepared to relax and stay awhile. Once she starts explaining, she doesn't like to be interrupted. Her husband, James, who has suffered her lectures for 40 years, leaves the house to cut the grass in a drizzly rain rather than endure another session. "James tolerates me," says Moyer, dragging her little barking dog Polly out of the room. "Polly bites."

Thousands of books and thousands more Internet sites have been devoted to the seemingly endless, impossibly intricate conspiracy theories surrounding the Kennedy assassination in Dallas 40 years ago this month. Moyer, a white-haired, retired high-school teacher, is intimately familiar with all the ideas out there. "I've read every word of everything," she says, and she's not kidding. At age 72, Moyer is one of the leading amateur experts on the assassination, a passion that has consumed the last four decades of her life and shows no signs of abating. Her modest home is stuffed with countless books, pictures, letters, journals, videotapes and documents, including copies of the investigative files of the Dallas Police Department and all 26 volumes of the Warren Commission results, the government's widely discredited official report on the assassination. Moyer has read and reread every word of everything, committing great chunks of it to her prodigious memory.

She also owns duplicates of the bullets that killed Kennedy and a replica of the murder weapon, a 6.5 mm Italian-made Mannlicher-Carcano bolt-action rifle. She has a color copy of the bootleg home movie showing Kennedy's head exploding in a red, mushy mist as the bullet tears through his brain. The film was shot by a bystander who was recording the Presidential motorcade when Oswald struck and the world changed.

"Would you like to see it?" she asks.

"No, thanks."

She also has a complete set of black-and-white autopsy photographs of the naked, dead Oswald, and another of him in his casket.

"Would you like to see those?" she asks.

"No, thanks."

Experts invite Moyer to share her encyclopedic knowledge of the assassination at conferences around the country. Larry Hancock, who chairs an annual Dallas meeting of what he calls "serious, scholarly researchers," says Moyer is well-respected by the international research community. These are the people who study the assassination by doing their own original research, conducting their own interviews, and scouring medical evidence and legal testimony. He calls Moyer a valuable source for anyone researching the multitude of bewildering conspiracy theories. As she says, "There's a lot of nutty people in on this."

Moyer's research specialty is the life and troubled times of Dallas strip-club owner Jack Ruby, the shadowy character who gunned down Oswald on live television while Oswald was being led to jail in handcuffs. In 1998 she published an exhaustive report chronicling Ruby's every known movement from November 20 through his arrest on November 24. Ever wonder where Jack Ruby was at 9 p.m. on November 21? He was with his friends Beverly Oliver and Lawrence Meyers at the Cabana Hotel, and he talked to a woman in a sequined dress. An hour later, he was eating a steak dinner at the Egyptian Lounge. "Martha was a great help in directing me to little-known info about Jack Ruby for my own book," Hancock says.

> *[Martha A.] Moyer's research specialty is the life and troubled times of Dallas strip-club owner Jack Ruby, the shadowy character who gunned down Oswald on live television. . .*

Mark Shaw, local author of 12 books (and no relation to yours truly), discovered Moyer while researching a book on the life of San Francisco attorney Melvin Belli, who represented Ruby during his trials. "I interviewed hundreds of people for this book and was repeatedly directed to Martha," Shaw says. "She's highly respected. She knows everything. She is one of the top Ruby authorities in the country." Originally, Shaw intended to write a straight biography of Belli, a peripheral but significant player in the assassination's aftermath. After discussing the matter with Moyer and poring over her massive Ruby research, he refocused the book, called it *Melvin Belli: The Lawyer. The Legend, the Defender of Lee Harvey Oswald Assassin Jack Ruby*, and will publish it next year. Shaw asked Moyer to review the completed manuscript and check for factual errors.

"Mark wrote that Jack Ruby bought his gun in Chicago. He didn't. He bought the Cobra pistol at Ray Brantley's hardware store in Texas," Moyer says. "I told Mark he needed to correct that." At this point, she directs her husband to stop cutting the grass in the rain and pop the assassination tape into the VCR. "I don't know how to work the VCR, but James does. You need to see this tape," she says.

"I'd rather not."

"You must," she insists.

Moyer's improbable odyssey into the assassination netherworld began November 22, 1963, when she was driving home for lunch and heard on the radio that the President had been shot. For the next four or five days, she was consumed with watching, reading, listening to and absorbing every scrap of information about the assassination and its dramatic aftermath. She insisted that James and their three small children do the same, though they haven't matched her sustained enthusiasm for the subject.

Though she had been a secretary at the Veterans Administration Hospital, Moyer's casual interest in history intensified with Kennedy's death and propelled her to Ball State University, where she earned bachelor's and master's degrees in history. She began teaching at Mississinewa High School in Grant County in 1972. Her interest in the JFK assassination expanded from hobby to obsession. To the mountain of newspaper clippings, she added books, reports and every other imaginable document on her way to assembling a library-quality collection.

Moyer retired from teaching in 1991 and began meticulously organizing, footnoting, cross-referencing, annotating, time-lining and cataloging the mass of material. She also began writing articles for various JFK assassination journals and Internet sites, work that brought her to the attention of other experts in the field worldwide, who applauded the clarity of her research. Naturally, she has visited Kennedy's grave, every significant assassination-related location in Dallas and the National Archives in Washington.

Being a historian, former schoolteacher and stickler for accuracy, nearly every time Moyer makes a statement, she reaches for a book or report and points to the relevant passage, reading while pacing around her living room, addressing her hapless interviewer like a class of one. After a couple hours, she is surrounded by documents. "Now, in this book by KGB Colonel Oleg Maximovich Nechiporenko, who knew Lee Harvey Oswald, he maintains . . .," she lectures with increasing intensity. Then she directs my attention to the pile of scrapbooks. "This is Oswald's autopsy photo. Here's a picture of Marina—lovely lady—she first called me when I was taking a shower, and James thought it was a joke. This is Oswald's rooming house in Dallas. This is Jack Ruby's brother Earl," she continues, flipping through page after page of photographs.

"Would you like to see the blueprints of Dealey Plaza in Dallas?" she asks as James, a retired tool-and-die maker, finally stops cutting grass and turns his attention to the VCR and the assassination film. But when James turns on the VCR, Elmer Fudd dances across the screen. Exasperated, James rifles through a pile of tapes as Judge Joe Brown appears on the screen. He finally gives up on Elmer Fudd, Judge Joe Brown, the elusive death tape and the whole VCR situation and marches out of the room, only to return with a box of bullets and the replica of the murder rifle. James, it turns out, is practiced in describing the rifle minutiae.

"Okay, you have to understand, only two people saw Oswald go into the building with a package under his arm," James says, while Moyer nods in agreement. "They say it was 25 to 26 inches long. Well, the gun that was found, this gun, is 40.2 inches long and breaks down to only 34.8 inches, and you can't get it under your arm."

What does this mean?

"Draw your own conclusion," says Moyer. "If you decide to really get into this, come back and we'll start at the beginning." I ask bluntly: Who does Moyer believe killed Kennedy and why? Answering that would take a couple of books, Moyer says, and besides, "I'm a researcher. I just deal in facts, not conclusions." When pressed, she says, "I think the assassination was a mob hit. Oswald was involved, but so were others. We'll probably never know, but we'll be studying it 500 years from now."

The Good Spy

How the quashing of an honest C.I.A. investigator helped launch 40 years of JFK conspiracy theories and cynicism about the Feds.

By Jefferson Morley
The Washington Monthly, December 2003

It was 1:30 in the morning of Nov. 23, 1963, and John F. Kennedy had been dead for 12 hours. His corpse was being dressed at Bethesda Naval Hospital, touched and retouched to conceal the ugly bullet wounds. In Dallas, the F.B.I. had Lee Harvey Oswald in custody.

The lights were still on at the Central Intelligence Agency's headquarters in Langley, Va. John Whitten, the agency's 43-year-old chief of covert operations for Mexico and Central America, hung up the phone with his Mexico City station chief. He had just learned something stunning: A C.I.A. surveillance team in Mexico City had photographed Oswald at the Cuban consulate in early October, an indication that the agency might be able to quickly uncover the suspect's background.

At 1:36 am, Whitten sent a cable to Mexico City: "Send staffer with all photos of Oswald to HQ on the next available flight. Call Mr. Whitten at 652-6827." Within 24 hours Whitten was leading the C.I.A. investigation into the assassination. After two weeks of reviewing classified cables, he had learned that Oswald's pro-Castro political activities needed closer examination, especially his attempt to shoot a right-wing JFK critic, a diary of his efforts to confront anti-Castro exiles in New Orleans, and his public support for the pro-Castro Fair Play for Cuba Committee. For this investigatory zeal, Whitten was taken off the case.

C.I.A. Deputy Director of Plans Richard Helms blocked Whitten's efforts, effectively ending any hope of a comprehensive agency investigation of the accused assassin, a 24-year-old ex-Marine, who had sojourned in the Soviet Union and spent time as a leftist activist in New Orleans. In particular, Oswald's Cuba-related political life, which Whitten wished to pursue, went unexplored by the C.I.A. The blue-ribbon Warren commission appointed by President Johnson concluded in September 1964 that Oswald alone and unaided had killed Kennedy. But over the years, as information which the commission's report had not accounted for leaked out, many would come to see the commission as a cover-up, in part because it failed to assign any motive to Oswald, in part because the government's pre-assassination

From *The Washington Monthly* 35, no. 12 (2003): 40–44. Copyright © 2011 by *The Washington Monthly.* Reprinted with permission. All rights reserved.

surveillance of Oswald had been more intense than the government ever cared to disclose, and finally because its reconstruction of the crime sequence was flawed.

Both the story of Oswald and the C.I.A., and the way in which it leaked out in bits and pieces fueled a generation of conspiracy-minded authors, journalists, and filmmakers who mined Richard Helms's dubious legacy—a rich vein of ominous ambiguity and unanswered questions about one of the most jarring events of modern American history. The untimely end to Whitten's investigation, which prevented a public airing of what the government actually knew, also contributed to a generation of public cynicism about Washington—to a national mythology of skullduggery, and the suspicion that secret agencies in Washington were up to no good and the truth never gets out. In the decades since Kennedy's death, the "rogue C.I.A. assassin" has become a stock Hollywood character, his villainy engrained in spy movies and the popular culture.

> *Both the story of [Lee Harvey] Oswald and the C.I.A., and the way in which it leaked out in bits and pieces fueled a generation of conspiracy-minded authors, journalists, and filmmakers . . .*

Whitten's story, told here for the first time, has an uncomfortable new resonance today, as the Bush administration tries to thwart investigations into, among other things, what our intelligence agencies knew about Saddam's WMD programs before we went to war with Iraq. Whitten was a rare C.I.A. hero in the Kennedy assassination story whose personal odyssey is a poignant but unsettling reminder that inquiries into a national tragedy can be compromised early on. Intelligence mandarins, seeking to protect their positions, can override independent subordinates. Official deceptions can take decades to unravel. Embarrassing secrets, however, don't simply go away; eventually, they filter out, as the Kennedy case shows, often doing more harm to the country than they would have had the public known the truth earlier.

Stumbling into history

John Moss Whitten was born in 1920 to an itinerant Navy family and grew up in Annapolis, Md. After graduating from the University of Maryland with straight As, he did a stint as a captain in U.S. Army intelligence during World War II, interrogating captured German officers. After the war, he studied law at the University of Virginia, and after graduating in 1947 went to work at the newly formed C.I.A. He was a confident, well-built man with sandy hair and a pompous manner. Serving in Washington and Vienna, he built a reputation as an effective, if sometimes abrasive, officer and a skilled interrogator. In March 1962, Whitten was recalled to Washington to work in the agency's Western Hemisphere division. At his home in south Bethesda, Whitten struck neighbors as a genial State Department hand and amiable dinner-party host. At work, he was regarded as more than competent. In March 1963, he was again promoted, this time to be chief of all C.I.A. covert operations in Mexico and Central America.

Hours after the president's assassination, Whitten found himself at the center of history. The press reported that Oswald had lived for 32 months in the Soviet Union and that an anti-Castro student group claimed he had served as a spokesman for a pro-Castro organization, the Fair Play for Cuba Committee. With a shocked nation wondering if the assassination was a communist-inspired act of war, Helms called a meeting in his office, ordered his senior staff not to discuss the assassination, and announced that Whitten would review all internal files on Oswald.

The following morning, while he was being transferred to a more secure jail in Dallas, Oswald was shot dead by nightclub owner Jack Ruby. At the same moment, Helms was delivering Whitten's preliminary finding—that Oswald had acted alone—to President Lyndon Johnson. Whitten's investigation continued—for the next couple of weeks, he and a staff of 30 worked almost around the clock, doggedly plowing through C.I.A. cables from all over the world, scouring for new information. He forwarded the most interesting material to the White House, under Helms's name. He drafted a report on what the C.I.A. knew about Oswald and began circulating drafts to the various offices in the operations directorate that had tracked Oswald at one point or another. Nothing he learned in these first few weeks changed Whitten's original assessment, that Oswald had shot President Kennedy without anyone else's help or command.

But in the first days of December, Whitten abruptly learned that Helms had not been providing him all of the agency's available files on Oswald. On Dec. 6, he and a colleague went to the White House to read a report the F.B.I. had been preparing on Oswald. When he finished, he walked out into the cold sunny morning, feeling stunned: The bureau, he realized, possessed information about Oswald's past political activities that Helms had known but had never shared with him. "Oswald's involvement with the pro-Castro movement in the United States was not at all surfaced to us [meaning him and his staff] in the first weeks of the investigation," he later told investigators.

At a meeting soon after Dec. 6, Whitten complained to Helms and James Angleton, the chief of counter-intelligence staff, who outranked even Helms. Oswald's involvement with pro-Castro groups, he argued, made his initial conclusions "completely irrelevant." Analytically, Whitten had a point. Bureaucratically, he was out of line. Angleton, a pinched, brainy alcoholic who was responsible for keeping track of American defectors to the U.S.S.R. including Oswald, quickly concluded that Cuba was unimportant to the investigation, and decided to focus his inquiry narrowly on his own theories about Oswald's life in the Soviet Union.

Whitten felt sandbagged when Helms turned the Oswald investigation over to Angleton. Helms told him his services would no longer be needed, and Whitten was sent back to his Latin America duties. His ideas for investigating Oswald's Cuban connections were abandoned.

The secrets Dick Helms kept

What Whitten didn't know was that Helms's reluctance to investigate Oswald's connection to the pro-Castro movement had little to do with unraveling the Kennedy assassination—and a lot to do with hiding the potentially embarrassing performance of Helms's top anti-Castro operatives in regards to Oswald.

In the 12 weeks prior to Nov. 22, the agency had been keeping tabs on the man who would later assassinate the president. In August, Oswald had tried to insinuate himself into the ranks of the anti-Castro Cuban Student Directorate, then turned around and started handing out pamphlets for the Fair Play for Cuba Committee. What the C.I.A. failed to disclose for more than 30 years was that the Directorate's leaders in Miami were receiving $25,000 a month at the time. As I reported in the *Miami New Times* two years ago, an undercover agency officer working for Helms named George Joannides was guiding and monitoring the group's activities at the time of its contacts with Oswald.

In September, one of the agency's Latin American operatives had stood in line next to Oswald in New Orleans as he applied for a visa to travel to Mexico City where, two weeks later, Oswald visited the Cuban consulate. His arrival there was recorded by C.I.A. photo and audio surveillance teams reporting to a highly-regarded career officer named David Atlee Phillips, perhaps Helms's most accomplished protégé. Reports of Oswald's presence in Mexico City went back to Langley, where they were reviewed by Helms's top aide, Tom Karamessines. Had the agency's investigation of Oswald proceeded the way Whitten wanted, the accused assassin's connections to Cuba would have been fully reviewed, forcing the agency to account, at least internally, for what Joannides, Phillips, and Karamessines knew about Oswald.

Helms may have also feared that having John Whitten running loose in the C.I.A. files might expose his ongoing effort to arrange Castro's assassination. Under Helms's direction, C.I.A. agents had been encouraging Rolando Cubela, a charismatic young commandante who had come to power with Castro in 1959 but had later become disillusioned, to consider simply killing Castro himself. Cubela was an important asset at the heart of the Cuban government, memorably code-named AMLASH. On the day Kennedy was killed, Helms had sent an aide to bring a pen, fixed to deliver deadly poison, to Cubela in Paris. Even after Kennedy was dead, Helms continued to pursue Castro's murder. He did not call off the AMLASH plot.

Whether Helms actually punished Whitten for attempting to pursue the Oswald investigation, we cannot tell; Whitten's job evaluation from 1963 remains classified. But in the following years, while Helms went on to become Director of Central Intelligence, Whitten's career stalled. In 1965, he was kicked sideways into an unimportant job reviewing operations. He would not get a senior position, but his brilliance could not be denied. In 1970, he was awarded the Distinguished Intelligence medal, the agency's highest honor. He retired and moved his family to Vienna, where he pursued a new career as a singer.

There he found refuge in the calmer glories of Johann Strauss. Whitten became the first American to be accepted into the Vienna Men's Choral Society, the venerable singing group whose New Year's concerts are televised around the world. On concert nights, he sang first tenor. In his free time, he served as tour director. Gerhard Track, director of the society and a close friend of Whitten's, told me that

Whitten had wished to leave his life in America behind and never spoke about his espionage work. An honest bureaucrat, Whitten had stumbled into the middle of perhaps the greatest scandal related to one of the most momentous events in American history, but he never sought to rat on the institution which had shunted him aside. Neither a conspiracy theorist nor an apologist, he remained loyal to Langley.

The spy who sang

The agency's dossier on Oswald, which Whitten had tried to draw upon, would of course leak out anyway over the next two decades, tarnishing both the agency and Helms's reputation. In 1973, President Richard Nixon, mistrusting Helms's role in the Watergate burglary scandal, forced him out of the director's chair. Details about Helms's role in the assassination plots began to leak out. In May 1976, the C.I.A. connection with Rolando Cubela became public knowledge. With public outrage running high, Congress sliced the agency's budget and reined in its activities. The Justice Department indicted Helms for misleading lawmakers about the agency's part in overthrowing a leftist government in Chile. In 1978, Congress reopened the JFK investigation.

Whitten reluctantly returned from self-imposed exile to testify in secret session. As a former senior official who had once enjoyed access to virtually all of the agency's files on Oswald, he greatly interested the House Select Committee on Assassinations (HSCA). On May 16, 1978, two investigators and a stenographer recorded seven hours of Whitten's testimony about what he knew of the agency's Oswald investigation.

At the beginning, Whitten raised his right hand and swore to tell the truth. When asked to give his name, he replied, "John Scelso," which had been a code name he used in C.I.A. cables. But his testimony was remarkably candid. A less self-confident man might have minced his words. Not John Whitten. He sang.

Asked whether he thought Helms had acted properly by failing to disclose the Cubela plot to the Warren Commission, Whitten replied, "No. I think that was a morally highly reprehensible act, which he cannot possibly justify under his oath of office or any other standard of professional service."

Whitten said that he believed Oswald was a "pro-Castro nut," but he was aware of no evidence that Oswald had conspired with others. Yet he added that Helms had thwarted two important lines of inquiry: Oswald's Cuba-related activities and the AMLASH/Cubela imbroglio. Had he known about the latter, Whitten said he would have polygraphed Cubela, which might have put to rest suspicions that the malcontent commandante could have been Castro's double agent. Had he not been kept in the dark by Helms, Whitten said he would also have taken the investigation to the C.I.A. station in Miami, preempting decades worth of public speculation about what C.I.A. officials knew about Oswald and when they knew it.

Had Whitten been permitted to follow these leads to their logical conclusions, and had that information been included in the Warren Commission report, that report would have enjoyed more credibility with the public. Instead, Whitten's secret testimony strengthened the HSCA's scathing critique of the C.I.A.'s half-hearted investigation of Oswald. The HSCA concluded that Kennedy had been killed by Oswald and unidentifiable co-conspirators.

The insistence of the C.I.A. that all of the records of the HSCA investigation be kept secret for 50 years stoked more suspicion and cleared the way for Oliver Stone's 1991 movie *JFK*, which portrayed the assassination as the work of high-level C.I.A. and Pentagon conspirators. The Washington press corps ripped Stone for taking liberties with the historical record. But polls show that the general public found his interpretation of Kennedy's death more believable than the government's. The loss of investigatory nerve that first showed in John Whitten's reassignment culminated in permanent damage to the credibility of the U.S. government.

Until death do you declassify

In 1996, Whitten's 192-page deposition was finally declassified by the Assassination Records Review Board, an independent civilian panel created by Congress after the "*JFK*" furor. The board's chairman, federal judge John Tunheim, describes the deposition as "one of the most important" new JFK records. At Whitten's request, however, the board did not then declassify his true name. Whitten died in a Pottstown, Pa., nursing home in January 2000. Whitten's nemesis survived him. In retirement, Richard Helms lived quietly in Washington's Foxhall neighborhood, his number listed in the phone book. He had worked off the notoriety of the 1970s during the Reagan years when his hard-line posture became more fashionable and his legal troubles were forgotten. He was a fixture on the social circuit, attending events at the Kennedy Center and lunching with friends at the Sulgrave Club in Foggy Bottom, steadily working to rehabilitate his reputation with selected historians and journalists.

Helms never deigned to discuss "John Scelso," the C.I.A. man who spoke so critically about him. He flicked off my requests for interviews in the late 1990s with world-weary ease. When I asked him about "John Scelso," he said, perhaps truthfully, "I don't think I recall the name." Helms died at his home on Garfield Street in Washington on Oct. 22, 2002. Seven days later, the C.I.A declassified John Whitten's name.

4

Government Machinations: Political Conspiracy Theories

(Time & Life Pictures/Getty Images)

President Clinton was under intense scrutiny during his second term for his personal relations with White House intern Monica Lewinsky as well as his real estate investments in the Whitewater Development Corporation.

The Clinton Conspiracies

By Paul McCaffrey

The words became part of the national vocabulary almost as soon as they were spoken: In a January 1998 interview with Matt Lauer on NBC's *Today*, First Lady Hillary Rodham Clinton declared her husband, President Bill Clinton, the victim of a "vast right-wing conspiracy." At the time, the president was the target of an ongoing probe by Special Prosecutor Kenneth Starr. Initially, the investigation centered on the president and first lady's involvement in a failed Arkansas real estate venture called Whitewater Development Corporation. Over time, the inquiry's purview expanded and Starr's office took on the task of examining the apparent suicide of Vincent Foster, an advisor to the Clintons, and eventually the president's relationship with a White House intern, Monica Lewinsky. The Lewinsky revelations had only recently surfaced when the first lady made her comments to Lauer. Though the evidence uncovered by Starr about Clinton's liaisons with Lewinsky led ultimately to the president's impeachment by the House of Representatives, the US Senate subsequently acquitted him of the charges, allowing Clinton to retain his office and serve out his second term. How these events would play out was still very much uncertain that January morning.

In the days that followed, the first lady's salvo was characterized by the media as a coordinated counterattack on the part of the White House, and it produced the anticipated reaction: The Clintons' political opponents dismissed the charges as an example of the first couple's paranoia and mental instability, while their supporters found them entirely apt and rallied around the embattled president. The incident and its underlying causes illustrated a larger interplay, however, revealing how the presidency was both a magnet for conspiracy theories as well as the target of potential conspiracies.

In December 1992, a month after Clinton was elected president, the conservative magazine *American Spectator* held its twenty-fifth anniversary dinner. Though the conservative movement had suffered a setback on election day, the mood was jubilant. The emcee for the evening, journalist P. J. O'Rourke, heralded the magazine's "return to political opposition," declaring, "What a relief to be on the attack again. No more gentle sparring with the administration. No more striking with the flat of our sword. No more firing blanks. Ladies and gentlemen, we have game in our sights. Clinton may be a disaster for the rest of the nation, but he is meat on our table."

The magazine became a regular antagonist of the Clinton White House, running stories sourced to Arkansas state troopers about the president's alleged extramarital affairs while governor and containing lurid accusations concerning the first lady and Vincent Foster. At times, the *American Spectator* implied that the Clintons had a hand in Foster's death. Soon the magazine's anti-Clinton efforts grew more ambitious. Funded largely by one of the *Spectator*'s principal financial backers, Richard Mellon Scaife, the magazine set up the Arkansas Project, the purpose of which was to uncover evidence of corruption during Clinton's tenure as governor.

The Arkansas Project's efforts first concentrated on the Whitewater controversy. The man they relied on to direct them in their investigation was David Hale, a former municipal judge in Arkansas who accused Clinton of Whitewater-related malfeasance. The project also engaged in considerable conjecture about the death of Vince Foster, continually connecting the Clintons to their longtime friend and advisor's demise. Starr would conclude after his own inquiry that, contrary to conservative conspiracy theories, Foster had indeed taken his own life.

As time wore on, Arkansas Project operatives failed to dig up anything truly damaging to the president and first lady, so it changed direction. During the early days of 1995, the Arkansas Project turned its gaze to Mena Airport, an isolated landing strip in western Arkansas, where one informant, an Arkansas state trooper named L. D. Brown, alleged Clinton had run a gunrunning and drug distribution operation, flying weapons to Nicaragua and bringing back supplies of cocaine. Brown also connected Clinton to murder. The *Spectator* published many of Brown's accusations in the August 1995 issue. The story did not generate much in the way of follow-up from other media outfits. The allegations, incredible though they were, were thinly sourced, based solely on the claims of a lone informant.

By the time the Lewinsky scandal emerged in January 1998, the Arkansas Project had spent $2.4 million but yielded little in the way of concrete evidence against the Clintons. The operation had served as a powerful generator of Clinton conspiracy theories, yet hadn't proven any of its breathless accusations. Soon, the tables were turned, as the Arkansas Project and the *Spectator* became the focus of left-wing conspiracy theories. An investigation by another media outlet, *Salon*, in a March 1998 report, claimed the Arkansas Project had funneled money to David Hale to influence his testimony against the Clintons in the Whitewater matter. These were grave accusations and had the potential to result in jail time for those involved.

Taking the *Salon* charges seriously, the Clinton Justice Department requested that Ken Starr look into the accusations and probe the *Spectator*. In the subsequent fourteen-month inquiry, after subpoenaing many of the project's operatives, investigators were unable to uncover evidence of a direct quid pro quo between the Arkansas Project and Hale.

In the end, the Arkansas Project probably caused more problems for the *American Spectator* than it did for the White House. The most damaging accusations it uncovered came off as farfetched and poorly sourced and were ignored by the mainstream media. Moreover, the project's financial and legal costs were catastrophic to the magazine's bottom line and ultimately alienated the publication from Scaife, its longtime benefactor, who subsequently cut off his funding. Whatever the truth of its Clinton-related conspiracy theories, the Arkansas Project did not bring down the president. But it nearly did bring down the *Spectator*.

While conservatives might claim the Arkansas Project was just an expensive and sophomoric attempt at investigative journalism—"a Keystone Kops operation" in the words of conservative writer Byron York—for Clinton supporters, the Arkansas Project offered proof of the "vast right-wing conspiracy" to which the first lady had originally referred. A wealthy opponent of the president, unable to unseat him at the polls, hired conservative hatchet men to dig up the dirt necessary to remove him from office. When the necessary dirt could not be found, this characterization goes, it was invented, whether through well-compensated "witnesses" or mere speculation.

But Bill Clinton is hardly the first—or last—president to be the subject or target of conspiracy theories. As the JFK assassination and 9/11 attacks demonstrate, conspiracy theories and the presidency often go hand in hand. Some of the speculation can be rather outlandish. For example, by virtue of the number of letters in his first, middle, and last name—six each—President Ronald Wilson Reagan, some conspiracists thought, could be the Antichrist spoken of in the New Testament's Book of Revelation. By comparison, the suggestion that Clinton was involved in arms dealing, drug trafficking, and murder comes off as rather tame.

Rarely are presidential conspiracy theories so monumental—and rarely is the president only the subject of one. Reagan was also front and center in the Iran-Contra affair, a conspiracy to fund the Nicaraguan Contras, a right-wing militia, with the proceeds from arms sales to Iran in the 1980s, though the president's knowledge of the effort was never established. There was also the "October surprise" conspiracy theory, in which it was alleged Reagan's backers made contact with Iranian officials to ensure that American personnel held hostage there would not be released before election day in 1980, thus helping Reagan defeat President Jimmy Carter.

Presidents George W. Bush and Barack Obama have each also been the subject of widespread conspiracy theories. The exceedingly close 2000 general election, which saw Bush narrowly win the presidency even after his opponent, Vice President Al Gore, secured over half a million more votes, proved an ideal recipe for conspiracy theories, especially since the deciding state, Florida, was then governed by Bush's brother Jeb. Four years later, in 2004, similar alarms were sounded when Bush defeated Senator John Kerry. Though Bush had outpolled Kerry by over three million votes, some suggested that based on exit polls indicating a Kerry victory, something was rotten in Ohio, the state that sealed the president's reelection in the Electoral College.

Questions of legitimacy resurfaced with Bush's successor, Barack Obama, as well. Unlike Bush, however, Obama had won a convincing victory in 2008, leaving little to no question of chicanery at the polls. Most of the theories concentrated not on his showing at the ballot box but rather on his birth certificate. A sizeable segment of the population—over a quarter in some polls—stated they believed the president was not born in the United States and that his birth certificate, listing Honolulu, Hawaii, as his birthplace, was a forgery. The release of Obama's long-form birth certificate in April 2011 stole much of the momentum from the "birthers," as they came to be known, but a not-insignificant minority of Americans still question the president's citizenship and thus his right to hold the nation's highest office.

While in the United States, presidents are often the central focus of political conspiracy theories, other officeholders are far from immune. Frequently, an accidental death leads to sinister speculation. In the past twenty years, Ron Brown, a cabinet secretary under President Clinton, and Senator Paul Wellstone, of Minnesota, for example, died in plane crashes that have become fodder for conspiracists.

At other times the subject of a political conspiracy theory does not focus on any one individual but on a party or an agenda. During Democratic presidencies, for example, gun-rights advocates are more inclined to believe that the government is intent on taking away their firearms, while under Republican presidencies, pro-choice activists tend to worry that the right to an abortion will be curtailed. In another vein, as the climate change debate has become part of our political dialogue, some contend that there is a conspiracy afoot among government officials and academics to manufacture data that supports the existence of global warming. Others say that traditional energy companies and their political allies have, in turn, doctored evidence in order to cast doubt on the impact of climate change.

Then there are the more grandiose political conspiracy theories that transcend individual actors and issues. For decades now, the threat of a so-called North American Union (NAU) has been a regular subject for conspiracists. The NAU would unite Mexico, the United States, and Canada into one integrated superstate, eroding the sovereignty of the individual nations and ushering in a euro-like economic zone. Akin to the NAU conspiracy theory is that of the New World Order (NWO), which anticipates the implementation of an authoritarian one-world government.

Unless more hard evidence is uncovered, the reality of such conspiracies will have to remain a matter of individual perception. That is, the Clintons and their supporters will likely conclude that the Arkansas Project was part of a coordinated and nefarious plot by their political opponents to sabotage the legitimacy of the administration and bring down the president. Meanwhile, Arkansas Project operatives and those assured of the Clintons' corruption will continue to view the endeavor as a good-faith effort to uncover a criminal conspiracy that did in fact exist, whether or not the supporting evidence was available. In the end, short of a smoking gun, the conspiracy is all in the eyes of the beholder.

Citing 'Sideshow,' Obama Offers Full Birth Certificate

By Susan Page and Jackie Kucinich
USA Today, April 28, 2011

President Obama, trying to squelch an escalating and distracting controversy, released on Wednesday a long-form birth certificate from 1961 that showed just what he has always insisted: He was born at Kapiolani Maternity & Gynecological Hospital in Honolulu.

So is the issue settled?

Even Obama doesn't think the signed-and-sealed document will convince some "birthers" who suspect he was born abroad and therefore might be ineligible to be president.

"I know that there's going to be a segment of people for which, no matter what we put out, this issue will not be put to rest," the president said in an extraordinary morning appearance in the White House briefing room. "But I'm speaking to the vast majority of the American people as well as to the press: We do not have time for this kind of silliness . . . We've got big problems to solve. And I'm confident we can solve them, but we're going to have to focus on them—not on this."

In New Hampshire, real estate mogul Donald Trump, who has used the birther issue to fuel a possible presidential campaign, bragged that he had "accomplished something that nobody else was able to accomplish" in forcing the document's release.

The notion that Obama lied about his birthplace has become one of those persistent conspiracy theories in American political life, from who-shot-JFK to the forces behind the 9/11 attacks.

"There is fertile ground for these kind of charges" about Obama, says Robert Goldberg, a historian at the University of Utah and author of *Enemies Within: The Culture of Conspiracy in Modern America.* "Knowing how Americans love conspiracy theories, this plays into American fears and anxieties, whether about black people or about the world around them."

Such controversies are stoked by skepticism about information from the government and other institutions, the vitriol and polarization in American politics, the echo chamber of cable news and the Internet, and even the profusion of movies and TV shows that depict governmental and global conspiracies, Goldberg says.

The release of official documents or reports by commissions rarely settle such issues for everyone.

Joseph Farah, CEO of the conservative website WorldNetDaily and publisher of a new book that investigates whether Obama is eligible to be president, says the issue isn't over.

"Assuming it is completely legitimate and the real deal, I think it raises more questions than it answers," he says of the birth certificate, saying the fact that Obama's father wasn't a U.S. citizen also could raise questions about his eligibility for the presidency. And Farah says he wants to see "the original document."

It remains in a bound volume at the state Department of Health in Hawaii in files that aren't open to public view.

Gaining traction

A USA TODAY/Gallup Poll released Monday indicated the issue has been gaining traction.

Only 38% of Americans said they thought the president was "definitely" born in the United States; 18% said he "probably" was. Nearly one in four, 24%, said he was probably or definitely born in another country. Nineteen percent said they didn't know enough to say.

Those who think the president was born outside the United States tend to be among his fiercest critics. Most are Republicans, conservatives and supporters of the Tea Party movement. Three of four disapprove of the job he is doing as president.

Trump raised the "decibel level" so high that the White House couldn't ignore it, says Al Cardenas, chairman of the American Conservative Union.

Only 38% of Americans said they thought the president was "definitely" born in the United States . . .

"I think he had somewhat of an arrogance before, in thinking he wasn't going to respond to an accusation of this nature, but obviously if it warranted that much national attention he should have dispensed with it and moved on," he says. "You scratch your head wondering why it took the president so long to put this to rest, if indeed that long form puts it to rest."

Democratic consultant Phil Singer says the White House release was smart.

"This is a non-issue that, for whatever reason, takes up space that would otherwise be dedicated to the good things that the president is doing. So it makes every piece of sense in the world to try to take the issue off the table," says Singer, a spokesman for Hillary Rodham Clinton when she ran against Obama in the 2008 Democratic primaries.

"It probably would have been a good thing if they'd done it when the issue first surfaced," he says, "but better late than never."

During the 2008 campaign, when initial questions were raised about where Obama was born, he requested a copy of his birth certificate from Hawaii and posted it on his campaign's website.

The "Certification of Live Birth" answered the questions then, White House communications director Dan Pfeiffer says.

That changed in recent weeks, as the issue was revived by Trump and others who questioned why Obama hadn't released the longer "Certificate of Live Birth" from Hawaii. It includes some additional information, such as the name of the hospital, and is signed by the mother, the doctor and the local registrar.

The White House had tried to ignore the issue, dismiss it and use humor to ridicule it. When Obama was introduced at the annual Gridiron Dinner last month in Washington, the president stopped the band as it played *Hail to the Chief* and said, "Can we go with that song we talked about?"

A refrain of Bruce Springsteen's *Born in the USA* followed, to laughter from the audience of journalists and officials. "Some things just bear repeating," Obama quipped.

But the issue seemed to be gaining velocity. "Essentially the discussion transcended from the nether regions of the Internet into mainstream political debate in the country," Pfeiffer says.

Obama said he decided it was time to respond when the debate over the deficit-reduction plans advanced this month by the White House and House Republicans was overshadowed by the birther debate. Getting the long-form certificate required Obama to write a letter to Hawaian officials seeking a waiver for its release.

His personal attorney, Judy Corley, flew to Honolulu to pick up two copies of the certificate, returning to Washington on Tuesday.

"We're going to have to make a series of very difficult decisions" on federal spending and deficits, Obama said. "But we're not going to be able to do it if . . . we get distracted by sideshows and carnival barkers."

Actually, a weekly analysis of leading news outlets by Pew's Project for Excellence in Journalism found that the economy commanded 39% of coverage the week the deficit plans were released, compared with 4% on the Obama administration and the birther issue.

On the other hand, last week Trump ranked second only to Obama as a newsmaker.

'A strong lineage of race'

Civil rights leaders see what Jesse Jackson calls "a strong lineage of race" in the questions raised about Obama, the nation's first African-American president.

"This was a bogus issue and untrue accusations designed to take away President Obama's legitimacy, the heart of his integrity," Jackson says, adding that birthers' message to the president is that "you are not born here, you are not one of us, you are a liar."

Rep. James Clyburn, D-S.C., the highest-ranking African American in Congress, also sees a racial overtone, likening it to the scrutiny Jackie Robinson faced when he became the first black player in major league baseball in 1947.

Obama "has not put the issue to bed," Clyburn says. "All he did was lay out the truth for everyone to see."

Farah denies racism is a factor, calling the allegation "the last refuge for scoundrels who have run out of arguments."

In its politics, the birther issue was a bigger problem for Republicans than for Obama, Pfeiffer argues. It has divided GOP ranks and put the spotlight on an issue that is secondary for most Americans.

Some Republican presidential hopefuls, including former Massachusetts governor Mitt Romney, have steered clear of the birther issue. But former House speaker Newt Gingrich took a skeptical tone when told of the document's release.

"All I would say is, why did it take so long?" he told a reporter for TPM.com. "The whole thing is strange."

Former Alaska governor Sarah Palin posted a mocking tweet that read, "Media: admit it, Trump forced the issue."

"If that's as good as it gets on the Republican side to run a candidate for president, I can't wait for this election," says Sen. Dick Durbin, an Illinois Democrat close to Obama. "It is almost a comic variety of political campaigning when you consider the serious issues facing our nation, that that's the best they can do."

Obama portrayed himself as trying to address the big challenges facing the country on jobs and the economy while his critics engage in a sideshow.

Still, the birther issue was a distraction for him, too.

"The fact that the president of the United States has to bend toward these conspiracy theorists, has to accept on some level their premise and take valuable time out of his schedule to confront this—that's startling," Goldberg says. "My sense is that is only going to entice them and energize them."

Trump sounded like a candidate undeterred by the loss of the issue that had drawn him attention, saying he would announce his decision whether to run for president later this month on the finale of his TV reality show, *Celebrity Apprentice*.

"I think if I do run, I'll do very well," Trump said. "I think I'd beat Obama."

Then he pivoted to another issue involving Obama's personal qualifications, saying he had read that Obama was a poor student at Occidental College and asking how he had won admission to Columbia University and Harvard Law School.

"I don't know why he doesn't release his records" from his school days, Trump said.

Latest Conspiracy Theory—Kerry Won—Hits the Ether

By Manuel Roig-Franzia and Dan Keating
Washington Post, November 11, 2004

The e-mail subject lines couldn't be any bigger and bolder: "Another Stolen Election," "Presidential election was hacked," "Ohio Fraud."

Even as Sen. John F. Kerry's campaign is steadfastly refusing to challenge the results of the presidential election, the bloggers and the mortally wounded party loyalists and the spreadsheet-wielding conspiracy theorists are filling the Internet with head-turning allegations. There is the one about more ballots cast than registered voters in the big Ohio county anchored by Cleveland. There are claims that a suspicious number of Florida counties ended up with Bush vote totals that were far larger than the number of registered Republican voters. And then there is the one that might be the most popular of all: the exit polls that showed Kerry winning big weren't wrong—they were right.

Each of the claims is buoyed by enough statistics and analysis to sound plausible. In some instances, the theories are coming from respected sources—college engineering professors fascinated by voting technology, Internet journalists, election reform activists. Ultimately, none of the most popular theories holds up to close scrutiny. And the people who most stand to benefit from the conspiracy theories—the Kerry campaign and the Democratic National Committee—are not biting.

"At this point the number of irregularities brought to our attention is not going to change the outcome of the election," said DNC spokesman Jano Cabrera. "The simple fact of the matter is that Republicans received more votes than Democrats, and we're not contesting this election."

The Ohio vote-fraud theory appears to stem from the curious ways of the Cuyahoga County Board of Elections. During even-numbered years the county's canvassing board posts vote totals that include the results from outside the county from congressional districts that spill over Cuyahoga's borders. The quirk made it look as if the county had 90,000 more votes than voters.

The disparities were spotted, and urgent mass mailings began: "Ohio precincts report up to 1,586% turnout . . . 30 Precincts in Ohio's Cuyahoga County report 'over' 100% turnout!" Later, the county added a disclaimer to its Web site in an attempt to explain the numbers.

"It takes me about three times to explain" why the fraud allegation is untrue, said Kimberly Bartlett, community outreach specialist for the Cuyahoga County Board of Elections. "You have to ask them why no top Democrat is making these charges."

There also have been reports of more votes counted than voters in some counties in Florida and North Carolina. Steve Ansolabehere of the Caltech-MIT Voting Technology Project said the preliminary results do not add up. "We'll see if there's anything dramatic or widespread once we see the full certifications come in," he said.

> *The people who most stand to benefit from the conspiracy theories—the Kerry campaign and the Democratic National Committee—are not biting.*

The Florida case is more nuanced than the Ohio voting battle. Numerous bloggers have noted that President Bush's vote totals in 47 Florida counties were larger—in some cases much larger—than the number of registered Republican voters in the same counties. A widely distributed piece on Consortiumnews.com said the results "are so statistically stunning that they border on the unbelievable."

The article's main numbers are correct. But the central premise—that there is something suspicious about Bush getting more votes than the number of registered Republicans in rural counties, which use paper ballots—may not be suspicious at all.

It is does not account for thousands of independents or for voters who do not list party affiliation. It is also common for Florida Democrats, particularly the "Dixiecrats" in the northern reaches of the state and the Panhandle, to vote for Republicans, a pattern that is repeated in much of the Deep South.

"Florida has always been the land of the Dixiecrats," said Walter R. Mebane Jr., a professor of government at Cornell University who specializes in voting issues. "In Florida, as you go north, you go south."

Despite its apparent flaws, the Florida theory raises some interesting questions. For instance, a further look at Florida voting patterns shows that the number of counties with more Bush votes than registered Republicans jumped from 32 in 2000 to 47 in 2004. Bush's improved performance might be explained by Al Gore, a southern moderate, having had more appeal to Dixiecrats four years ago than Kerry, who is from Massachusetts, did in this election.

The theories on exit polls are even more slippery. Because the early exit polls that were leaked and caused so much excitement among Democrats are not publicly distributed, the criticisms have not been based on statistics. Instead there are comments such as those from Zvi Drezner, a professor at the California State University at Fullerton business and economics school, who wrote that "the exit polls did not 'lie'" and described "a gut feeling that the machines did not report the correct count."

Many voting experts say the theory that the exit polls were correct is deeply flawed because the polls oversampled women. MIT political scientist Charles Stewart III also has said focusing solely on the early polls favoring Kerry in Ohio and

Florida is the wrong approach because exit polls in some Democratic-leaning states tilted toward Bush, evening out the national picture.

The U.S. Justice Department, which handles complaints fielded by a bipartisan commission formed after the 2000 election chaos, said the allegations of vote buying and voter-registration fraud were no different than the pattern of previous elections. But other sources are documenting huge numbers of complaints. Verified Voting, a group formed by a Stanford University professor to assess electronic voting, has collected 31,000 reports of election fraud and other problems, but nothing that would overturn the Nov. 2 outcome.

Still, messages posted on the aptly named Quixotegroup discussion cluster—which takes its name from the literary figure Don Quixote who used his lance to tilt against windmills—urged members to send fraud evidence to the law firm of Kerry's brother, Cameron Kerry, to persuade the Democratic candidate to "unconcede."

A high-ranking Democrat, mindful of balancing respect for the complainers and a desire to move on, summed up the conspiracy theorists with a line from Alexander Pope: "Hope springs eternal in the human breast."

Those Pesky Voters

By Bob Herbert
New York Times, June 12, 2006

I remember fielding telephone calls on Election Day 2004 from friends and colleagues anxious to talk about the exit polls, which seemed to show that John Kerry was beating George W. Bush and would be the next president.

As the afternoon faded into evening, reports started coming in that the Bush camp was dispirited, maybe even despondent, and that the Kerry crowd was set to celebrate. (In an article in the current issue of *Rolling Stone*, Robert F. Kennedy Jr. writes, "In London, Prime Minister Tony Blair went to bed contemplating his relationship with President-elect Kerry.")

I was skeptical.

The election was bound to be close, and I knew that Kerry couldn't win Florida. I had been monitoring the efforts to suppress Democratic votes there and had reported on the thuggish practice (by the Jeb Bush administration) of sending armed state police officers into the homes of elderly black voters in Orlando to "investigate" allegations of voter fraud.

As far as I was concerned, Florida was safe for the G.O.P. That left Ohio.

Republicans, and even a surprising number of Democrats, have been anxious to leave the 2004 Ohio election debacle behind. But Mr. Kennedy, in his long, heavily footnoted article ("Was the 2004 Election Stolen?"), leaves no doubt that the democratic process was trampled and left for dead in the Buckeye State. Mr. Kerry almost certainly would have won Ohio if all of his votes had been counted, and if all of the eligible voters who tried to vote for him had been allowed to cast their ballots.

Mr. Kennedy's article echoed and expanded upon an article in *Harper's* ("None Dare Call It Stolen," by Mark Crispin Miller) that ran last summer. Both articles documented ugly, aggressive and frequently unconscionable efforts by G.O.P. stalwarts to disenfranchise Democrats in Ohio, especially those in urban and heavily black areas.

The point man for these efforts was the Ohio secretary of state, J. Kenneth Blackwell, a Republican who was both the chief election official in the state and co-chairman of the 2004 Bush-Cheney campaign in Ohio—just as Katherine Harris was the chief election official and co-chairwoman of the Bush-Cheney campaign in Florida in 2000.

No one has been able to prove that the election in Ohio was hijacked. But whenever it is closely scrutinized, the range of problems and dirty tricks that come to

> *What's not shocking, of course, is that every glitch and every foul-up in Ohio, every arbitrary new rule and regulation, somehow favored Mr. Bush.*

light is shocking. What's not shocking, of course, is that every glitch and every foul-up in Ohio, every arbitrary new rule and regulation, somehow favored Mr. Bush.

For example, the shortages of voting machines and the long lines with waits of seven hours or more occurred mostly in urban areas and discouraged untold numbers of mostly Kerry voters.

Walter Mebane Jr., a professor of government at Cornell University, did a statistical analysis of the vote in Franklin County, which includes the city of Columbus. He told Mr. Kennedy, "The allocation of voting machines in Franklin County was clearly biased against voters in precincts with high proportions of African-Americans."

Mr. Mebane told me that he compared the distribution of voting machines in Ohio's 2004 presidential election with the distribution of machines for a primary election held the previous spring. For the primary, he said, "There was no sign of racial bias in the distribution of the machines." But for the general election in November, "there was substantial bias, with fewer voting machines per voter in areas that were heavily African-American."

Mr. Mebane said he was unable to determine whether the machines were "intentionally" allocated "to create these biases."

Mr. Kennedy noted that this was just one of an endless sequence of difficulties confronting Democratic voters that stretched from the registration process to the post-election recount. Statistical analyses—not just of the distribution of voting machines, but of wildly anomalous voting patterns—have left nonpartisan experts shaking their heads.

The lesson out of Ohio (and Florida before it) is that the integrity of the election process needs to be more fiercely defended in the face of outrageous Republican assaults. Democrats, the media and ordinary voters need to fight back.

The right to vote is supposed to mean something in the United States. The idea of going to war overseas in the name of the democratic process while making a mockery of that process here at home is just too ludicrous.

A Week of Fear

But not in the GOP's convention hall

By Byron York
National Review, September 27, 2004

"Are Americans going to react to a message of fear, or respond to a message of hope?" asked Tom Vilsack, the Democratic governor of Iowa. Vilsack was speaking at his party's "rapid response" center at the Republican convention in New York, where he, along with other Democratic officials, spinmeisters, and sympathetic pundits, spent much of convention week repeating one simple point: Democrats represent "the politics of hope," as senior Kerry adviser Tad Devine put it, while Republicans represent the "politics of fear."

But if one ventured outside the confines of Madison Square Garden and its media center, a far different story emerged. Supporters of John Kerry staged dozens of events—protests, plays, book readings, concerts, and parties—designed to counter the message of the convention. And those events were, by and large, almost desperate expressions of fear, in which participants pronounced themselves terrified of George W. Bush and what might happen to the United States if he were elected to a second term.

"I'm scared," the actress Rosie Perez told a crowd gathered at Crobar, a stylish Chelsea nightclub, on the night before she joined 200,000 anti-Bush demonstrators in the pre-convention protest march. "I'm f***ing scared out of my pants right now, and if you're not, wake up." A few minutes later, the comedian Chevy Chase took the stage to say of George W. Bush, "He's frightening. He's scaring the crap out of me." Chase said the president "makes Barry Goldwater look like Pollyanna," but then realized that some in the mostly young crowd didn't get the comparison. "I remember 1964. You hadn't been born yet," the 60-year-old Chase told the audience, with a slight tinge of bitterness in his voice.

Chase and Perez did not say exactly why they were so frightened. Of course it had to do with Bush, but what, precisely, was it that was so terrifying? A few days later, the *New York Times* columnist Paul Krugman offered an answer.

At a New York University forum entitled, "The Books on Bush," Krugman said the president is the front man for a decades-old, far-reaching, right-wing conspiracy to gain control of the U.S. government. "We probably make a mistake when we place too much emphasis on Bush the individual," Krugman said. "This really isn't about Bush. Bush is the guy that the movement found to take them over the top."

Krugman explained that the conspirators who placed the president in power were the same ones who tried to remove Bill Clinton from office. But the conspiracy itself began far earlier. "There's complete continuity going back, really, I think—but this is my next book—you really need to go back to Goldwater," Krugman said. "A lot of this has to do with civil rights, and the people who don't like them." (Krugman's audience, older than the crowd at Crobar, seemed to know who Goldwater was.)

As Krugman reached the end of his talk, he came to the question of what might be done to avert a rightwing takeover. Of course it's important to defeat George W. Bush, Krugman said, but that's not enough. "The answer, I think, my great hope now, is that we need an enormous unearthing of the scandals that we know have taken place," Krugman explained. "We need a mega-Watergate that rocks them back." The audience, which had given Krugman a standing ovation before he even began speaking, loved it.

Still, there were undoubtedly some Democrats who enjoyed Krugman's analysis but found it a bit, er, *understated*. For them, the hot ticket of convention week— the true anti-Bush hard stuff—was the double-billing of playwright Tony Kushner's *Only We Who Guard the Mystery Shall Be Unhappy* and New York University professor Mark Crispin Miller's *Patriot Act: A Public Meditation*, at the New York Theatre Workshop in the East Village.

Kushner's play is a "work in progress" in which First Lady Laura Bush, played by Academy Award-winning actress Holly Hunter, reads to a group of Iraqi children. Early on, Mrs. Bush discovers that the children are in fact ghosts, since all had been killed by American bombs (the situation is explained to the First Lady by an angel, played by *Sex and the City* actress Cynthia Nixon). As the play goes on, Mrs. Bush fights the realization that her husband is a terrible, remorseless man responsible for thousands of needless deaths, not only from the war in Iraq, but from capital punishment in Texas. "My husband, he executed everyone they told him to, everyone they let him, I should say," Kushner's Mrs. Bush tells the audience. "My God, a hundred-and-something people and he never even missed his early, early bedtime, nor for that matter, from what I could see as I sat up reading and rereading Dostoyevsky, ever even stirred in his sleep!"

> **[Paul] Krugman said the president is the front man for a decades-old, far-reaching, right-wing conspiracy to gain control of the U.S. government.**

In *Patriot Act*, Miller presented a far less melodramatic, and, if possible, even more menacing, Bush. Analyzing the president's misstatements, gestures, and policies, Miller told the audience that the president has a plan for "the transformation of the United States into a theocracy" and the "replacement of the Constitution by the first five books of the Old Testament." In Bush's new America, Miller explained, the justice system would be based on Leviticus, with Americans being sentenced to death for adultery, homosexuality, and premarital sex, among many other capital offenses. "It's hard to understate the extent to which this administration is driven by the theocratic agenda," Miller said.

Miller spoke in all apparent seriousness, and his audience appeared to listen in the same spirit. At one point, on the screen behind him, Miller projected a lineup of photographs of the leaders of the theocratic coup. In the upper left, there was the late theologian R. J. Rushdoony, who believed in the rule of Biblical law; next was conservative California philanthropist Howard Ahmanson; next was Marvin Olasky, of "compassionate conservatism" fame; and then came Sen. Trent Lott, televangelists Jerry Falwell and James Robison, the Traditional Values Coalition's Rev. Louis Sheldon, and, finally, radio host Oliver North. In Miller's narrative, they were all intimately connected, and the audience was supposed to understand that all those connections led to George W. Bush, the White House, and the imposition of theocracy. And indeed, most of the overwhelmingly friendly audience seemed to get it; they gave Miller a rousing ovation when he finished (his last bit had been a warning that Bush intended to postpone, steal, or possibly even cancel this year's election).

By the end of convention week, the anti-Bush, pro-Kerry performers had sent a clear message: Be very, very afraid. Yet Democrats continued to maintain that they were on the sunny side of the hope/fear issue. Paul Krugman himself said so, when he wrote—just days after warning darkly of a right-wing takeover of the United States—that Barack Obama, the keynote speaker at the Democratic convention, had delivered "a message of uplift and hope," while George W. Bush "intends to run a campaign based on fear."

Perhaps some Democrats truly believed that. But in New York, Krugman, Miller, Kushner, Hunter, Nixon, Chase, Perez, and their fellow anti-Bush celebrities spent more time appealing to fear than anyone speaking from the podium of the Republican convention.

Whatever It Is, Bill Clinton Likely Did It

Without proof, foes say he's tied to lurid crimes

By Greg Ferguson and David Bowermaster
U.S. News & World Report, August 8, 1994

Sitting in a cozy parlor and wearing a red cardigan, Larry Nichols looks into the camera like an earnest Mr. Rogers and tells of "countless people who mysteriously died" after having run-ins with Bill Clinton. Nichols, an Arkansas state employee fired in 1988 for making hundreds of calls to the Nicaraguan Contras from his office, says it's all part of Clinton's "evil society."

So goes "Bill Clinton's Circle of Power," a video made earlier this year by Citizens for Honest Government, a California-based conservative group headed by television producer Pat Matrisciana. The video is filled with dark suggestions that as president and governor, Clinton was connected to the murders and beatings of several people, including political opponents. The Rev. Jerry Falwell promoted the video during a month of TV infomercials, and it has sold more than 100,000 copies, according to its makers. They hope its sequel, "The Clinton Chronicles," which repeats the charges at greater length, might outsell the first, even without Falwell's help.

Beyond last week's congressional Whitewater hearings and the ferment over Paula Corbin Jones's sexual harassment lawsuit, attacks against Clinton have taken a decidedly sinister turn. Televangelists, conservative talk-show hosts, political opponents and some computer bulletin-board aficionados are suggesting that Clinton could be tied to dozens of deaths, from a pneumonia case in Delaware to three of the four federal agents killed in the raid on the Branch Davidian compound in Waco, Texas.

Weird Era

Even at a time of great national anxiety and confusion, the intense, fecund and often bizarre charges leveled against Clinton are startling. He has unusually high negative ratings in many polls, but even that fails to explain fully the extreme nature of the charges leveled at him. "These attacks have reached a level of invective and viciousness that is unparalleled," complained White House counsel Lloyd Cutler during last week's Whitewater hearings. "There are a great many people who would like to bring President Clinton down who will stop at practically nothing."

No episode seems beyond Clinton's reach in the world of conspiracy buffs. A *Wall Street Journal* editorial in March chastised the "respectable press" for showing "little-to-no appetite for publishing anything about sex and violence" in Whitewater-related matters. It proceeded to report that while working on a story for the *New Republic* about incestuous relationships between business leaders and politicos in Arkansas, writer L. J. Davis opened the door to his Little Rock hotel room and remembered next awakening face down on the floor with a hefty bump on his head and "significant" pages of his notes missing. The implication was that some sinister elements had tried to quash Davis's piece. But Davis soon admitted drinking at least four martinis that night. No pages were missing from his notebook, and he had no idea how he ended up on the floor. "I certainly wasn't about to conclude that somebody cracked me on the head," Davis said at the time.

Even the most serious charges are characterized by serious deficiencies in corroborating evidence. In a letter to congressional leaders, former Rep. William Dannemeyer lists 24 people with some connection to Clinton who have died "under other than natural circumstances" and calls for hearings on the matter. On Dannemeyer's list is James Wilhite, a friend of White House adviser Thomas "Mack" McLarty who suffered fatal head injuries in December 1992 when he skied into a tree in Colorado. Clinton was nowhere near the scene. Dannemeyer also mentions Paul Tully, a chain-smoking, overweight Democratic strategist who, according to Little Rock police spokesman Lt. Charles Holladay and the Pulaski County coroner's report, died of a heart attack in 1992. Next is Jon Walker, an administrator in the Resolution Trust Corp. office probing Madison Guaranty; Walker died last year when he jumped from a Northern Virginia apartment building. Tom Bell, a detective with the Arlington, Va., police, says Walker was a "particularly clear case of suicide because there was a witness."

Others on the Dannemeyer list are more curious but completely lack evidence implicating Clinton. In March, a plane piloted by 72-year-old Herschel Friday, head of a prestigious Little Rock law firm, crashed on approach to a private runway near Friday's home. Friday served on Clinton's presidential campaign finance committee, and his widow, Beth, says the Clintons were "good friends." However, rumors about a link between Whitewater and Friday's death began circulating soon after the crash. The National Transportation Safety Board has not issued its final report on the crash, but so far investigators have given the family no indication the plane had mechanical problems. Mrs. Friday is confident her husband's death was "purely an accident." Dannemeyer admits that Clinton may have had no involvement in Friday's death and some of the others, but he insists that the "number goes beyond coincidence." He says he merely wants them investigated.

"The Clinton Body Count"

Dannemeyer's list of "suspicious deaths" is taken largely from one compiled by Linda Thompson. She is an Indianapolis lawyer who in 1993 quit her one-year-old general practice to run her American Justice Federation, a for-profit group that promotes pro-gun causes and various conspiracy theories through a shortwave radio program, a computer bulletin board and sales of its newsletter and videos. Her list, called "The Clinton Body Count: Coincidence or the Kiss of Death?" and updated biweekly, now contains 34 names of people she believes died suspiciously and who had ties to the Clinton family. Thompson admits she has "no direct evidence" of Clinton killing anyone. Indeed, she says the deaths were probably caused by "people trying to control the president" but refuses to say who they were. Thompson says her allegations of murder "seem groundless only because the mainstream media haven't done enough digging."

Earlier this year, Thompson released two videotapes and a folksy music video purporting to show that the February 1993 shootout in Waco, Texas, was a conspiracy in which three agents from the Bureau of Alcohol, Tobacco and Firearms were "executed" in the Branch Davidian's armory by their own men because of what they might have witnessed as Clinton's bodyguards. Though the men did help the Secret Service guard Clinton a few times, the Treasury Department's report in the Waco standoff refutes the charge: "Contrary to some publicly disseminated accounts, none of the agents that entered the armory was killed." According to the report, the men were killed in different locations around the compound. ATF spokesman Les Stanford says, "Her videos are replete with falsehood and errors."

> *Televangelists, conservative talk-show hosts, political opponents and some computer bulletin-board aficionados are suggesting that Clinton could be tied to dozens of deaths . . .*

Of the "suspicious deaths" listed by Thompson and endorsed by Dannemeyer, many victims have only the most tenuous ties to Clinton—four members of Marine Helicopter Squadron One, for example. The unit is responsible for transporting the president. The four marines died in May 1993 when the Blackhawk helicopter they had taken out for a maintenance-evaluation flight crashed. According to a Marine spokesman, Chief Warrant Officer Robert Jenks, faulty installation of a spindle pin allowed the helicopter's engines to produce too much power until an overspeed protection device shut them down. There was no evidence of sabotage. Clinton had set foot in the aircraft on only one occasion, two months before, when he traveled from the White House to the USS *Theodore Roosevelt*. Thompson concedes, "I don't know what Clinton's motive was." But she speculates that they "could have been privy to information about Clinton's plan for Bosnia."

Foster's Death

The starting place for all Clinton murder theorists seems to be Vincent Foster, the deputy White House counsel whose death last year unleashed a torrent of speculation. Jerry Falwell, Pat Robertson, Rush Limbaugh and others have suggested that Foster was probably murdered. On the anniversary of Foster's death, July 20, Foster's family made a public appeal to end the speculation. The death has been ruled a suicide in two separate investigations. Foster's family says they fully accept that verdict. That hasn't stopped Clinton's attackers, however. Many have dismissed the report by Whitewater investigator Robert Fiske Jr., a former U.S. attorney for New York under Presidents Ford and Carter and a highly respected private attorney, calling Foster's death a suicide. In rejecting more macabre theories about Foster, these critics say, Fiske—a Republican—was simply doing Clinton's bidding. "Fiske was appointed by Janet Reno at the suggestion of Bernard Nussbaum," says Falwell. "It's like putting Hillary Clinton in there." Testifying last week before Congress, Nussbaum said he never mentioned Fiske or anyone else to Reno as a potential special counsel.

There are other suicides that the conspiracy buffs tie to Clinton. In May, Sherwood, Ark., police officer Bill Shelton found his live-in girlfriend, Kathy Ferguson, slumped on the couch in his apartment, dead from a self-inflicted gunshot wound. A month later, Shelton was found on Ferguson's grave, a bullet hole through his head, a gun by his side and a suicide note in his truck.

Less than a week before Ferguson's death, her ex-husband, Danny, was named as a codefendant in Paula Jones's lawsuit against the president. Rumors began swirling that her death—and later Shelton's—was tied to the president's alleged infidelities. But police have found no reason to think so. The relationship between Ferguson and Shelton had reportedly fallen on hard times, and Ferguson's daughter told police her mother had been upset about a note from Shelton. The only people hinting at ties to Bill Clinton are in the media, police say. "It's like they want me to say something [about a connection]," says Sherwood Police Department spokesman Ray Snider. "It was suicide, period."

Luther "Jerry" Parks's death last September is almost as disputed as Foster's. Indeed, Parks's case is the only murder on Dannemeyer's list that law enforcement authorities do not consider solved. Parks's security company guarded Clinton's campaign headquarters in 1992. His son, Gary, asserts in both "Circle of Power" and "The Clinton Chronicles" that his father collected a secret file of the president's alleged indiscretions. Shortly before the elder Parks was shot to death while driving his car, Gary says, the file was stolen. Lieutenant Holladay says there is no evidence of such a file, nor any evidence that Clinton had anything to do with Parks's death. Gary, he says, "is grasping at straws. We have found his allegations to be baseless." Jerry Parks reportedly had many enemies after he was fired from two Arkansas police departments and after a bitter falling out with a business partner. Still, Larry Nichols says he is helping Gary Parks bring a wrongful death suit against "someone close to Clinton who doesn't have presidential immunity."

One recent death is that of Stanley Huggins, who died in June. In 1987, Huggins examined the loan practices of the thrift, Madison Guaranty, at the center of the Whitewater storm. His 400-page report has never been made public. But Dr. Richard Callery, Delaware's top medical examiner, says Huggins died of viral myocarditis and bronchial pneumonia. Lt. Joel Ivory of the University of Delaware police says his "exhaustive" investigation of Huggins's death turned up "no sign at all of foul play."

The flood of accusations shows no sign of abating. And to all conspiracy buffs, official sources are suspect. Falwell asks how the Arkansas police could investigate the deaths: "The police in Arkansas brought Clinton's girlfriends to him." He also says that guilty or innocent, Clinton encourages suspicion: "He's trying to get the courts to postpone his sex harassment suit. If he gets by with that, O. J. Simpson should run for president."

5

From Bombed Levees to Blood Libel: Religious and Ethnic Conspiracy Theories

People wait for rescue in the flooded Lower Ninth Ward in New Orleans, Louisiana, on August 29, 2005.

"Myths of the Unloved" and Myths of the Majority

By Paul McCaffrey

Recent history is rich with examples of religious and ethnic conflicts fueled, at least in part, by widespread belief in conspiracy theories. The ongoing disputes between Israelis and Palestinians, and the long-running "Troubles" in Northern Ireland between predominately Roman Catholic republicans and mostly Protestant unionists, have each featured elaborate conspiratorial speculations on both sides. The same is true of the bloodshed in the former Yugoslavia among Catholic Croats, Greek Orthodox Serbs, and Bosnian Muslims. In the African nation of Rwanda, the embrace of conspiracy theories helped motivate the Hutu-led genocide of ethnic Tutsis in the 1990s.

Thankfully, ethnic and religious conspiracy theories rarely result in the sort of violence described above. Yet the potential for such violence exists, and thus these forms of speculation must be dealt with carefully; understanding the underlying elements at play is essential. Most ethnic and religious conspiracy theories are motivated by fear and uncertainty, sometimes justified, often not. The degree to which populations believe in such theories is very much influenced by attendant circumstances: During periods of economic or political turmoil, conspiratorial speculation tends to have a more receptive audience.

Unfortunately, one peculiarity about ethnic and religious conspiracy theories is just how common they are. Wherever there are pronounced ethnic and religious differences among populations living in proximity to one another—and in an increasingly globalized and interconnected world everyone is proximate—conspiracy theories tend to emerge. It is safe to say that virtually every individual ethnic or religious group has one conspiracy theory or another associated with it. Like all rumors, they travel and evolve over time, though just because they are widely heard does not mean they will be widely believed.

There are two major varieties of religious and ethnic conspiracy theory: ones that originate in historically marginalized and oppressed communities to explain their marginalization and oppression at the hands of the majority, and ones that originate in dominant majority groups, blaming various real or imagined social ills on a particular ethnic or religious minority.

Cinqué Henderson, writing in the *New Republic*, described the first variety of speculation as "Myths of the Unloved." A key theme in such theories is the underlying powerlessness of the targeted demographic in the face of the amorphous power structure that persecutes it. Though to the uninitiated, this sort of speculation can sound fantastic, even offensive, myths of the unloved frequently have some basis in truth, some historical precedent that renders their seemingly farfetched claims more believable, if not entirely provable.

In the United States, this type of conspiracy theory has flourished in the African American community. The African American experience departs in dramatic ways from the conventional American narrative, tempering the story of "the land of freedom and opportunity" with the legacy of slavery and Jim Crow. Though slavery was abolished in the nineteenth century, and the civil rights movement of the 1950s and 1960s led to tangible advances, social and economic conditions in the African American community continue to lag behind the American average. Conspiracy theories often provide explanations for this divergence.

Two of the more illustrative conspiracy theories of this sort to emerge in recent years concern the HIV/AIDS epidemic and Hurricane Katrina. According to some polls, a small but significant proportion of African Americans believe that HIV/AIDS was created by the government. Fully 15 percent held the view that HIV/AIDS has been used as a genocidal weapon against the black community. Similarly, a sizeable minority of respondents believed that in the aftermath of Hurricane Katrina, certain New Orleans levees were purposely breached, flooding predominantly poor and African American neighborhoods in order either to save richer and whiter ones or to implement a form of nature-induced ethnic cleansing, deliberately sacrificing poorer, blacker areas to force their populations out.

Though these suspicions may sound shocking, they are not without verifiable, real-world precedents. For forty years, beginning in 1932, the US Public Health Service, in conjunction with the Tuskegee Institute, conducted a study on untreated syphilis in African American men. Nearly four hundred participants were not told they had the disease, nor did they receive proper medical care. Without their knowledge or consent, they spent the next four decades as unwitting human guinea pigs, with researchers recording the mounting toll the disease took on them. In return for their participation, they were given regular medical checkups, burial insurance, and an occasional free meal. In 1947, when penicillin emerged as a widely used cure for the malady, it was never administered to the Tuskegee test subjects. As the disease went untreated, it was unknowingly spread to wives and offspring. Many study participants died as a result of the illness. Only in 1972 did the government's malfeasance come to light, and subsequently the test subjects and their survivors received reparations for their mistreatment. In 1997, twenty-five years after the initial revelations, President Bill Clinton issued a formal apology on behalf of the American people. When viewed through the prism of the Tuskegee experiments, the idea of an HIV/AIDS conspiracy becomes less implausible.

Looking further back, to the Great Mississippi Flood of 1927, the notion that the government may have demolished levees during Hurricane Katrina, inundating poorer neighborhoods on purpose to preserve wealthier ones, is not so incredible either. The 1927 flood was one of the most devastating natural disasters in American history, leaving much of the American South underwater and displacing hundreds of thousands of people. As the deluge approached New Orleans, many worried what impact the flooding of the city would have on the regional economy. A group of prominent citizens lobbied the US Army Corps of Engineers to dynamite a levee in the town of Caernarvon, about thirteen miles south of New Orleans, thus wiping out a series of poor rural communities, but saving New Orleans itself from destruction. The Corps signed on to the plan and, using twenty-nine tons of dynamite, blasted a hole in the Caernarvon levee. New Orleans did avoid the worst of the flooding, though not because of any manmade levee break, but because naturally occurring breaches upstream channeled the worst of the deluge away from the city. As for those flooded out by the dynamited levee at Caernarvon, they were promised compensation for their lost homes, but it was slow in coming, and for a good many it never came at all. In view of the government's actions in 1927, it requires a smaller leap of faith to suppose something similar may have occurred in 2005. Whether there is hard evidence to support such a suspicion is, of course, a matter of debate.

The other main type of religious and ethnic conspiracy does not originate in minority communities; it targets them. And unlike myths of the unloved, these conspiracy theories, which one might call "myths of the majority," have a marked tendency to lead to widespread bloodshed, resulting in inquisitions, lynchings, pogroms, and worse.

Of this variety, anti-Semitic conspiracy theories are both unique and instructive. Few other forms of ethnic and religious speculation have had such a long history, shown such a propensity to evolve and shift over the centuries, and resulted in so much bloodshed. Among the more shocking claims of anti-Jewish conspiracy theories is the blood libel—the belief that Jews murder gentile children so that their blood can be used in Jewish ceremonies. There are also more secular theories, claiming covert, coordinated Jewish control over important levers of social power, whether the banking system or the media. Since the establishment of the state of Israel in 1948, new variations have entered into these sorts of conspiracy theories.

Anti-Semitic speculation also intersects with 9/11 conspiracy theories, through unsubstantiated claims that some four thousand Jewish workers mysteriously did not show up to work in New York on the day of the attacks. Today, the Middle East is a major hub of these sentiments. But dismissing anti-Semitic conspiracy theories as solely a regional affair is ill-advised. The history of the twentieth century, let alone the past two thousand years, amply demonstrates how widespread, insidious, and protean these beliefs are. As just one example, anti-Semitic conspiracy theories were used to justify the Holocaust, the systematic murder of six million Jews by Nazi Germany, then in later years to deny that the Holocaust ever occurred.

Anti-Semitic conspiracy theories have a singular provenance with few historic parallels. A more typical example of a myth of the majority, however, is speculation that has emerged in the United States and other Western countries over the past few years focused on Muslims. Fears of "creeping sharia," a stealth campaign to introduce Islamic law into legal statutes, have reached such a pitch that certain states, Oklahoma among them, have taken action. In Oklahoma, legislators introduced a ballot initiative that outlawed state courts from using sharia law as a basis for any of their decisions. The public approved the measure with 70 percent of the vote, though the constitutionality of the law has been challenged in federal court.

Trepidation over creeping sharia is unusual, especially in a state like Oklahoma, where there is a minuscule Muslim population. Some have suggested that the creeping sharia conspiracy theories are better understood as an unhealthy and bigoted reaction to global events, the 9/11 attacks, and the wars in Iraq and Afghanistan, in particular. Controversy over the "Ground Zero Mosque," a proposed Muslim community center near the site of the World Trade Center, may also have contributed to their emergence. Whatever the origins of this speculation, proponents of this conspiracy theory point to examples in US courts where religious laws, sharia among them, are recognized, whether in divorces, loan agreements, or other contracts, provided they don't violate civil statutes. Many fear that soon this practice will morph into more widespread applications of Islamic law as it relates to marriage, crime and punishment, and other areas.

Of course, these are only a small sampling of the countless conspiracy theories that have circulated around the globe at one time or another. Though they are each distinct, their similarities are obvious. They can each serve as both a form of bigotry as well as a justification for that bigotry. There is a profoundly alienating quality to them that can broaden the divisions between people of different backgrounds and ultimately lead to violence.

Blame It on the Jews

Anti-Semitism and the History of Jewish Conspiracy Theories

By Phil Molé

Skeptic, November 3, 2003

Not long after the World Trade Center attacks of September 11, 2001, the Internet teemed with legends and rumors about the cause of the tragedy. An alarming number of these legends implicated Jews in the attacks. The American website Information Times, using misinformation propagated by Lebanon's Al-Manar Television, claimed that 4,000 Jews were mysteriously absent from their jobs at the World Trade Center on September 11.[1] This fictitious story was a clear attempt to demonstrate Jewish foreknowledge of the terrorist attacks, and possibly even blame them for planning the acts of terrorism as a means of prompting American retaliation against Israel's Muslim enemies. More fantasies about the evil intentions of Jews would follow during the coming months. In March 2002, the Saudi-Arabian daily newspaper *Al-Riyadh* ran an article by Dr. Umaya Ahmad Al-Jalahma of King Faisal University in Al-Dammam claiming that Jews kill non-Jews and use their blood to make Passover matzos.[2]

To many in the West, these claims are puzzling. However, Western Christian culture was the birthplace for many of the anti-Semitic attitudes currently expressed by Islamic extremists. The claim published in *Al-Riyadh* that Jews need Gentile blood for rituals, for instance, was popular in Europe throughout the Middle Ages. And even in contemporary Western culture, one occasionally finds hints of Jewish conspiracy theories, such as the common belief that Jews control the media.

The "media control" theory illustrates the difficulties involved in assessing the causes of anti-Semitic ideas. Although Jews represent only about 2% of the American population, they are dramatically prominent in the newspapers, television and film industries. The reason for this is traceable to complex social and historical factors, such as the large numbers of European Jews who arrived in the United States during the formative years of Hollywood, the cultural preferences of Jews for these occupations, and the social desire for Jews to live and work with their friends and relatives. Thus, notions of Jewish "domination" of the media aren't entirely ridiculous, but they are also far from completely rational. Jewish over-representation in the media has certainly not resulted in frequent depictions of specifically Jewish issues on television. Jews working in the media need to appeal to a broad demographic base, and hardly find it prudent to promote pure "Jewish" interests foreign to most members of their target audience. Depictions of Jewish rituals such as bar-mitzvahs and Hanukah celebrations are much less frequent than corresponding depictions of such Christian cultural hallmarks as Christmas parties and church wedding ceremonies.

To realistically assess the causes of anti-Semitic theories, we need to carefully examine the specific times and places in which the theories originated, and avoid comforting oversimplifications of complex issues.

Beginnings: The Christian and Medieval Context

Many ancient peoples such as Egyptians and Romans expressed hostility toward Jews. This hostility could properly be considered anti-Semitic when it focused on perceived "Jewish" traits such as exclusiveness. Still most modern anti-Semitic attitudes can be traced to the development and eventual success of the Christian religion, although this does not necessarily indicate that Christianity has been the most important factor determining expressions of anti-Semitism. Jesus was a Jew who claimed that his mission was to fulfill Jewish law, not to replace it. His followers also understood his role in human history in terms of the Jewish scriptures collected in the Septuagint, or Greek version of the Hebrew Bible. Christianity, in its early stages, was a fringe religion embraced by small groups of both Jews and Gentiles who saw in Jesus the embodiment of an ideal religious life.[3]

Since Rome had crushed an uprising of Jewish revolutionaries in 70 CE, Christians did not wish to provoke further Roman wrath by publicly blaming the Roman procurator Pontius Pilate for the death of Jesus. Thus, the gospel authors were rather generous in their portrayals of Romans. According to the author of the Gospel of Luke, both Pilate and the Roman centurion present at the crucifixion proclaim the innocence of Jesus. Pilate even offers to release Jesus, finding he has done nothing wrong, but the Jewish crowds reject his offer (Luke 23: 4–5).[4] The author of the Gospel of John also emphasizes Pilate's failed attempts to free Jesus, and the bloodlust of the Jews in demanding his death. But John goes further in designating "the Jews" as a people different from Jesus and hostile to his mission. In John 8:44, Jesus tells "the Jews" that, far from being the children of Abraham or God, they are actually the children of Satan.[5] Jesus, of course, could not have been making an ethnic or racial classification about all Jews, since he was also Jewish. But these distinctions would be lost in later times, when Christians would be fully separated from the Judaic roots of their religion and perceive "the Jews" more readily as a separate community. Jews, as a people, would be judged guilty of deicide.

After Rome officially recognized Christianity in the 4th century CE, Judaism was its main intellectual and spiritual rival. Many of the early church fathers frequently took opportunities to denounce Jews as the main contributors to Christian heresies such as Arianism (the belief that Jesus was not fully divine), and as general obstacles to the spread of Christian faith. One of the most persistent critics of these "Judaizing" tendencies in Christian thought was John Chrysostom. In many eloquent orations, he emphasized the dangers of Jewish religious beliefs, and reminded his listeners of the role Jews played in the arrest and execution of Jesus. While John did not seem to display any deep hatred for Jews in his personal interactions with them, there is no doubt that his sermons contributed considerable ideological grist for the anti-Semites of later times.[6] Those who wished to view Jews as "Christ-killers" would often turn to Chrysostom's sermons for confirmation of their biases.

Through its early conflicts with Judaism, Christianity acquired a certain set of attitudes and doctrinal assertions regarding the inferiority of Judaism. These attitudes did not always lead to acts of hatred, and actual expressions of anti-Semitism varied greatly between times and places. Still, Christian beliefs about Jews were often far more hostile than those expressed by adherents of other religions. For instance, the Islamic conquests of the Holy Land in the 7th century and the strong Muslim presence in Spain beginning in the 8th century placed many Jews under direct Muslim political control. Many more Jews flooded into the Islamic Ottoman Empire after their expulsion from Catholic Spain in 1492. Jews did not have full political and civil rights under either Muslims or Christians, and encountered restrictions on their occupations and places of residence. There were some instances such as the attacks on the Jews of Granada in 1066 and 1090 when Muslims treated their Jewish subjects with considerable violence. Yet, their treatment as subjects of Islam seldom approached the worst moments of their lives in Christian nations.[7] There are few events in the history of the Jews in Muslim countries before the 20th century comparable to the acts of hatred and intolerance they endured in Christian Europe.

Much of the differences in fortune between the Jews of Islam and those of Christendom can be traced to the differences in perception of Jews between the two religions. Muslims knew that Jews conspired against Mohammed, but they also knew that the Jewish plots ended in failure. Jews were a nuisance, but not a serious threat to most Muslims.[8] Theoretically, Christians should also have perceived what they saw as Jewish actions against Jesus as fruitless, since alleged Jewish plots did not prevent Jesus from fulfilling his role as the Messiah. In practice, however, Christians dwelled on the sinister portrayals of Jews found in the New Testament and the teachings of the church fathers. To Christians, Jews were more likely to appear as menacing conspirators with a special mission to undermine the religious legacy of Jesus. This sinister image of Jews allowed Christians to develop various paranoid fantasies about diabolical Jewish rituals and conspiracies.

One of the racier charges against Jews resulted from, of all things, the adoption of the church dogma of transubstantiation—the literal transformation of the Eucharistic bread and wine into the body and blood of Christ. The magical aspects of this Church ritual spawned a variety of popular myths and legends. Not surprisingly, some of these myths involve nefarious schemes by Jews to steal hosts (and thus steal the body of Christ), and then mock or defile the host in rebellion against Christianity. According to one widely discussed account, two Jews in Passau in 1478 successfully schemed to obtain eight Eucharistic hosts.[9] They stabbed the hosts until blood oozed from them and threw them into a fire, but they would not burn. Instead, an image of the Christ child appeared, and several doves and angels miraculously escaped from the flames. This host desecration charge would resurface with slight variations many times, and would find expression in popular art of the period.

However, the most sinister allegation against Jews in Medieval times was the charge of "ritual murder." According to anti-Semitic theorists, Jews kidnapped Christian children and drained them of their blood, often killing the children in the process. Jews would then use the blood to perform religious or occult rites. Some Christians maintained that Jews used this ill-gotten blood to bake Passover matzos or anoint rabbis, while others argued that Jews needed the magical powers of Christian blood to remove the foul smell allegedly inflicted upon them by God for killing the messiah.[10] Still more outlandishly, some believed that God cursed male Jews by making them weak and effeminate because of their complicity in the death of Jesus. Male Jews were supposedly so feminine that they menstruated, and required Christian blood to stop bleeding.[11]

Table 1 shows the frequency of ritual murder charges in various European countries from the 12th through the 16th centuries. The first documented ritual murder accusation occurred in 1148 in England, and spread most quickly through German-speaking Europe, partially because large populations of Jews expelled from other areas of Europe had resettled in Germanic lands. One of the most famous ritual murder charges was the Simon of Trent affair of 1475, in which a 25-year old local Jew was blamed for the unexplained death of a 2-year old boy. Under heavy torture, the Jew "admitted" he had killed the boy and drained his blood for use in magic rituals. Such coerced confessions provided solutions for unresolved tragedies, and allowed neglectful or abusive parents to find scapegoats for the deaths of their children.[12] Such charges would remain common until the 16th century, when Protestant polemics labeled belief in ritual murder as Catholic superstition, helping to discredit these allegations.

The reduced number of ritual murder charges during the 14th century was not due to any decrease in anti-Semitism. Instead, new conspiracy theories about Jews spreading the Black Death temporarily distracted popular attention from ritual murder paranoia. As in ritual murder trials, torture played a prominent role in extracting bogus confessions from Jews. Subjected to actual or threatened torture, Jews confessed to spreading the deadly disease by poisoning wells and public fountains. The charges linking Jews to the onset of the plague seemed to originate in southern France and in Spain, where a large share of Europe's Jews lived prior to the expulsion edict of 1492. Soon, mob violence against Jews erupted in many European towns, including Barcelona, where 20 Jews were slaughtered and much property destroyed.[13]

We must try to understand these expressions of anti-Semitic hatred in a larger context. Most acts of violence against the Jews originated in the underclasses, and not with incitement by church or government authorities. Sometimes, in fact, mob actions against Jews were part of larger reactions against the existing order. This was certainly true of the Cossack leader Bogdan Chmielnicki, who led an uprising against Polish overlords who exploited the peasantry. Many Jews died in the Chmei-lnicki uprising, but largely because they were visible targets as financial mediaries responsible for collecting payments from the peasant classes.[14] Official authorities were certainly not free of prejudice by modern standards, but they seldom condoned mob violence and often punished the perpetrators. During the height of the ritual murder accusations, for example, Austrian emperors placed Jews under their protection and sometimes explicitly forbade further ritual murder charges against them. Still, popular prejudice against Jews remained, and would nurture the development of a new kind of anti-Semitic theory in the 18th century.

TABLE 1—FREQUENCY OF RITUAL MURDER CHARGES

Century	12th	13th	14th	15th	16th	Totals
German-speaking lands	2	15	10	14	12	53
England	2	7	0	0	0	9
France	2	1	4	0	0	7
Spain	1	1	0	0	4	6
Italy	0	0	1	6	0	7
Bohemia	1	0	1	0	3	5
Poland	0	0	0	2	8	10
Hungary	0	0	0	1	3	4
Totals	8	24	16	23	30	101

Adapted from R. Po-chia Hsia, 1988, *The Myth of Ritual Murder: Jews and Magic in Reformation Germany*, London: Yale University Press.

The Growth of Conspiracy: Jews in the Modern World

Throughout the Middle Ages and early modern period, many anti-Semites portrayed Jews as bogeymen who plotted to harm Christians through ritual murder, well poisonings and various black arts. Those who were not inclined to attribute such magical and diabolical traits to Jews still tended to regard them as social undesirables who profited in peddling and money lending. But these ideas were not yet modern conspiracy theories, with their imagined secret networks of individuals controlling the politics and economies of entire nations. To understand how these theories arose, we need to examine the historical context of the period before and after the Enlightenment of the 18th century.

Before the late 17th century, national and religious identities were intertwined. Most people assumed (as some members of the Christian Right still do) that a nation containing people of different religious affiliations would lack the bonds of spiritual and intellectual affinity necessary to survive. For if some citizens pursued a religious identity separate from the majority faith of their nation, they would not feel the same spirit of kinship shared by their countrymen. They would worship in different places and follow different religious rituals and holidays, reducing their communal ties with other citizens and compromising their suitability for civil and military service. For all these reasons, religious minorities were considered potential sources of subversion, and did not enjoy equal rights in any country.[15]

Jews, of course, were a well-known and conspicuous minority. Partly because of the prohibitions limiting their choices of occupations and residence, and partly because of cultural and social ties characteristic of most minority groups, Jews were largely a separate people. They did not scatter diffusely across the population of Europe, but tended to concentrate within particular towns and communities. Their range of occupations was broader than contemporary accounts would have us believe, but nonetheless, large numbers of Jews did enter professions such as banking and usury. There were many factors influencing these occupational choices. Civil service positions and many other occupations were closed to Jews, and difficulties in obtaining land (coupled with the threat of expulsion by local governments) discouraged trades such as agriculture that required large investments in land and property.[16] Cultural preferences for jobs shared by other members of their community was another important consideration. Jews, therefore, were culturally distinct from the larger society in which they lived.

Beginning in the late 17th century, a new generation of political thinkers challenged existing bonds between religion and state. To a growing number of modern thinkers, society was based on a contract between rational individuals seeking to safeguard basic rights and qualities of life. One could not justify the existence of a given society based on arguments from tradition and political or religious authority. The influence of these thinkers would spread throughout Europe during the Enlightenment of the 18th century.

Enlightened Europeans often discussed their new philosophical ideas in salons or social clubs. Some of these clubs were professional associations of tradesmen, and adopted rituals of membership to establish their uniqueness. The Freemasons, originally an association of professional tradesmen such as stoneworkers (hence the name "masons"), was one such organization. With time, however, the society downplayed its professional affiliations to attract more members. By the mid-18th century, the Freemasons were primarily a philosophical club in which the latest intellectual trends would be discussed. Because of the society's relative exclusiveness and involvement in political thought, many prominent political leaders were members. Eventually, a number of other new societies would model themselves after the Freemasons, with the Bavarian Illuminati being among the most famous of them.[17]

The existence of these "secret societies" would intersect in important ways with the development of modern conspiracy theorists and their preoccupation with Jews. The democratic revolutions that swept through the West during the 18th century gave the new breed of political theorists a chance to put their ideas into practice. These revolutions caused social upheaval on unprecedented levels, and many people tried to understand the underlying reasons for the changes affecting their lives. The actual causes, of course, involved a complicated mixture of politics, religion, economics, and the contingencies of history. But most of us cannot, with any satisfaction, shake our fists in anger at impersonal social forces. We need to blame people for the perceived ills of society, and we need to imagine that these people are acting with established motives.

To many people, secret societies such as the Freemasons and Bavarian Illuminati seemed to be behind the sweeping changes occurring in their societies. After all, some prominent leaders belonged to these organizations, and political ideas were known topics of discussion at their meetings. As secret societies continued to spread and diversify across Europe, former members added to the growing paranoia by publicly "revealing" hysterically sordid details about life among their lodge brothers.[18] Their motives in spreading these exaggerated revelations varied from spite to ambitions of political favor, but in either case they filled the public mind with fantasies about secret rituals, dark oaths, and evil plots.

It was also at this time that public attention began turning toward the political rights of Jews. The ideals of the Enlightenment declared that societies should be open to participation by all men, regardless of their religion. But in practice, political leaders questioned whether Jews could become fully integrated members of their larger nations. The "enlightened despot" Joseph II granted some civic rights to Jews in southern Austria in 1782, but the possibility of full political emancipation would not arise until the French Revolution.[19] Many leaders, reviewing the isolation and perceived moral deficiencies in Jewish societies, expressed doubts that Jews could become ideal citizens. Others feared the power Jews already seemed to have, and argued that giving them more freedom would harm gentile society. Despite protests such as this, political citizenship would come to French Jews in 1791, and other European countries would follow the French example. Still, many persisted in thinking of Jews as a separate and hostile social entity made all the more dangerous through their newly acquired rights. The phrase "state within a state" would increasingly be used to indicate the sentiment that Jews were a community unto themselves, and lacked full loyalty to their native countries.[20]

Not surprisingly, Jews soon began to displace Freemasons and Illuminati as the prime suspects of conspiracy theorists. One of the first linkages of Jews to the new political conspiracy theories arose in 1806, when Napoleon convened a special assembly of rabbis to discuss potential obstacles to Jewish assimilation. At this time, the French Jesuit Abbé Augustin Barruel circulated a forged letter blaming the Jews for the French Revolution. In an earlier pamphlet, Barruel had attributed the cause of the Revolution to a conspiracy organized by Freemasons, but he had no logical difficulty in updating his theory to match the times.[21] By mid-19th century, the notion of a Jewish world conspiracy was also appearing in popular literature. Hermann Goedsche's novel *Biarritz* (1868) included a chapter called "In the Jewish Cemetery in Prague" depicting a secret meeting of representatives of the twelve tribes of Israel. At the end of this fictional meeting, a rabbi gives a long speech expressing the hope that Jewish world domination will be complete by the time of the next gathering one hundred years hence. This speech, eventually known as "The Rabbi's Speech," would circulate independently through Europe in the late 19th century, although later copies would fail to mention its fictional origin.

Belief in Jewish conspiracies gained further plausibility from the appearance of prominent Jews and Jewish organizations in European society. The Alliance Israelite Universelle, founded in France in 1860 to help persecuted Jews in Russia and Rumania, soon became an object of suspicion and derision. For the first time, some Jews also earned high-ranking offices in government. In Britain, Lionel Rothschild entered the British Parliament in 1858, and Benjamin Disraeli became Prime Minister about a decade later. Although baptized a Christian, Disraeli possessed Jewish ancestry and continued to consider himself a Jew throughout his life. He also seemed to consider Jews a superior race with powerful influences on world politics and economics. In his novel *Coningsby*, the Jewish character Sidonia proclaims that "the world is governed by very different personages from what is imagined by those who are not behind the scenes"—a reference to the hidden levers of Jewish domination.[22] The increasing prominence of certain Jews such as the famous Rothschild family seemed to verify Disraeli's words. The Rothschilds were extremely influential in international affairs and exerted powerful influences on national policies. Thus, beliefs in growing Jewish power over international affairs were not entirely without foundation, however exaggerated they may have been.

Suspicions of Jewish power would eventually lead to the most infamous of all conspiracy theories: *The Protocols of the Elders of Zion*. The theory started in France but developed in Russia, a country where Jewish assimilation continued to lag behind Western Europe. In Russia, Jews constituted a "state within a state" more than anywhere else. Most Russian Jews still lived within the so-called Pale of Settlement, and constituted a culturally and physically distinct population. Russian Jews overwhelmingly spoke Yiddish instead of their country's native tongue—a feature distinguishing them from the much more culturally assimilated Jews of German-speaking countries. While certain Russian Jewish communities (especially those of Odessa) achieved high degrees of cultural distinction, many others were very poor.[23] For this reason, leftist revolutionary groups often contained significant numbers of Jews who wished to remodel the existing society into one more open to Jewish aspirations. Although the majority of Jews did not belong to these groups Gentiles paid special attention to those who did.[24]

In 1881, revolutionaries assassinated Russian Czar Alexander II in Russia. Some Jews seem to have played a role in the assassination plot, along with many Gentiles, but popular outrage often focused exclusively on the dangers of the "Jews" to Russian society. A wave of Jewish persecutions started in Russia, often involving "pogroms," or mob attacks on entire Jewish communities.[25] Jewish shock at the violence committed in these pogroms was a major inspiration for the birth of the Zionist movement, which sought to establish a Jewish homeland in Palestine where Jews could finally be free of the restrictions and persecutions they had known in Christian states. Led by the Austrian Jew Theodore Herzl, the Zionists held their first congress in Basel in 1897.[26]

This is the context in which the Russian Sergey Nilus published the most popular edition of the *Protocols* in 1905. Most probably inspired by the continuing circulation of earlier anti-Semitic tracts such as "The Rabbi's Speech," the *Protocols* consists of 24 lectures allegedly given by the leader of a secret Jewish government regarding Jewish plots for world domination. According to this Elder, the Jews would accomplish this by amassing wealth at the expense of the Gentiles and ultimately bringing about the financial and political collapse of Gentile society. According to the sixth protocol, the Elder declares:

> Soon we will start organizing great monopolies—reservoirs of colossal wealth, in which even the large fortunes of the Gentiles will be involved to such an extent that they will sink together with the credit of their government the day after a political crisis takes place . . . We must use every possible kind of means to develop the popularity of our Supergovernment, holding it up as a protection and recompenser of all who willingly submit to us.[27]

Following the outbreak of World War I, the *Protocols* spread throughout Europe and were translated into many languages. Still, not everyone accepted them with equal enthusiasm. In 1921, the *London Times* definitively proved the *Protocols* were a forgery based on an 1865 political tract by the Frenchman Maurice Joly called *Dialogues in Hell Between Machiavelli and Montesquieu.*[28] A political tract criticizing Napoleon III, Joly's book had absolutely nothing to do with Jews or their alleged conspiracies. It contained a fictional dialogue between the liberal political philosopher Montesquieu and the more cynical Machiavelli on the advantages and disadvantages of liberal democracies.[29] Members of the Russian secret police apparently forged the *Protocols* by extracting some of "Machiavelli's" statements about the need to manipulate the masses in order to maintain stable societies, attributing them to the Elders of Zion. In many places, the *Protocols* are almost an exact plagiarism of Joly's text. Still, those who wanted to believe in the *Protocols* found reasons to consider them genuine. Confusing cause and effect, they could claim that the best proof of the truth of the *Protocols* was that their "predictions" about the changes in European society had been verified. (Of course, the *Protocols* originated at a time when these changes had already occurred, so this was no "prediction" at all). True believers could even claim, falsely, that Maurice Joly was a Jew, and his original text really was an exposé of the Jewish conspiracy after all.[30]

> **With the triumph of Hitler and the Nazi Party, the myth of the Jewish world conspiracy would become, in the words of one eminent historian, a "warrant for genocide."**

The *Protocols* found a particularly attentive audience in Germany after World War I. Prior to this period, Germany had actually been one of the more hospitable places for European Jews to live. Jews were largely assimilated into German culture, making many important contributions of their own, and enjoyed a large measure of political rights. Almost all observers, Gentile or Jew, agreed that Germany was a much better place for Jews to live than the more repressive societies of Russia and Rumania.[31]

The Jewish situation in Germany would change only after disillusionment with the Versailles Treaty and the economic depression of the mid-1920s led to growing dissatisfaction with the Weimar Republic. Some dissatisfied elements of the population came to regard Jews as the chief agent of Germany's misfortunes, and interest in the message of the *Protocols* increased. One of the most fervent believers in the truth of the *Protocols* was Adolf Hitler, as seen in *Mein Kampf*:

> To what extent the whole existence of this people [the Jews] is based on a continuous lie is shown incomparably by the *Protocols* of the Wise Men of Zion, so infinitely hated by the Jews. They are based on a forgery, the *Frankfurter Zeitung* moans and screams every week: the best proof that they are authentic. What many Jews may do unconsciously is here consciously exposed. And that is what matters. It is completely indifferent from what Jewish brain these disclosures originate; the important thing is that with positively terrifying certainty they reveal the nature and activity of the Jewish people and expose their inner contexts as well as their final ultimate aims.[32]

With the triumph of Hitler and the Nazi Party, the myth of the Jewish world conspiracy would become, in the words of one eminent historian, a "warrant for genocide."[33]

Epilogue: The Continuing Appeal of Anti-Semitic Conspiracy Theories

The development of Jewish conspiracy theories depended upon a number of historical factors interacting in novel ways with the activities and culture of Jews. While these factors are complex, our analysis allows us to reach several general conclusions.

First, much has been made in recent years of alleged direct links between Christian doctrine and anti-Semitism.[34] There is no doubt that Christian portrayals of Jews as Christ-killers found in the New Testament and the writings of the early church fathers created an undercurrent of hostility toward Jews in Christian culture. However, this hostility was often more latent than active. If Christianity was the primary cause of anti-Semitism, we should expect to find equal expressions of anti-Semitism among all of the Christian states of Europe. This is not the case. Anti-Semitic violence was rare in the Christian nations of Norway, Sweden, Britain, Italy or Denmark—a hard fact to explain if Christianity is the major determinant of anti-Semitism. Anti-Semites may have tapped into Christian tradition for inspiration to nourish their hatred, but the motivations for their hatred were products of particular times and places.

Similarly, we cannot accurately explain the final culmination of Jewish conspiracy theories in the Holocaust by pointing to anything uniquely anti-Semitic in German culture. To be sure, many Germans did not like Jews, but some degree of aversion to Jews was common in virtually every European country. Not all of these countries developed a Final Solution. Germany prior to 1917 was in many ways a model of Jewish cultural assimilation, and lacked the outbreaks of mob violence characteristic of turn-of-the-century Russia. We must seek explanations for the Final Solution in the contingencies of Germany's post-WWI history instead of seeing it as the fruition of centuries of unalloyed anti-Semitism, as some recent historians have done.[35]

Finally, modern Jewish conspiracy theories arose as people tried to explain the widespread changes in European society beginning in the late 18th century. Belief in conspiracies allows us to feel moral outrage against human enemies, instead of impotence in the face of impersonal historical forces beyond our control. To many, the growing prominence of Jews in late 19th century Europe was intricately linked to the changes in society. The explanation available to modern historians—that Jewish emancipation was simply a result of the same social forces driving the democratic revolutions—was not as emotionally satisfying as blaming the Jews for the social upheavals in Europe.

This need to explain unpleasant realities in emotionally appealing terms may well be the most important cause of anti-Semitic conspiracy theories, and may enhance the effects of the other factors. As a case in point, the most violent anti-Semitic conspiracy theories of today originate with militant Middle Eastern Muslims and other ideological opponents of Israel. Although Islamic doctrinal assessments of Jews had always lacked the special animosity of the Christian tradition, anger over the continuing existence of Israel now causes many Muslims to perceive Jews as a diabolical threat. Since these once mighty nations of Islam cannot drive out the "intruders" in their midst, some Muslims find something supernaturally evil in the Jewish character that enables them to resist defeat.[36] It is surely no coincidence that Arabic translations of the *Protocols* began to appear after Israel's victory in the Six Day War, and mainstream Arabic newspapers now often resurrect medieval legends about Jewish ritual murder practices. Comic strips depicting the horrible consequences of continued Jewish power are also common in the Middle East. American right-wing extremist groups such as the Church of the Creator even blame Israel for 9/11.

Jewish conspiracy theories have gone from being a special lunacy of Western countries to an international problem. Unfortunately, it seems quite possible that all those disenchanted souls who reject certain aspects of the modern world will continue to view Jews with suspicion, and seek refuge in blaming familiar enemies.

Acknowledgment

The author would like to thank Professor Albert S. Lindemann of the University of California, Santa Barbara for his generosity in reviewing a draft of this article and offering helpful suggestions.

Notes

1. Curtis, Brian. 2001. "4,000 Jews, 1 Lie: Tracking an Internet Hoax." http://slate.msn.com/?id = 116813.

2. Beichman, Arnold. 2002. "Blood Libel Lives." *The Washington Times*, March 19.

3. Meeks, Wayne. 1984. *The First Urban Christians: The Social World of the Apostle Paul*. London: Yale University Press.

4. Meeks, Wayne and Bassler, Jouette M. 1993. *The HarperCollins Study Bible: New Revised Standard Version with Apocryphal/Deuterocanonical Books.* Helms, Randel McGraw. 1990. Gospel Fictions. Buffalo: Prometheus Books.

5. Meeks and Bassler, 1993.

6. Chrysostom, John. 1979. *Discourses Against Judaizing Christians.* Washington: Catholic University of America Press. Wilken, Robert Louis. 1983. *John Chrysostom and the Jews: Rhetoric and Reality in the Late Fourth Century.* Berkeley: University of California Press.

7. Lewis, Bernard. 1999. *Semites and Anti-Semites: An Inquiry into Conflict and Prejudice.* New York: W.W. Norton.

8. Lewis, 1999.

9. Hsia, R. Po-chia. 1988. *The Myth of Ritual Murder: Jews and Magic in Reformation Germany.* London: Yale University Press. Rubin, Miri. 1999. *Gentile Tales: The Narrative Assault on Late-Medieval Jews.* London: Yale University Press.

10. Hsia, 1988.

11. Horowitz, Elliott. "Jews, Stereotypes of." In Lindahl, Carl, McNamara, John and Lindow, John. 2002. *Medieval Folklore: A Guide to Myths, Legends, Tales, Beliefs and Customs.* Oxford: Oxford University Press.

12. Hsia, 1988.

13. Cantor, Norman F. 2001. *In the Wake of the Plague: The Black Death and the World It Made.* New York: Free Press.

14. Lindemann, Albert. 1997. *Esau's Tears: Modern Anti-Semitism and the Rise of the Jews.* Cambridge: Cambridge University Press.

15. Palmer, R.R. *The Age of the Democratic Revolution* (Vol.1). Princeton: Princeton University Press.

16. Katz, Jacob. 1973. *Out of the Ghetto: The Social Background of Jewish Emancipation 1770–1870.* Cambridge: Harvard University Press.

17. Roberts, J.M. 1972. *The Mythology of the Secret Societies.* New York: Charles Scribner's Sons.

18. Roberts, 1972.

19. Katz, 1973. Lindemann, 1997.

20. Katz, Jacob. 1980. *From Prejudice to Destruction: Anti-Semitism, 1700–1933.* Cambridge: Harvard University Press.

21. Cohn, Norman. 1996. *Warrant for Genocide: The Myth of the Jewish World Conspiracy and the Protocols of the Elders of Zion.* London: Serif Books.

22. Disraeli, Benjamin. 1844. *Coningsby; or, the New Generation.* Leipzig. Rather, R.J. 1986. "Disraeli, Freud, and Jewish Conspiracy Theories." *Journal of the History of Ideas,* 47(1), 111–131.

23. Zipperstein, Steven J. *The Jews of Odessa: A Cultural History, 1794–1881.* Stanford: Stanford University Press. Lederhendler, Eli. 1992. "Modernity Without Emancipation or Assimilation? The Case of Russian Jewry." In Frankel, Jonathan and Zipperstein, Steven J. *Assimilation and Community: The Jews in Nineteenth-Century Europe.* Cambridge: Cambridge University Press. Fishman, David. 1989. "The Politics of Yiddish in Czarist Russia." In Jacob

Neusner, et al., (eds.) *From Ancient Israel to Modern Judaism*, vol. 4. Atlanta: Scholar's Press, 1989, 155–71.

24. Lindemann, 1997.
25. Cohn, 1996. Lindemann, 1997.
26. Lacquer, Walter. 1972. *A History of Zionism: From the French Revolution to the Establishment of Israel*. New York: Henry Holt.
27. Cohn, 1996.
28. Lacquer, 1972.
29. Cohn, 1996. Maurice Joly's original book is, judging by the excerpts I have read, an astute work of political philosophy deserving rediscovery. At the time of this writing, Lexington Books will soon publish a new English translation by John Waggoner.
30. Cohn, 1996.
31. Lindemann, 1997.
32. Hitler, Adolf. *Mein Kampf.* (1925) 1999. Translated by Ralph Manheim. New York: Mariner Books.
33. Cohn, 1996.
34. See for instance, Carroll, James. 2001. *Constantine's Sword: The Church and the Jews*. New York: Houghton Mifflin Company. Despite glowing reviews from such eminent historians as Garry Wills, Carroll's book is little more than a haphazard collection of facts intended to prove an already established conclusion, with very little attempt at dispassionate analysis.
35. The most obvious example of this trend is Goldhagen, Daniel Jonah. 1996. *Hitler's Willing Executioners: Ordinary Germans and the Holocaust*. New York: Vintage Books. Contrary to Goldhagen's thesis, the Holocaust was not a predestined conclusion of German history.
36. Lewis, 1999.

ZOG Ate My Brains

Conspiracy theories about Jews abound. Chip Berlet unpacks their appeal.

By Chip Berlet
New Internationalist, October 1, 2004

If you surf the web, you may have encountered the claim that the Israeli spy agency Mossad warned 4,000 Jews who worked in the World Trade Center to stay home on 11 September 2001; or that a handful of Jewish lobbyists control US foreign policy; or the world is run by the Zionist Occupation Government (ZOG). All these claims are patently false, yet they have devoted defenders.

The idea that a secret group of powerful people is conspiring to control world events is centuries old, and it is seeing a troubling resurgence on the political Left. Unlike most progressive theories about political power that stress systemic, institutional or structural analyses, conspiracy theories claim a handful of sinister plotters are mucking things up. This often devolves into charges that 'The Jews' are behind some sinister plan for global subversion. Where do these ideas come from?

Sticking to Protocols

In the early 1900s, Czar Nicholas II's *Okhranka* (secret police) in Russia promoted a hoax document called the *Protocols of the Learned Elders of Zion*—claimed to be the minutes of a secret 'cabal' of Jews who manipulated world events through the Freemasons and other groups. *The Protocols* were translated into many languages and circulated around the world. Author Norman Cohn titled his study on this fake *Warrant for Genocide*, because it was used to justify pogroms in Russia and the scapegoating and murder of Jews in Nazi Germany.

The specific allegations change based on time and place, but the basic elements of destructive conspiracy theories remain the same:

- **Dualistic division:** The world is divided into a good 'Us' and a bad 'Them.'

- **Demonizing rhetoric**: Our opponents are evil and subversive . . . maybe subhuman.

- **Targeting scapegoats**: 'They' are causing all our troubles—we are blameless.

- **Apocalyptic timetable:** Time is running out and we must act immediately to stave off a cataclysmic event.

Brenda Brasher, a sociologist at the University of Aberdeen, Scotland, notes that in this model, 'People are cast in their roles as either enemy or friend, and there is no such thing as middle ground. In the battle with evil, can you really say you are neutral?'

Conspiracy theory is sometimes called conspiracism. Michael Barkun, author of *A Culture of Conspiracy: Apocalyptic Visions in Contemporary America*, contends that conspiracism attracts people because conspiracy theorists 'claim to explain what others can't. They appear to make sense out of a world that is otherwise confusing.' There is an appealing simplicity in dividing the world sharply into good and bad and tracing 'all evil back to a single source, the conspirators and their agents.' Barkun notes that 'conspiracy theories are often presented as special, secret knowledge unknown or unappreciated by others.' For conspiracists, 'the masses are a brainwashed herd, while the conspiracists in the know can congratulate themselves on penetrating the plotters' deceptions.'

Conspiracism often gains a mass following in times of social, cultural, economic, or political stress. Immigration, demands for racial or gender equality, gay rights, power struggles between nations, and war can all can be viewed through a conspiracist lens. Conspiracism started as a way to defend the *status quo*, but it spawned a flipside where the conspiracy is perceived as controlling the government. This was a central motif of the 1950s 'Red Scare' when fears of global communist subversion were a common conspiracist script. Today, Arabs and Muslims are portrayed in a similar demonizing way as conspiring against Western culture. Sadly, as tensions in the Middle East have boiled over, an increasing number of Arabs and Muslims have grabbed onto antisemitic conspiracy theories to explain devastating struggles over land and power. This is evidenced by the popularity of *The Protocols of the Elders of Zion* in the region where they have been repackaged into a television series broadcast from Lebanon and Egypt.

Antisemitic conspiracism is aggressively peddled to progressives by several rightwing groups including the international network run by Lyndon LaRouche, a frequently unsuccessful US presidential candidate. While LaRouche rhetoric can seem bonkers, his followers are successful in recruiting students on college campuses and in networking with some Black Nationalist groups. Sometimes Arab publications circulate articles from LaRouche group analysts. When LaRouche publications condemn the neoconservative policy advisers to President Bush as the 'Children of Satan', it echoes historic antisemitic rhetoric about evil Jewish conspiracies tracing back to medieval Europe.

Lobby Libel

Why would progressives embrace conspiracism? In the 1980s, isolationists on the Right, and anti-war activists on the Left grew suspicious of President Ronald Reagan's support for covert action overseas and political repression at home. As they interacted, some progressive groups began circulating allegations about 'Secret Teams,' 'Shadow Governments,' or 'The Octopus,' that echoed historic antisemitic conspiracy theories found in rightwing publications. With the collapse of communism in Europe many rightists shifted scapegoats to claim a New World Order conspiracy was manipulating the US Government. Again, some leftists adapted this rhetoric. During the first Gulf War, some anti-war activists spoke of a 'Jewish Lobby' in ways that blended stereotyping with conspiracism.[1]

'When we blame US foreign policy on Israel or some Jewish cabal,' it 'takes the heat off those who

> *Out on the furthest conspiracist limb are race hate groups and neo-Nazis who are obsessed with the Zionist Occupation Government (ZOG)...*

are the real decision makers,' says Penny Rosenwasser, a board member of US-based Jewish Voice for Peace. 'We need to aim our criticism at the proper targets. US foreign policy is influenced more by corporate interests, the Christian Right and the arms manufacturers than by the Israeli Government.' Rosenwasser points out that it is US foreign policy that needs to be challenged: 'Blaming scapegoats diverts us from our work for human rights and justice.' She sees that some people 'blur the distinction between the Jewish people and the policies of the Israeli Government.' That's what happens with phrases like 'the Jewish Lobby' where the work of Jews seeking justice for Palestinians is simply erased.

The story about the Jews avoiding the Twin Towers on 11 September? Every aspect of this tale is false. Reporters traced it back to a series of rumours and claims by unnamed sources that bounced around the internet getting more elaborate with each retelling. To take this story seriously, you would have to be willing to assume that if 4,000 random Jews were told of an impending terrorist attack, not one would step forward with a public warning. To believe this about any religious, racial or ethnic group raises serious questions about lingering prejudice.[2]

Mad about ZOG

Out on the furthest conspiracist limb are race hate groups and neo-Nazis who are obsessed with the Zionist Occupation Government (ZOG)—an idea that is the modern incarnation of the infamous *Protocols*.

But such ideas are by no means the preserve of the extremist fringe. Brasher says: 'We tend to look at apocalyptic and conspiracist belief and laugh it off and push it aside. Yet in many ways it is pervasive. I came back to visit the United States after the attacks on 9/11 and was amazed to see apocalyptic rhetoric being spun out by elected officials and people on the Right and Left.'

There are powerful forces that shape our reality. Conspiracies do take place. How we approach the workings of élite groups and individuals, however, is crucial if we are to avoid traversing down the conspiracists' path.

G. William Domhoff, author of several books on how powerful élites try to shape political and economic policies, distinguishes his techniques for researching power structures from those used by conspiracists. Domhoff complains: 'There is no falsifying a conspiracy theory. Its proponents always find a way to claim the élite really won, even though everyday people stop some things, or win some battles.' Author Holly Sklar agrees: 'When I write about influential élite planning groups such as the Trilateral Commission, I don't portray them as omnipotent puppet masters manipulating politicians and policies in a vast conspiracy. When progressives grab on to conspiracy theories it undermines effective strategic analysis, planning and action.'

Even when conspiracy theorists proclaim they are not targeting Jews, conspiracism creates a milieu in which antisemitism can flourish. Many progressives, conservatives, New Agers—even UFO groups—have spoken out against antisemitic conspiracy theories. And an increasing number of activists suggest that conspiracism itself needs to be opposed, especially on the political Left. Lee Quinby, author of *Anti-Apocalypse*, complains that 'Progressive thought falters under the weight of apocalyptic and conspiratorial thinking,' because 'disagreement and dissent are disallowed, democratic debate is precluded, and differences of opinion are penalized.' Domhoff agrees: 'Conspiracism is a disaster for progressive people because it leads them into cynicism, convoluted thinking, and a tendency to feel it is hopeless even as they denounce the alleged conspirators.'

Robert Alan Goldberg writes about this in *Enemies Within: The Culture of Conspiracy in Modern America*. He believes: 'Healthy scepticism of authority is essential to democracy. The key is to maintain logical consistency while demanding evidence in support of an argument. Conspiracy theories are slippery in their logic and careless of facts and assumptions. They work from a premise or preconception of conspiracy and deny other possible explanations of events. Circumstance, rumour and hearsay serve as evidence and are deemed sufficient for proof.'

Mark Fenster, author of *Conspiracy Theories*, cautions that we should not fear popular activism or avoid finding simple ways to explain current political issues, 'but don't embrace them without understanding their downside risk. And always educate about the complex structures that affect what often appear to their victims as simple dynamics.' Fenster warns that if our 'simple, populist narrative slips and becomes racist or antisemitic or exclusionary, then its power to affect positive social and economic change disappears.'

Chip Berlet is a Senior Analyst at Political Research Associates (PRA) in Boston, Massachusetts and has been writing about the political Right for over 20 years.

Notes

1. For a detailed analysis of Right-Left alliances and conspiracism around the first Gulf War, see: Chip Berlet, *Right Woos Left: Populist Party, LaRouchite, and Other Neo-fascist Overtures To Progressives, And Why They Must Be Rejected*, http://www.publiceye.org/rightwoo/rwooz9.html
2. For a detailed analysis of the origins of the 4,000 Jews libel, see: http://slate.msn.com/id/116813/ and: http://www.snopes.com/rumors/israel.htm

The Tuskegee Experiment's Long Shadow

By Paul Ruffins
Black Issues in Higher Education, October 29, 1998

Have you checked the numbers on your social security card yet? Rumor has it that the federal government keeps track of Black folks by assigning them social security numbers that contain an even number in the fifth digit.

If you are now rifling through your wallet looking for your social security card, stop. The rumor is untrue. But it is one of several that have been burning up the Internet in recent months, causing African Americans of all walks of life to wonder, if only momentarily, about the validity of these conspiratorial rumors.

Conspiracy theories are as American as apple pie, according to Dr. Anita Waters, a sociologist at Denison University, who describes such theories as "ethnosociologies." Yet, what makes Black belief in conspiracy theories so difficult to interpret and evaluate is that in many recent cases the rumors are based in fact.

Black America's willingness to entertain beliefs in conspiracy theories, sometimes referred to as "urban legends," has been widely studied and analyzed by a variety of scholars—most particularly, by those in the fields of folklore, political science, medicine, and public health.

Most who investigate these tales believe that they are a significant phenomenon in African American culture dating back to the earliest contact between Africans and Europeans.

Dr. Patricia Turner, a professor of African American studies at the University of California, Davis has made an exhausting compilation of African American rumors and conspiracy theories. She believes that from Black Americans' encounter with racism, "folklore emerges in which individuals translate their uneasiness about the fate of the group as a whole into more concrete, personal terms."

Whether scholars think that the widespread interest in rumors is a problem for African Americans also varies by academic discipline. In general, folklorists, cultural anthropologists, and sociologists tend to see these rumors, legends, and conspiracy theories as just another product of the same cultural creativity that produced the blues, jazz, and rap music. In effect, a way to confront, interpret, and resist the dominant culture.

However, political scientists and medical researchers who understand the history and fears that serve as a backdrop for these tales, tend to view these urban legends more negatively.

"The problem with conspiracy theories is that they don't really help people formulate specific politics for actual change," notes Professor Clarence Lusane of American University, author of *Pipe Dream Blues: Racism and the War on Drugs*.

Medical researchers go even further, saying that the widespread willingness to entertain conspiracy theories about AIDS and medical experiments represent a major threat to the health and well-being of African Americans.

How Many True Believers?

It is impossible to know exactly how many African Americans believe in some sort of conspiracy. However, various studies have found that at least some of these beliefs are quite widespread.

In 1991, the *American Journal of Public Health* reported that, as part of an attempt to educate African Americans about the dangers of AIDS and HIV infection, the Southern Christian Leadership Conference surveyed 1,056 Black church members in the South and Midwest. Thirty-five percent of the respondents believed that AIDS was a form of genocide, and another 30 percent were unsure.

Forty-four percent believed that the government is not telling the truth about AIDS, while 35 percent were unsure. An additional 34 percent believed that AIDS is man-made.

Additional evidence comes from a lengthy New York Times/WCBS-TV poll that queried 408 African Americans about popular conspiratorial theories. The survey found that 77 percent of Black respondents thought there was some truth to the statement, "the government deliberately singles out and investigates Black-elected officials to discredit them in a way it doesn't do with White officials." Seventy percent of respondents believed that "the government deliberately makes sure that drugs are easily available in poor Black neighborhoods to harm Black people." And 29 percent believed that "the virus that causes AIDS was deliberately created in a laboratory to infect Black people."

Ever since Richard Hofstadter's investigation of right-wing conspiracy theorists—featured in his article "The Paranoid Style in American Politics"—many academics have accepted the assertion that believers are marked by a sort of personal or cultural paranoia that engenders feelings of powerlessness and victimization that interferes with their participation in mainstream social change.

On the other hand, since African Americans have been the targets of documented conspiracies, many folklorists and sociologists argue that believing in conspiracies may not only be rational, but even positive.

Freedom of Information Act documents have proven that during the Federal Bureau of Investigation's COINTELPRO program, the FBI did plant informants who helped destabilize organizations such as the Black Panthers. Similarly, the recently released Mississippi Sovereignty Commission papers conclusively revealed that there was at least a state government conspiracy to track and harass civil rights leaders.

Waters, says that "treating conspiracy theories as invariably mistaken is unrealistic in societies where concerted and secretly planned social action is an everyday accomplishment of industries and government agencies."

She has subjected Hofstadter's predictions to an empirical test and concluded that they don't hold true for African Americans. "African Americans who believe in conspiracies are better educated than those who do not believe, they are active politically, they are in touch with the community, and they are closer than are skeptics to the front line of both interethnic conflict and cooperation," she says.

"Conspiracy theories flourish, in part because they are ways to foster solidarity and collective action," says Theodore Sasson, a Black sociologist who has studied conspiracy theories in Boston's African American communities. "In several of the discussions in which conspiracy theories were discussed, participants explicitly urged one another to engage in one form or another of resistance against White oppression."

> **What makes Black belief in conspiracy theories so difficult to interpret and evaluate is that in many recent cases the rumors are based in fact.**

Turner goes much further, and argues that even conspiracy theories that are blatantly wrong or absurd—such as one asserting that Church's Fried Chicken makes Black men sterile—can still have positive effects.

"The fact that rumors function as a sort of self-imposed consumer harness within the African American community is laudable," she says. "The thought of precious dollars being spent on luxury-style consumer items produced by White corporations violates the community's sense of the value of financial independence and self-determination and inspires action."

Instruments of Political Manipulation or Social Change?

While theorists such as Turner, Waters, and Sasson argue that rumors can be useful, Lusane and others continue to maintain that the Black community's ready acceptance of conspiracies has largely negative political consequences.

"The biggest political problems with conspiracy theories in the Black community is that they almost always give Black politicians and leaders a kind of political shock absorber that allows them to avoid some responsibility for their mistakes," Lusane says.

"[A] good example of this concerns the Reverend Henry Lyons and the National Baptist Convention. It is now perfectly clear that Lyons was personally misusing Convention funds. However, there are many people close to him who may be innocent, but who will still lose out if he is removed. Even if they know he is guilty, it is still in their own best interest to perpetuate the idea that he is the victim of a government plot."

Dr. Earl Ofari Hutchinson, a psychologist and author of *The Crisis in Black and Black*, warns Black folks to reject succumbing to all-encompassing conspiracy theories.

"African Americans must recognize that many of the problems that confront African Americans are in reality American problems. This demands that great care always be taken not to substitute paranoia for caution and vigilance and risk [turning] potential friends among Blacks and non-Blacks into sworn enemies."

Many conservatives decry Black America's belief in plots as a defense mechanism to avoid taking responsibility for "real" problems—such as drug dealing and illegitimacy—that African Americans would prefer to deny.

Professor Shelby Steele, of the National Association of Scholars, for example, has stated that believing in conspiracies prevents people from really committing their efforts to achieve personal goals.

"If you actually believe that the society in which you live is feeding AIDS and drugs to you to eliminate you, you are not going to see your own possibilities in that society," Steele says. "You're not going to move into the American mainstream. It's a profoundly destructive belief."

Perhaps the only example of a major Black conspiracy theorist creating a positive change in terms of health involves the late Elijah Muhammad, the founder of the Nation of Islam. Muhammad widely promoted the theory that Europeans were plotting genocide against Blacks in various forms including selling them drugs, cigarettes, alcohol, and pork.

In response, Muhammad taught his followers to take steps to protect themselves. He authored *Eat to Live* which advocated a healthier, lower fat diet; and preached abstinence from alcohol, tobacco, and drugs. Muhammad showed that the one way conspiracy theories may be useful is if they help people make reasonable changes to avoid risks.

CONSPIRACIES EVERYWHERE

Sometimes it seems that African Americans see conspiracies everywhere.

The cover of journalist Barbara Reynolds's new book, *No, I Won't Shut Up*, prominently features a "Special Report: Dr. King, Ron Brown: Crimes, Cover-ups, and Conspiracies."

Commentator Tony Brown has published *Empower the People: Overthrow the Conspiracy That Is Stealing Your Money and Freedom*. Brown's alleged conspiracy involves an "evil cabal" that corrupted the Freemasons in the eighteenth century.

Educator Jawanza Konjufu has become an underground bestseller by publishing four different volumes of *Countering the Conspiracy to Destroy Black Boys*.

In her book, *I Heard it Through the Grapevine, Rumor in African-American Culture*, Dr. Patricia Turner—a professor of African American studies at the University of California, Davis who has made an exhausting compilation of African American rumors and conspiracy theories— discusses virtually all of the popular Black "urban legends." These include:

- The ubiquitous "Kentucky fried rat," found in a bucket of take out chicken;

- The belief that Church's Fried Chicken, Tropical Fantasy fruit drink, and KOOL Cigarettes contain a secret ingredient to make Black men sterile;

- The belief that Troop brand athletic clothing was owned by the KKK and if you cut open the lining, it contained the slogan, "To Rule Over Oppressed People;"

- The belief that Reebok sneakers were made in apartheid South Africa;

- The belief that Gloria Vanderbilt went on the *Oprah Winfrey Show* and said that she didn't want Black women wearing her designs;

- The belief that the National Centers for Disease Control was involved in the Atlanta Child Murders as part of an experiment to extract the cancer drug interferon from the tips of Black boys' penises;

- The belief that AIDS was created in Africa when a U.S. government biological warfare experiment got out of hand; and

- The belief that the government deliberately markets crack and other drugs in Black neighborhoods.

CONSPIRACY THEORIES ARE BAD FOR BLACK HEALTH

In the medical arena, at least, there seems to be incontrovertible evidence that conspiracy theories are a major impediment to Black health.

This is particularly true concerning AIDS, where at least one study found that those who feel that it is a genocide plot were not any more likely to protect themselves from HIV infection by using condoms or abandoning drugs. To make things worse, conspiracy theories can actually sabotage positive programs.

African Americans' fears of conspiracies also interfered with the population's participation in health and biomedical research.

Compared to other Americans, Black folks are at much higher risk for cancer, stroke, kidney failure, AIDS, and many other serious diseases and conditions. Yet, researchers in virtually every field of medicine have found it very difficult to attract and retain African Americans in clinical studies—even though in 1993, the National Institutes of Health Revitalization Act required all applicants for NIH and Alcohol, Drug, and Mental Health Administration grants to increase their efforts to include minorities in human subject research.

In a 1997 paper entitled "Why Are African Americans Under-Represented in Medical Research Studies," published in *Ethnic Health,* three researchers from the University of Iowa School of Medicine concluded that fear of being treated like a "guinea pig" was a major factor—and that memories of the Tuskegee Experiment played a major role in that fear.

The forty-year Tuskegee Experiment was designed to study the "terminal effects" of the microbe causing syphilis. Black men infected with the disease were deliberately left untreated to die, infect their wives, and ultimately, their children.

As Mark Smith, M.D., of the Johns Hopkins School of Medicine in Baltimore notes, the African American community is "already alienated from the health care system and the government and . . . somewhat cynical about the motives of those who arrive in their communities to help them."

He adds that the Tuskegee Syphilis Study "provided validation for common suspicions about the ethical even-handedness in the medical research establishment and in the federal government, in particular, when it comes to Black people."

Recently, a team of four researchers led by Philip Gorelick, M.D., MPH, tried to quantify how much of a role the fear of being a guinea pig plays in reducing African Americans' willingness to participate in medical trials. The team found: "The primary reason that patients withdrew from the study was concern about being the subject of experimentation and the possibility of being a guinea pig."

The researchers also noted: "When family or friends were consulted, 83 percent reinforced the patients' concern about medical experimentation."

In order to try and overcome African Americans' fear of participating in medical experiments, the researchers advocate forming a "recruitment triangle" that includes family members as well as the patient and his or her primary doctors and other medical personnel.

The shadow of Tuskegee also inhibits African Americans from becoming more actively involved in non-experimental programs, such as bone-marrow transplants that would save thousands of lives.

Between 1998 and 1996, more than 4,400 bone marrow transplants from unrelated donors were performed, but fewer than 3 percent involved Black patients. One reason was because only 7 percent of the volunteers in the National Marrow Donor Program are African American.

These small numbers are particularly serious because while Whites can find a close enough match 70 percent of the time, African Americans only have a 42 percent chance of finding a matching donor.

According to Robert Pinderhughes, the spokes-person for the marrow donor program, the specter of Tuskegee lurks as an impediment. He believes that every time a Black patient has a bad experience in a hospital, it reinforces fears of Tuskegee.

One optimistic sign is that after the National Marrow Donor Program launched a recruitment campaign in 1993, the Black match rate almost doubled, rising from 22 percent to 42 percent in 1996.

"Were moving in the right direction, but we have a long way to go," Pinderhughes said.

Were the Levees Bombed in New Orleans?

Ninth Ward residents give voice to a conspiracy theory

By Lisa Myers and the NBC Investigative Unit
MSNBC, December 7, 2005

It's become a strongly held belief by some in the storm zone—the idea that the destruction of New Orleans' heavily poor, heavily black Ninth Ward was neither an accident nor an act of nature.

Dyan French, also known as "Mama D," is a New Orleans citizen and community leader. She testified before the House Select Committee on Hurricane Katrina on Tuesday.

"I was on my front porch. I have witnesses that they bombed the walls of the levee, boom, boom!" Mama D said, holding her head. "Mister, I'll never forget it."

"Certainly appears to me to be an act of genocide and of ethnic cleansing," Leah Hodges, another New Orleans citizen, told the committee.

Similar statements, sometimes couched as rumors, have also been voiced by Louis Farrakhan, leader of the nation of Islam, and director Spike Lee.

"I don't find it too far-fetched," Lee said in a recent television interview, "that they try to displace all the black people out of New Orleans."

Harvard's Alvin Pouissant says such conspiracy theories are fueled by years of government neglect and discrimination against blacks: slavery, segregation and the Tuskegee experiments, during which poor blacks were used to test the effects of syphilis.

"If you're angry and you've been discriminated against," Pouissant says, "then your mind is open to many ideas about persecution, abandonment, feelings of rejection."

The latest theory is partly rooted in historical fact. In 1927, the levees were bombed to save parts of the city, and black neighborhoods were inundated.

But independent engineers investigating levee failures during Katrina say that's not what happened this time.

Prof. Robert Bea, from the University of California, Berkeley, studied the levee failures and his team issued a preliminary report.

> *The latest theory is partly rooted in historical fact. In 1927, the levees were bombed to save parts of the city, and black neighborhoods were inundated.*

"We didn't find any evidence that would indicate explosions," says Bea.

New Orleans columnist Lolis Eric Elie says the federal government badly neglected black Americans during Katrina, but he does not believe the levees were blown up.

"One of the problems with that theory," Elie says, "is that there were a whole lot of other areas of the city, including some that are predominantly white, where there was flooding."

Harvard's Pouissant also says that latching on to conspiracy theories is a way for the powerless to cope with terrible losses — incendiary claims born of an enormous tragedy.

Lisa Myers is NBC's Senior Investigative Correspondent.

For Critics of Islam, 'Sharia' a Loaded Word

By Michelle Boorstein
Washington Post, August 27, 2010

Protesters of the proposed Islamic center near Ground Zero waved signs there Sunday with a single word: sharia.

Their reference to Islam's guiding principles has become a rallying cry for those critical of Islam, who use the word to conjure images of public stonings and other extreme forms of punishment in countries such as Saudi Arabia or Afghanistan and argue that those tenets are somehow gaining a foothold in the United States.

Blogs with names such as Creeping Sharia and Stop Shariah Now are proliferating. A pamphlet for a "tea party" rally last weekend in Fort Walton Beach, Fla., asked: "Why do Muslims want to take over the world and place us under Shariah law?" Former GOP House speaker Newt Gingrich amplified that point in a much-publicized speech a few weeks ago, exploring what he calls "the problem of creeping sharia."

The fact that the word has become akin to a slur in some camps is an alarming development to many religious and political leaders. "We are deeply saddened by those who denigrate a religion which in so many ways is a religion of compassion," Peg Chamberlin, president of the National Council of Churches, said in a statement this month signed by 40 national religious leaders.

Sharia in Arabic means "way" or "path." Muslims agree that sharia is God's law, but there is little consensus on the particulars. To some, sharia is a set of rules that are codified and unchanging. To others, it's a collection of religious principles that shift over time.

Imam Yahya Hendi, Muslim chaplain at Georgetown University and spokesman of the Islamic Jurisprudence Council of North America, describes Muslims as being divided into two camps: "Those who see sharia mandating that we live as Muslims did 1,300 years ago, and those who say sharia doesn't have a specific format as to how you live your life, that Islam gives you paradigms."

This question of how to define sharia has become a more urgent issue for Muslims around the world in recent decades as, according to some estimates, one-third of them live outside Muslim-majority countries for the first time in history. Conferences are held where scholars debate what it means for a government or a person to be "sharia-compliant."

Imam Feisal Rauf, a Sufi Muslim who is spearheading the controversial mosque center, runs something called the Shariah Index Project, which seeks to create a more progressive benchmark for measuring the "Islamicity" of a state. Daisy Khan, Rauf's wife, said the couple believe the word "sharia" primarily refers to several broad principles

A pamphlet for a "tea party" rally last weekend in Fort Walton Beach, Fla., asked: "Why do Muslims want to take over the world and place us under Shariah law?"

called "maqasid sharia," which include the protection of life, property and religion, among others. These principles are believed to be the foundation of the faith.

Others say "sharia" refers to the specific words of the Koran (Muslims' holy book of God's revelation passed orally to the prophet Muhammad) as well as all the hadith, which are the actions and statements attributed to Muhammad that have been passed down, analyzed, interpreted (and sometimes tossed out) over the centuries.

Many of the harshest, most controversial writings are in the hadith, such as those giving lower status to non-Muslims and mandates to stone adulterers (including a much-publicized stoning this month in Afghanistan, meted out by the Taliban). Muslims have debated their accuracy for centuries.

Another key source is fiqh, the collection of opinions scholars have written to determine how the will of God can be carried out in daily life. Some people include all fiqh as well when they refer to "sharia" or "Islamic law."

Daniel Pipes, a conservative Middle East scholar controversial for his focus on extremism among Muslims, said sharia refers to something "enormously specific," which he compared to the U.S. Constitution. The danger, he said, is when Muslims "want to implement sharia in every detail on everyone in a stringent way."

The Rev. Canon Julian M. Dobbs, who oversees Muslim engagement for the umbrella group of conservative Anglicans who broke away from the Episcopal Church in North America, referred to stonings as being part of sharia. "Islamic scholars must stop the self-deception which claims that Islam is 100 percent peace, and with honesty, recognize the violence that continues to exist within their religion today," he said.

Geoff Ross, a Navy veteran who organized the tea party event in Florida last weekend, said the word means "the law that practicing Muslims follow to lead their daily lives." He became involved with anti-sharia events last year.

"I study the Koran, I study the Internet. I look at sources on the Internet and try to vet that information," he said. "I'm not anti-Islam. I'm anti-terrorist. But if you take quotes from the Bible and compare them to the Koran, the Bible might say, 'Turn the other cheek,' while the Koran would say, 'Strike your enemies down and kill them.'"

There is also great disagreement—and sometimes contradiction—across the Muslim world about what it means to implement sharia, or, to use a frequent term, to be a sharia-compliant country.

Recent polling in the Muslim world shows people can say that they believe sharia should be a source for crafting legislation but simultaneously believe that religious leaders should play no role in drafting laws.

Dalia Mogahed, executive director of the Gallup Center for Muslim Studies, said most constitutions in the 57 members of the Organization of Islamic Conference Member States "mention sharia as a source of legislation. But that means very different things."

Pipes said three countries claim they are implementing sharia: Saudi Arabia, Iran and Sudan.

Those who decry what they call "creeping sharia" are concerned about Muslims in the West winning more public accommodations. Examples they cite include Harvard University recently creating women-only hours at one of its swimming pools; banks offering products that comply with Islam's ban on charging interest; and female police officers wearing head coverings when entering mosques.

"Some Islamists employ mass-murder attacks while others prefer a gradual march through our institutions—our legal, political, academic, and financial systems, as well as our broader culture; the goal of both, though, is the same," Andrew McCarthy wrote in a *National Review* piece July 31 called "It's about sharia."

6

Science Fictions? Roswell, the Moon Landing, and Beyond

(WireImage)

A sign outside the top secret United States Air Force base Area 51 in Nevada.

The Roswell Mystery and Its Legacy

By Paul McCaffrey

On June 14, 1947, while walking with his son on an isolated sheep ranch outside of Roswell, New Mexico, William Ware "Mac" Brazel came upon something unusual. In a press account published the next month, Brazel described what he found as "a large area of bright wreckage made up [of] rubber strips, tinfoil, a rather tough paper and sticks." Strewn over an area of ground about two hundred yards across, the material gathered together, Brazel estimated, would have been around the size of a table top. He did not tell authorities about his discovery for several weeks, however, and in the meantime, a number of unidentified flying objects (UFOs) were reported across the country. The flurry of sightings commenced on June 24, when pilot Kenneth Arnold spotted a group of nine as he flew his plane over the Cascade Mountains in Washington State. The objects moved "like a saucer," in Arnold's words, and according to his calculations, traveled at supersonic speeds. As news of Arnold's "flying saucers" spread, UFO sightings increased. Before long, citizens in Roswell spotted something in the skies that they could not explain.

Brazel returned to the ranch site on July 4 with his wife and family and collected some of the debris. The following day, Brazel heard about the UFO reports and, thinking the wreckage he found might have something to do with these sightings, decided to contact George Wilcox, the local sheriff. After Brazel informed him of his intriguing find, Wilcox called officials at nearby Roswell Army Airfield. Major Jesse A. Marcel and intelligence officer Sheridan Cavitt were sent over to investigate. They gathered the last of the material from the crash site and, in Brazel's home, tried to reconstruct the object without success. Subsequently, Marcel transported all the wreckage back to Roswell Army Airfield before shipping it to the Eighth Air Force, stationed in Fort Worth, Texas, for further examination.

On July 8, 1947, under orders, Walter Haut, the press officer of the 509th Bombardment Group, Marcel's unit, issued a press release that went out across the country. Haut announced that the 509th had recovered a flying saucer. A media deluge ensued, and Roswell was inundated with calls from inquiring reporters.

The next day, Brigadier General Roger Ramey of the Eighth Air Force issued a retraction, telling the media that the wreckage was not that of a UFO, but of a weather balloon. Embarrassed by the uproar his discovery had caused, a chastened Brazel commented, "If I find anything else besides a bomb they are going to have a hard time getting me to say anything about it." Nevertheless, he took issue with General Ramey's explanation. Brazel had found weather balloons in the area before and, he remarked, "I am sure what I found was not any weather observation balloon."

Whether true or not, Ramey's retraction had the desired effect. In the days and weeks that followed, the Roswell story fell out of the public eye and stayed largely forgotten for the next thirty years. That is, until a physicist and amateur UFO re-searcher named Stanton Friedman managed to locate Major Marcel.

Stanton Friedman met Marcel by chance in 1978, in Baton Rouge, Louisiana. Though three decades had passed, Marcel remained convinced that the 509th press release had been accurate, that whatever Brazel had found that day outside of Roswell, it was not of earthly origin. Friedman commenced a more in-depth investigation and grew convinced that an enormous government conspiracy had concealed the truth about Roswell from the public. With two other authors, Charles Berlitz and William Moore, Friedman published his findings in *The Roswell Incident* (1980). Spurred on by these revelations, other researchers delved into the matter, and Roswell became a central focus of UFO researchers and conspiracy theorists alike.

As UFO researchers—also called "ufologists"—took up the case, they tracked down additional material and interviewed additional sources. Their leads piled up, and the implications of what happened at Roswell grew larger and larger. Soon the incident became wrapped up in stories of other alleged UFO activity in the area.

Another team of researchers—Kevin Randle and Don Schmitt—concluded that alien remains had in fact been found at the Roswell site. Glenn Dennis, a former Roswell mortuary worker who had earlier spoken with Friedman, told them that operatives from the air field had contacted him in early July 1947 with strange questions about child-size coffins and embalming procedures. A nurse from the base even revealed to him that she had participated in alien autopsies. This nurse, Nurse X as she is known among Roswell conspiracists, has never been adequately identified and remains one of the central mysteries of the case.

As the years progressed, additional witnesses came forward and their stories grew increasingly vivid. Under hypnosis, one claimed to have observed the wreckage of a UFO near the Roswell site. Eight aliens lay among the shattered remnants of the spacecraft. Seven of them were dead. One was still breathing. Before the witness could investigate further, military personnel ordered him to leave and suggested he forget what he saw.

In trying to weave together the various strands of the Roswell story and reconcile the conflicting accounts of the alleged witnesses, researchers have come up with a number of scenarios. Some theorize that a midair UFO collision took place, leading to two crash sites. Others believe the government may have held extraterrestrial crash survivors captive in order to learn more about their technology and to help reverse engineer their spaceships. There are skeptics, too. One noted UFO researcher, Kent Jeffrey, did some detective work on his own, talking his way into a reunion of the 509th Bombardment Group, where he interviewed pilots who were at Roswell in 1947. The pilots were unanimous: they had not heard a whisper about any crashed UFO until decades later. Further inquiries by Jeffrey led to similar dead ends. "In essence," he concluded, "the 1947 Roswell case has turned out to be a red herring, diverting time and resources away from research into the real UFO phenomenon."

Jeffrey is the exception rather than the rule among Roswell sleuths, however. While there are major disagreements among them, the general consensus is that the government has not been honest with the public and is responsible for a massive ongoing cover-up. Their complaints about government stonewalling and malfeasance have not gone unheard in the nation's capital. Responding to congressional pressure, the US Air Force has compiled and published two official reports on the matter. In July 1994, after interviewing all the surviving witnesses and conducting its own investigation, the Air Force concluded that the debris found by Mac Brazel came from a specialized high-altitude balloon outfitted with high-tech listening devices. The balloon was part of Project Mogul, a top-secret intelligence operation designed to monitor nuclear tests in the Soviet Union.

Ufologists greeted the Air Force's initial report with a great deal of skepticism. Their chief criticism was that it failed to address reports of alien bodies. The Air Force took up this issue in a 1997 study. Investigators declared that the descriptions of alien corpses matched those of mannequins the military used for testing purposes. There were documented cases in the 1950s of crash test dummies being dropped from aircraft and from high-altitude balloons over New Mexico. Consequently, witnesses could have observed the recovery of these mannequins and reinterpreted events over the decades to conclude that they had seen alien bodies near Roswell.

Whether plausible or not, these explanations fail to pass muster with Roswell conspiracists. Among the public as a whole, the results are not much more encouraging. In a 1997 poll taken around the fiftieth anniversary of the Roswell incident, fully 80 percent of US citizens believed the government was hiding evidence of alien life.

Though what really happened at Roswell will probably never be known, the suspicions that have surrounded the incident are not as unusual as they seem. Rather, they represent a form of conspiracy theory that became increasingly common in the post–World War II era. Rapid technological advancement—the development of nuclear technology and the achievements of the space program, for example—combined with the existential worries provoked by the Cold War created the ideal environment for a Roswell-like level of mistrust to develop. These conspiracies, with their emphasis on technology and extraterrestrials, share much with the world of science fiction. At the same time, they continue to overlap with other, more earthly conspiracies, echoing the underlying skepticism regarding government and the military found in 9/11, JFK, and other popular conspiracy theories. In fact, there is a distinct subset of JFK conspiracy theories that connect the murder of the president with aliens. Supposedly, ten days before he was assassinated, the president issued a secret memo requesting information about UFOs. There are those who draw a direct connection between this inquiry and subsequent events in Dallas.

Given its wide reach in popular culture and its influence on other forms of speculation, Roswell theorizing is a central nexus of science-fiction-oriented conspiracies. Assorted Roswell theories extend into other sectors of the genre. For example, the wreckage from Roswell was supposedly transported to the notorious Area 51, a top-secret military base in the Nevada desert. From the most mundane perspective, Area 51 is associated with advanced aerodynamic research. It is where the US

Air Force builds and tests its most cutting-edge and presumably classified weapons systems and aircraft. Conspiracists go further than this, however, and suggest that extraterrestrial technology, from Roswell and elsewhere, is reverse engineered at Area 51. Indeed, aliens may even be sequestered there and pressed into service, their knowledge and skills commandeered with or without their consent. There are also whispers of time-travel, teleportation, and weather-control experiments.

Along with the more grandiose speculations of the Roswell and Area 51 variety, there are also smaller-scale sci-fi conspiracy theories. Among these are ones pertaining to "chemtrails," or chemical trails. Visible in the sky, chemtrails resemble conventional contrails, or condensation trails, the long white lines left in the wake of a passing jet. Scientists claim that that is precisely what chemtrails in fact are—contrails, formed when the plane's emissions interact with the atmosphere. Conspiracists offer a more sinister explanation. In their view, chemtrails—which they say remain in the sky for much longer than contrails, and are often seen crisscrossing the sky in large numbers—are evidence of the release of chemical and biological agents into the atmosphere by governments or other entities without public knowledge or approval. What these substances are meant to achieve is subject to interpretation. Some maintain the chemtrails are used to influence the weather, others that they are a means of population control.

Embedded in these science-fiction conspiracy theories, whether about chemtrails or Roswell, is the obvious mistrust of government and advanced technology. Yet there is a form of the genre that subverts this dynamic, alleging that the technology in question does not exist at all, but is in fact an elaborate government-sponsored fabrication. For example, Neil Armstrong's famed "giant leap for mankind," the original moon walk in July 1969, is said by some to have been nothing but a giant deception. Those espousing the moon hoax scenario point to supposed discrepancies in the photographs or in the composition of moon rocks taken from the alleged moon landings, among other evidence, to suggest the missions never actually took place, that contrary to popular belief, man has never walked on the moon. As to what motivated the government to hatch such a complicated ruse, conspiracists offer differing explanations. Some claim it was a tool to intimidate the Soviets. Others that it was meant to distract the American public from the worsening conflict in Vietnam.

Between crashed aliens, reverse-engineered spacecraft, chemtrails, and the moon hoax, this form of conspiracy theory is an especially vibrant one, allowing conspiracists to extend their investigations beyond the confines of Earth—and beyond the confines of the human species. In the years ahead, it is safe to predict that even further dimensions will be added to sci-fi conspiracy theorizing.

Roswell, New Mexico, UFO Crash

By Brad Steiger and Sherry Steiger
Conspiracies and Secret Societies, 2006

The air force press release of July 8, 1947, that announced the retrieval of a crashed flying saucer outside of Roswell, New Mexico, has become the Mother of All UFO Conspiracies.

The alleged UFO crash outside of Roswell, New Mexico, on the night of July 2, 1947, is the one event that spawned nearly every UFO conspiracy theory extant today. Here is what generations of UFO researchers contend happened at Roswell:

An extraterrestrial craft developed mechanical problems and crashed on a ranch located about sixty miles north of Roswell.

Major Jesse Marcel—winner of five air combat medals in World War II, intelligence officer for the 509th Bomber Group, a top-security, handpicked unit—was ordered to go to the site and salvage the remains of the unknown aircraft reported by Mac Brazel, a rancher who had discovered the debris on his land.

In 1980 Marcel, long retired, recalled that he and his men found wreckage from the UFO scattered throughout the area of the crash. He admitted that he had no idea exactly what he and his men were supposed to retrieve—and, forty years later, he still didn't know.

The strange, weightless material discovered by the 509th Bomber Group was difficult to describe. The pieces varied in length from four or five inches to three or four feet. Some fragments had markings that resembled hieroglyphics. Although the material seemed to be unbreakable, the military investigators thought that it looked more like wood than metal. Marcel put his cigarette lighter to one of the rectangular fragments, but it would not burn. He and his crew brought as many pieces of the crashed UFO back to Roswell Army Air Base as they could gather. Lewis Rickert, who in 1947 was a master sergeant and counterintelligence agent stationed at the air field, was among the military personnel present at the crash site. In 1994 he recalled that the jagged, flexible fragments were no more than eight or ten inches long and six or seven inches wide and they could not be broken.

On July 8, 1947, Walter Haut, the public affairs officer at Roswell Army Air Base, sent out a release announcing that the air force had "captured" a flying saucer. The announcement was transmitted to thirty U.S. afternoon newspapers that same day, and the entire nation was electrified as word spread that a military team had actually recovered debris from the crash of one of those mysterious airborne discs that people had seen buzzing around the country ever since a civilian pilot named Kenneth Arnold claimed to have had an encounter with "flying saucers" near Mount Rainier, in Washington State, on June 24.

On the very next day, July 9, the press office at the air field released a correction of its previous story. It had not been the debris of a flying saucer that had been recovered, after all. It was nothing but the remains of a downed weather balloon. Also on July 9, the *Roswell Daily Record* carried the story of Mac Brazel, the rancher who had found the "saucer," who said that he was sorry that he had told anyone about the crashed junk in the first place.

In the 1980s Kevin Randle, a former captain in U.S. Air Force Intelligence, together with Don Schmitt, director of the J. Allen Hynek Center for UFO Studies, found new evidence indicating that the crash actually occurred on July 4, 1947, rather than July 2, as is commonly stated. It was on July 5, according to Schmitt and Randle, that Mac Brazel visited Sheriff George Wilcox and informed him of the peculiar discovery he had made near his ranch the day before. The military unit under the command of Major Marcel retrieved the crash debris and alien bodies on July 5. On July 8 Walter Haut issued the press release stating that the army had captured a flying saucer. Almost immediately thereafter, the official cover story of a collapsed weather balloon failing to earth in the desert was heavily promoted by the military.

Numerous civilians who claimed to have arrived at the crash site remembered seeing the corpses of small, hairless beings with large heads and round, oddly spaced eyes.

Barney Barnett, a civil engineer employed by the federal government, said that he had seen alien bodies on the ground and inside the wrecked spaceship. He described them as small, hairless beings with large heads and round, oddly spaced eyes. Barnett stated that a military unit arrived on the scene and an officer ordered him off the site with the stern admonition that it was his patriotic duty to remain silent about what he had seen.

The press officer Walter Haut was given direct orders by his base commander, Col. William Blanchard, to prepare the official press release refuting the flying saucer account. The cover story of the weather balloon initiated the military/government conspiracy to keep the truth of a crashed extraterrestrial UFO from the public.

The nuclear physicist Stanton Friedman contends that Major Marcel was very familiar with all kinds of weather and military balloons and would not have mistaken such ordinary debris for that of a downed alien spaceship. Nor would any of the military personnel have mistaken alien bodies for diminutive human remains. After the wreckage was properly identified as extraterrestrial in nature, Friedman claims, the official cover-up was instigated at both the Roswell base and the headquarters of the Eighth Air Force in Fort Worth, Texas, by the Eighth Air Force's commandant, Brig. Gen. Roger Ramey, on direct orders from Gen. Clement McMullen at Strategic Air Command headquarters in Washington, D.C.

At least one of the alien crew survived the crash and was shipped, along with the debris of the vehicle, to Wright Field in Dayton, Ohio, thus becoming a resident of the infamous "Hanger 18" at Wright-Patterson. Most eyewitness accounts speak of five alien bodies found at the impact site and state that four corpses were transported to Wright Field and the fifth to Lowry Field, Denver, to the air force mortuary service. Numerous secondary accounts of the incident assert that one of the UFOnauts survived the crash and was still alive when the military arrived on the scene. Some UFO researchers maintain that circa 1986 the alien being was still alive and well treated as a guest of the air force at what is now Wright-Patterson Air Base.

Don Schmitt and Kevin Randle, in their book *UFO Crash at Roswell*, include an interview with Brig. Gen. Arthur Exon, who told them that, in addition to debris from the wreckage, four tiny alien cadavers were flown to Wright Field.

A number of civilians were threatened by the military to keep their mouths shut about what really occurred at Roswell. During an interview with a granddaughter of Sheriff George Wilcox in March 1991, Schmitt and Randle were told that the sheriff saw the debris of a UFO and "little space beings." Later, military men "who were not kidding" visited Wilcox and his wife and warned them that they would be killed if they ever told anyone what he saw at the crash site. Not only would they be murdered, but their children and grandchildren would also be eliminated.

Randle and Schmitt located a Ms. Frankie Rowe, who had been twelve years old at the time of the mysterious occurrences outside Roswell. Her father, a lieutenant with the fire department, told his family at dinner on the night of the UFO crash that he had seen the remains of what he had at first believed to be an airplane. He also saw two little bodies in body bags and a third alien entity walking around in a daze. He described the beings as about the size of a ten-year-old child. Later, a group of military men arrived at the house and made it clear that if they ever talked about the incident again, the entire family would be taken out in the desert and "no one would ever find us again."

In the November 1994 issue of *American Funeral Director*, Glenn Dennis recalled the telephone conversation that he had with the mortuary officer at Roswell Army Air Base on Tuesday, July 8, 1947, when he was asked if he could provide three- or four-foot-long hermetically sealed caskets. A short time later Dennis was on the base in his capacity as an ambulance driver, transporting an injured airman to the base hospital. As he drove past two field ambulances, he looked into their open back ends and saw an enormous amount of a silvery, metallic material, two chunks of which were curved at the bottom in the manner of a canoe. He also noticed that the pieces were covered with odd markings, which he assumed were some kind of hieroglyphs.

Dennis stated in the article that he was a familiar figure at the air base, even accepted as an honorary member of its officers club. On this occasion, however, two MPs grabbed him and brought him to a red-haired officer who warned him that somebody would be picking his bones out of the sand if he ever shot his mouth off about seeing the peculiar material. As the MPs were escorting Dennis back to his ambulance, they met a female nurse in the hallway. The nurse, with whom he was well acquainted, held a towel over the lower part of her face, and Dennis at first thought that she had been crying. Alarmed by his presence, she told him to leave at once before he was shot. Dennis indicated his two-man armed escort and said that he was leaving the base. As he was being ushered rudely down the hall, Dennis saw two men who also had towels over their noses and mouths.

The next day, the nurse arranged to meet Dennis at the officers club. There she told him that a flying saucer had crashed in the desert and the army had recovered bodies of three dead aliens. Until the bodies were

She told him that a flying saucer had crashed in the desert and the army had recovered bodies of three dead aliens.

frozen, she said, their smell had nauseated the medical staff. Dennis said that the nurse became extremely emotional while describing smallish beings with large heads and big eyes. He never saw her again. He was informed that she had been transferred to a base in England. Later, he was told that she had been killed in an airplane crash.

Other Roswell conspiracy theories with slightly different interpretations of the event were not long in surfacing: An extraterrestrial craft did crash at Roswell in 1947, and through reverse engineering of the advanced alien technology at secret air bases such as Area 51, our scientists and engineers have accomplished aeronautical breakthroughs decades ahead of when we might have expected them. Artifacts found with the crashed extraterrestrial space vehicle were discreetly farmed out to major U.S. corporations that were able to back-engineer many technological advances, to the benefit of all world citizens.

The alien kept alive in Hangar 18 at Wright-Patterson Air Force Base has been acting as a liaison between a secret agency within the government and the extraterrestrials, actually exchanging humans for advanced technical data. In secret underground military and commercial facilities, aliens have been seen working side by side with earthling scientists and engineers developing additional technological advances derived from extraterrestrial technology.

Witnesses to such activity report subterranean laboratories where the extraterrestrials seek to create part-alien, part-human beings. Others tell horror stories of having observed "large vats with pale meat being agitated in solutions" and large test tubes "with humans in them."

On June 24, 1997, the Pentagon held a special briefing conducted by the U.S. Air Force—timed to coincide with the fiftieth anniversary of Kenneth Arnold's 1947 sighting of flying saucers—in order to release the document entitled *The Roswell Report: Case Closed*. This publication, stated Col. John Haynes, would be the air force's final word concerning fifty years of accusations that the government was hiding evidence of extraterrestrial visitation.

The debris found at the crash site outside of Roswell was from a Project Mogul balloon, a top-secret intelligence-gathering device, hence the cover-up was for purposes of national security. The alleged bodies seen around the crash site were not those of extraterrestrial beings—or of any living beings. They were actually dummies, roughly the size of humans, that were used in experiments with high-altitude parachutes that began in 1953. After the experimental drops, air force personnel would retrieve the simulated human forms, and it must have been at certain of these recovery missions that folks around Roswell got the idea that they saw military types picking up "alien" bodies.

For those who wondered how witnesses could confuse dummies dropped over the desert near Roswell in 1953 with humanoid corpses scattered near a specific crash site in 1947, Colonel Haynes explained this confusion as a manifestation of the mental phenomenon of "time compression," wherein the memory melds events separated by many years into "compressed" segments of time. That is, civilians who witnessed the crash site of a weather balloon in 1947 and, six years later, saw air force personnel retrieving crash dummies dropped from the skies recall the two events as one in their compressed memories. With all the controversy regarding flying saucers and aliens, the witnesses remember the balloon fragments and the dummies as the debris from a crashed spacecraft and the corpses of its extraterrestrial crew.

On October 25, 1998, an interview in the newspaper *The People* (London) with Dr. Edgar Mitchell, the sixth person to walk on the moon, startled UFO buffs and skeptics alike. Without hesitation, the former astronaut proclaimed, "Make no mistake, Roswell happened. I've seen secret files which show the government knew about it, but decided not to tell the public." Mitchell explained that because of his being a scientist and a former astronaut, military people with access to top-secret files were more willing to speak with him than to civilian researchers with shaky credentials. Although he had begun his inquiries as a cynic, he said, he became convinced of the existence of aliens after speaking with "the military old-timers" who had been in service at the time of Roswell. He added that the more government documentation he was told about, the more convinced he became.

Mitchell stated that he was shocked to learn the extent to which the UFO mystery had been covered up by the governments of the world, but in defense of such actions, he said that there were sound security reasons for not informing the general public of the truth about Roswell: "Quite simply, we wouldn't have known how to deal with the technology of intelligent beings advanced enough to send a craft to Earth. The world would have panicked if we'd know aliens were visiting us." He expressed his belief that those individuals who were in possession of top-secret documentation of alien visitors would soon begin to come forward and that full disclosures would be made within three or four years.

In July 1997 a CNN/Time poll taken to commemorate the fiftieth anniversary of the enigmatic event at Roswell indicated that 80 percent of the American public believes the government is hiding information about the UFO mystery. In addition, 54 percent of those surveyed are certain that life exists outside of Earth; 35 percent expect extraterrestrial beings to appear "somewhat" human; 64 percent are convinced that alien life forms have made contact with humans; and 37 percent are concerned that ETs are abducting humans.

Bibliography

Berlitz, Charles, and William L. Moore. *The Roswell Incident.* New York: Grosset and Dunlap, 1980.

Friedman, Stanton T., and Don Berliner. *Crash at Corona: The U.S. Military Retrieval and Cover-up of a UFO*. New York: Marlowe, 1992.

Korff, Kal K. *The Roswell UFO Crash*. New York: Prometheus, 1997.

Randle, Kevin. *Roswell UFO Crash Update: Exposing the Military Cover-up of the Century*. New Brunswick, NJ: Inner Light Publications, 1995.

Randle, Kevin D., and Donald R. Schmitt. *UFO Crash at Roswell*. New York: Avon, 1991.

U.S. Air Force. *The Roswell Report: Case Closed*. Washington, DC: Government Printing Office, 1997.

Did NASA Fake the Moon Landing?

By Ray Villard
Astronomy, July 2004

To quash any lingering doubts as to whether or not we went to the Moon, *Astronomy* is setting the record straight, once and for all.

The seven Project Apollo manned expeditions to the Moon will long be remembered as expressions of America's pioneering spirit and sheer technological prowess. That is, if the landings really happened.

For the past several decades, a small group of NASA-watching sleuths has repeatedly tried to pawn off the incredulous idea that the Apollo Moon program really was an elaborate, $30 billion hoax filmed in a movie studio. This group believes the United States needed to cement its world leadership during the Cold War by pretending to pull off what really was a technologically impossible stunt. Moon hoax proponents think they've come up with suspicious evidence that scientists, investigative reporters, and everyone else on Earth apparently has overlooked for more than thirty years. The far-out idea drew 15 million viewers when FOX-TV twice ran a documentary on this subject in 2003.

Seeds of doubt

In the October 30, 1938, theatrical radio adaptation of H. G. Wells's *War of the Worlds*, actor Orson Welles managed inadvertently to convince 1.2 million Americans that martians were invading Earth. So, for conspiracy theorists, it's easy to imagine that with $30 billion and the awesome power of the United States government, the world could be made to believe almost anything. If Hollywood can fake perfectly believable dinosaurs, space aliens, and fantasy planets, why not a visit to the Moon?

A former aerospace technical writer, Bill Kaysing kicked off the Moon conspiracy idea in 1975 in a self-published book with the blunt title *We Never Went to the Moon*. Several copycats have followed him—*Moongate: Suppressed Findings of the U.S. Space Program* by William L. Brian [1984], Ralph Rene's *NASA Mooned America* [1994], and *Dark Moon-Apollo and the Whistle-Blowers* by Mary Bennett and others [1999].

But don't expect to find these books on *The New York Times* bestseller list. According to a 1999 Gallup poll, an inconsequential 5 percent of the population in the United States actually believes we never went to the Moon. (Coincidentally, this is the same percentage of the population estimated to be intoxicated at any given

From *Astronomy* 32, no. 7 (2004): 48–53. Copyright © 2011 by *Astronomy.* Reprinted with permission. All rights reserved.

time.) However, 42 percent of the American population believes the government routinely hides information from us. This generalized suspicion keeps the Moon hoax idea popping up like a zombie in some cult-classic horror film: You blow its brains out, but the monster just keeps lumbering along.

Fuzzy logic

It doesn't help Moon conspiracy theorists that not one person from the Apollo era's 35,000 NASA employees or 200,000 contractors has ever stepped forward with "whistle-blowing" insider testimony or "smoking-gun" memos about a staged event. Conspiracy theorists also need to explain how the Hollywood special-effects wizards who presumably pulled off Academy-Award-winning moonwalk scenes have managed to remain stone silent for decades (despite the fact it would look great on their resumes!). This lack of proof forces conspiracy theorists to counter that the government scared and murdered potential tattletales, including its own astronaut-heroes in a reprehensible assertion that the tragic 1967 Apollo 1 fire was rigged. A casual browse through Moon conspiracy Internet sites is a mind-numbing journey into the dark side of common sense. The conspiracy theorists are their own worst enemies. They serve up a witch's brew of paranoia, lamebrain science, goofy amateur photo-analysis, and gaping contradictions in logic you could sail the *Titanic* through. *Dark Moon* author Mary Bennett purportedly uncovered "secret" documents that show Apollo was a hoax. Bill Brian (*Moongate*) agrees Apollo was a scam but, suspects we reached the Moon with the aid of a secret, anti-gravity device that NASA reverse-engineered by copying parts of a captured, alien flying saucer.

Mission implausible

Under cold scrutiny, everyday logic, and low-level science, Apollo conspiracy theories implode faster than a black hole. NASA's own actions are inconsistent with how anyone would attempt to pull off a Moon hoax. If what actually happened during the Apollo program was scripted, the government showed a penchant for gambling and brinkmanship. For example, the government "pretended" to almost kill one of the crews (Apollo 13) to boost television ratings. NASA also had an astronaut "pretend" to break a camera (Apollo 12) after squandering billions of dollars on Hollywood special effects.

The scientific samples, photographic evidence, and telemetry from the Moon are incontrovertible. For this to be otherwise, the world's foremost planetary scientists would have to be dead wrong (imagine the book: *Moon Rock Analysis for Dummies*). Or even more fantastic, scientists have their own international conspiracy to pawn off phony data—an idea even more impossible than a government conspiracy.

The hours of astronaut moonwalk video are far too complex to have been faked with 1960s motion-picture special-effects technology (unless the Apollo billions were really spent building a time machine to bring back from the future an image-rendering computer and powerful animation software).

Seeing is believing

One Moon conspiracy theorist claim is that you can't simply look at the Moon and directly see evidence of human visitation. The six lunar-lander descent stages left on the Moon are small compared to our satellite as a whole—only about 15 feet across. Even the eagle-eyed Hubble Space Telescope can see an object no smaller than 265 feet across at the Moon's distance. However, two researchers, Misha Kreslavsky of Brown University and Yuri Shkuratov of the Kharkov Astronomical Observatory in the Ukraine, recently uncovered the first direct visual evidence of human visitation to the Moon. They had been comparing the 1994 Clementine lunar orbiter images with Apollo images taken more than thirty years ago for evidence of fresh cratering activity. In doing so, they discovered a disturbed regolith (but no impact crater) around the exact location of the Apollo 15 landing site.

Five small, nuclear-powered stations left behind by the astronauts transmitted telemetry information from twenty-five separate experiments, yielding information about the Moon's seismic activity, subsurface temperature, rate of micrometeorite impacts, and other surface properties. In 1977, the experiments were turned off for budgetary reasons. However, the central station transmitters continue to send signals that have been used for spacecraft navigation checks, gravitational experiments, mapping planetary positions, and precisely measuring Earth's shape. The stations also include a small mirror array called a retroreflector that astronomers have used to bounce laser beams off the Moon for more than thirty years to precisely measure distances to an accuracy of three-quarters of an inch.

A casual browse through Moon conspiracy Internet sites is a mind-numbing journey into the dark side of common sense.

Some 842 pounds of Moon rocks—ancient anthracites, lava basalts, and breccias (agglomerations of fractured pieces from meteorite impacts)—have been shared with the worldwide geology community. Radioisotope dating of these samples indicates ages significantly older (4.4 billion years) than the oldest Earth rocks (3.8 billion years), meaning the rocks are very well preserved, partly because they are bone-dry. You simply don't walk down to the beach and pick up a 4.4 billion-year-old rock. Trying to fool the entire geology community is like trying to fool Mother Nature. Where did these rocks come from if not from the Moon's surface?

Fantastic voyage

Fundamental to the conspiracy theory is our supposed inability to go to the Moon. Some scientists were saying the very same thing at the time American pioneer Robert Goddard was launching rockets in a Massachusetts farm field. The thought of humans traveling to the Moon was so fantastic even early science-fiction writers didn't predict it happening for centuries to come.

Going to the Moon certainly was rocket science. But you don't need breakthrough physics or warp-drive to make the trip. The modern rocket engine is based on science principles formulated by Isaac Newton centuries ago. The hardest part of going to the Moon is climbing out of Earth's gravitational field. The immense launch complex at NASA's Kennedy Space Center in Florida and the extraordinary Saturn V rockets that hurled our astronaut pioneers to the Moon were what accomplished this task, and nothing was phony about them. Ask any one of the thousands of media or VIP guests who witnessed the mighty rockets climb majestically on Promethean flames into the topaz Florida skies.

Besides, NASA didn't need such a brawny rocket for a hoax. It could have launched a few small rockets (Saturn 1-B class) and explained it was assembling the Moon ship in low Earth orbit (a strategy considered in the 1960s). Also, hoaxers could have gotten away with a single vehicle. The actual lunar orbit rendezvous approach—requiring a separate orbiter and lander vehicle—was so complex it automatically invited scrutiny by doubters.

To the danger zone

To be sure, space travel is hazardous. One obstacle cited by detractors is the Van Allen radiation belts, which are caused by Earth's magnetic field. Electrons and protons zipping along magnetic field lines can degrade electronics on spacecraft. But rushing toward the Moon at 7 miles (11 kilometers) a second, the Apollo astronauts spent just a few hours within the belts.

The biggest potential threat for space travelers is from solar flares. The radiation from a giant flare is equal to 40 billion atomic bombs exploding at once. Fortunately, this amount of radiation is dispersed widely through space.

Also, the Sun was at a minimum in its 11-year cycle of activity during the Apollo years, so deadly flares were rare. A radiation sensor outside the Apollo 12 spacecraft registered one small solar flare, but no increase in radiation dose to the crewmen in the spacecraft was detected.

Another popular Moon conspiracy idea is that micrometeoroids would have sandblasted the spacecraft either in space or on the Moon's surface. This far-out claim has no basis in reality. It's well documented that even when Earth passes through a particularly intense meteoroid shower, nothing happens to spacecraft. The November 1999 Leonid meteor storm, the most intense since the dawn of the space age, dramatized this point. Not one of seven-hundred operational satellites was damaged during the Leonid meteoroid onslaught.

Is it real or computer graphics?

The crux of the conspiracy theory is the allegation that the moonwalks were filmed on a huge movie set. The argument for synthetic images seems very believable when you look at a film like *Red Planet* (2000), which offers convincing panoramas of astronauts trudging across Mars. Today we take all these fantasy scenes for granted thanks to the revolution in computer graphics and digital-image processing made possible by microcomputers. Now, images can be completely fabricated with precise control of all scene elements: lighting, texture, motion, and choreography.

Cinema special-effects technology of the 1960s was an emerging art and was truly primitive by today's awesome capabilities. No microcomputers, digital-image processing, or 3 D animation software existed. The decade's landmark space film, *2001: A Space Odyssey*, illustrates the pinnacle of special-effects capability in the 1960s. *2001*'s special effects took more than two years to complete, employed an army of technicians and some of the movie industry's top effects-experts, and swallowed a big chunk of the film's $10.5 million budget.

Even by 1977, all the fantastic *Star Wars* scenes were classic studio effects. Making the final film involved the laborious process of optical printing, where separated elements of a scene had to be assembled directly onto motion-picture film by repeated passes of the film through gigantic optical printers. The film pioneered the computer motion-controlled camera—critical for crafting space scenes as good as the Apollo footage.

Quiet on the Moon set

The first images from the 1969 Apollo 11 landing are so fuzzy it seems like almost anything could have been pulled off—except the effects of the Moon's 1/6 gravity on astronaut motion. A cinematically naive assertion by Moon hoax advocates is that all scenes were filmed in the Nevada desert. To do this, technicians would have needed to block out the sky—an inconceivable task to pull off without the use of a matte box in front of the lens to block some of the camera's view. This would have required that the camera remain stationary.

A key problem with a matte box is that shadows would have noticeably changed direction, shifting from west to east as the Sun moved across the sky during the hours of filming. (The Sun moves 15° per hour across Earth's sky, but 13° per day across the Moon's.)

Lunar photography 101

A boringly long and trivial list of conspiracy "proofs" exists that argues the moonwalks were artificially lit with classic Hollywood studio lighting. These claims prove only one thing—the conspiracy theorists know less about photography than a high school freshman joining the camera club. Despite truly boneheaded assertions to the contrary, all Apollo images are absolutely accurate and consistent with the reality of a single, really bright light source—the Sun. The only "fill" lighting is from sunlight reflecting off the lunar surface.

Allegations of multiple shadows from multiple lights are red herrings. You can duplicate the Apollo shadows by taking pictures of select foreground and background objects on a sunny day with a $10 camera. The shadows are always parallel but converge toward a point on the horizon as seen in wide-angle lenses.

Topping it off is the highly publicized "gotcha" that there are no stars in the lunar sky. Perhaps the accusers forgot it was daytime on the Moon when pictures were shot. Try photographing stars at midnight with a simple camera pre-set for a sunny day and see what develops. The film used in the primitive Apollo cameras—and

even that in the cameras on the space shuttle today—does not approach the dynamic range needed to capture faint starlight in a sunlit scene. As in *2001* and
other space movies, Hollywood special-effects wizards could have inserted stars for
artistic effect, but this would have been a dead giveaway the Apollo images were
fake.

Mirror on reality

NASA's choice of reflective coatings on helmet visors for the Apollo astronauts also
challenges the concept of a fraud. Any catalog photographer will tell you he or she
spends hours setting up the lighting to photograph a shiny object like a toaster. The
mirrored surface reflects the camera and studio, so a photographer must build a
"tent" around the object to reflect the light.

The astronaut helmets were not only reflective gold (for protection against ul-
traviolet radiation) but also curved, so they acted like wide-angle rear-view mirrors
(caution: cinematographer may be closer than he appears). The helmets would have
reflected the entire hoax setup: lighting, cameras, and the soundstage technicians.
Today, digital trickery allows for realistic reflections to be inserted onto visors. If the
Apollo footage really was faked, NASA never would have selected such helmets.
In all space movies—including *2001*—astronauts have clear, see-through helmets.
NASA could have done the same, and no one would have been any wiser.

Peter Pan on the Moon

I find it amazing that Moon conspiracy theorists obsess over nerdy details about
lighting but blithely ignore the precise motion of all objects in the Moon's 1/6-grav-
ity environment. This is the real nail in the coffin against faked Moon videos. Using
real actors, it is absolutely impossible to duplicate motion in the absence of gravity
or reduced gravity convincingly unless the shot is heavily reprocessed or synthesized
digitally.

Conspiracy theorists can't dismiss hours and hours of Apollo footage showing
all lunar objects following simple ballistic paths that appeared completely different than they would under the tug of Earth's gravity. This can't be done with slow
motion or other conventional film effects. Endless subtleties exist in the Apollo
scenes showing the precise, gentle pull of gravity on a true extraterrestrial world: the
way dust flew along long, shallow parabolic trajectories when it was kicked up; the
trajectories of myriad foil pieces blasted off the lander when the Apollo 16 ascent
module lifted off. A final tour de force is footage of the entire Moon rover bouncing
along on big arcs.

Curtain call

Thanks to FOX-TV's gambit for ratings, the Moon hoax got some time back in the
spotlight, but the effect was minimal. This way-out idea will always hover on the
dim periphery of basic common sense, alongside the outrageous collection of other
equally absurd "it-never-happened" conspiracy theories.

But the Moon conspiracy folks discredit American heroes, anger a lot of space engineers and scientists, and exasperate NASA spokespersons. The "we-never-went-to-the-Moon" authors come off to the vast majority of the thinking public as nothing more than fools.

For as long as there is a civilization on Earth, the intelligence, boldness, and bravery of the men and women behind the Apollo missions will be remembered. That will never be said for their detractors. All they have managed to do is try and put our national heritage up for sale—and for nothing more than TV ratings.

Seeing Red on Mars

By David L. Chandler
New Scientist, January 31, 2004

The rolling landscape of red soil is strewn with dark rocks. NASA's brace of rovers have certainly confirmed the picture we have come to expect of Mars. But take a closer look at the images they have been sending back. Is the Red Planet really, well, quite this red?

Welcome to the latest space conspiracy theory. The soft version of the story claims that in a bid to make an ordinary-looking, brownish Mars live up to its billing, NASA has been naughtily tweaking the colours in Spirit's digital images. The hard version has the evil NASA doctoring the colours so the rest of us won't notice evidence of life, such as patches of green.

Leaving aside the question of why NASA would want to hide such a momentous find, has it been taking liberties with the colours? Talk to NASA's image experts and you discover that getting the colours right is a surprisingly difficult—and, despite the technical wizardry involved, subjective—job. In fact, truly accurate results, the specialists agree, are not going to happen until people have been to Mars and seen its colours first-hand.

That said, there are problems related to these Mars rover images, some of them preventable. And in failing to make it clear just what we are seeing, NASA has naively allowed conspiracy theorists a field day.

Although there are standard red, green and blue (RGB) filters on board that can produce a fair approximation of "true" colour, these have hardly been used. Instead, most of the colour images displayed so far have been taken through green, blue and infrared filters (IR-GB). When the infrared gets rendered as red, the results are pretty close to true, but with some really glaring exceptions. Blue and green, in particular, just don't come out right. As far as we know, those colours don't exist anywhere on the surface of Mars. If they did, we would have noticed them in the few images that have been produced using a normal red filter.

But they are to be found on the spacecraft itself—hence the conspiracy theories. Standard blue and green paints, it turns out, are extremely reflective in the infrared, even though they hardly reflect any red light at all. So the red-yellow-green-blue colour targets installed on each rover, as well as the bright blue NASA logo, look very strange indeed. So does the blue insulation around much of the wiring. The blue paint reflects more than three times as strongly in infrared as it does in blue. So when the pictures taken with IR-GB filters are printed as RGB, the result is that the red pigment overwhelms the blue and you see a deep burgundy or even, with the insulation, a hot pink. Similarly, the green reflects more than twice as much infrared as it does green, so the green colour patch ends up a sort of mustard colour.

Is the Red Planet really, well, quite this red?

Why have they been doing this? Jim Bell of NASA tells me that it's because the important thing is to get the information the geologists need to distinguish rock types, and to tell dusty rocks from clean ones. And for that, infrared is much more useful than red; hence its use for the main panoramic images we have been seeing.

That's just part of it, though. Because of the reddish dust that is always in the air, the light falling on the surface of Mars is red to begin with; the effect is likely to be rather like terrestrial lighting close to sunset, when hills take on a pink or magenta hue. And the quality of Mar's red light will depend greatly on the level of dust as well as the time of day. That's a problem for NASA because the panoramas it has been showing us are mosaics assembled from dozens of separate frames. It may take months of fine-tuning to get the colours consistent between frames.

Still, Bell says, compared to the initial images from Viking, which were way too red, even the initial images from this mission have been closer to what things would really look like there. Better still for Bell, nobody is in a position to argue with him. Until of course someone goes there to check.

Is Baked Alaska Half-Baked?

Alaska's High-Frequency Active Auroral Research Program (HAARP) is a magnet for conspiracy theorists

By David Naiditch
Skeptic, 2003

The High-Frequency Active Auroral Research Program (HAARP), located near Gakona, Alaska, began in 1990. It consists of a high-power transmitter used to temporarily excite a limited area of the ionosphere, and a sophisticated suite of instruments used to observe the physical processes that occur in the excited region. When complete, 180 72-foot antennas will be distributed over about 33 acres, with a total transmitter power of about 3,600 kilowatts.

Background

HAARP has become a favorite target for conspiracy theorists and doomsayers. They have blamed HAARP for triggering catastrophes of biblical proportions, such as massive floods, devastating droughts, powerful hurricanes, tornadoes and thunderstorms, and devastating earthquakes in Afghanistan and the Philippines aimed to "shake up" Muslim terrorists.

HAARP has also been blamed for major power outages in the western United States, the downing of TWA flight 800, and mysterious diseases such as the Gulf War Syndrome and Chronic Fatigue Syndrome. Some claim HAARP is a mind control device that spurred the shootings at Columbine High School and elsewhere. (Devices are even being sold to block HAARP's mind-altering emissions.) HAARP has also been described as an impenetrable missile defense shield, a death ray capable of rendering the Earth uninhabitable, a machine that can interfere with the migratory paths of wild animals, a diabolical tool wielded by the forces of the Antichrist, a worldwide communications jammer, an apparatus that can cause the Earth to spin out of control, and a system linked to UFO activity.

Why is HAARP such an attractive target for conspiracy theorists? HAARP is a gigantic, high-energy, Pentagon-funded gizmo located in the remote Alaskan wilderness that plays around with the Earth's ionosphere, but whose purpose seems deeply mysterious to the scientifically uninformed. HAARP also involves physics resembling the alleged revolutionary work of a poster child of conspiracy theorists, Nikola Tesla, and is allegedly linked to physicist Dr. Bernard J. Eastlund's weird patent (#4,686,605) involving the use of Tesla technology for altering the Earth's energy fields.

The two main HAARP conspiracy and doomsday books are, *Angels Don't Play This HAARP: Advances in Tesla Technology* by Dr. Nick Begich and Jeane Manning, and *HAARP: The Ultimate Weapon of the Conspiracy* by Jerry E. Smith, the former Executive Director of the National UFO Museum. In addition, numerous websites can be easily located that describe all the alleged dire effects of HAARP.

Perhaps the best defense of HAARP is posted on the official HAARP website, especially on the page entitled "Some Frequently Asked Questions about HAARP." The site provides detailed descriptions of HAARP, its purpose, and its impact on the environment. According to this website, HAARP is a research facility whose goal is to "further advance our knowledge of the physical and electrical properties of the Earth's ionosphere which can affect our military and civilian communication and navigation systems." The ionosphere extends from 35 to 500 miles above the Earth's surface. It contains charged particles, called ions, and electrons that can destroy, reflect, and absorb radio signals. The behavior of these particles impacts communications, navigation, surveillance, and remote sensing systems. By better understanding Earth's ionosphere, the reliability and performance of these systems can be improved.

The quotations that follow are all taken from the HAARP website.

Is HAARP a secret project?

Although many conspiracy theorists claim that HAARP is a top secret project, the official HAARP website states, "The HAARP program is completely unclassified. There are no classified documents pertaining to HAARP." Indeed, why would a secret project provide so much public information on a website? Furthermore, HAARP is staffed by researchers from many different industries, and many universities, including UCLA, MIT, the University of Alaska, Stanford University, the University of Massachusetts, Clemson University, Penn State University, Dartmouth University, the University of Tulsa, the University of Maryland, and Cornell University. Such publicized wide participation is hardly a sign of a clandestine project. In addition, photographs of the HAARP facility are readily available and show no barriers or security fences, guards, surveillance equipment, or other indications of a secret operation. There are even occasional public tours of the facility.

Can HAARP be used for military purposes?

Although the Air Force and Navy jointly manage HAARP, officials claim HAARP is not designed for military purposes, but is a research facility whose specifications were developed by a consortium of (previously mentioned) universities.

The HAARP website does say that interest in ionospheric research includes "the unexplored potential of technological innovations which suggest applications such as detecting underground objects, communicating to great depths in the sea or earth . . ." This statement has led to reasonable speculation that HAARP-like technology is or may be used to communicate with deeply submerged submarines or to detect hidden underground military installations.

Are HAARP's emissions a health risk?

According to the HAARP website, "HAARP complies completely with all existing safety standards for electromagnetic radiation at all locations on or off the site," and an "Environmental Impact Study was conducted during 1992–93 in accordance with the National Environmental Policy Act (NEPA)." Furthermore, HAARP's emissions, even at the closest public access to the site, are claimed to be lower than emissions existing in many urban environments.

The HAARP website also addresses the concern that HAARP emits extremely low frequency (ELF) radiation that could produce health problems and affect our mental functions. While HAARP does not transmit signals in the ELF range, it is possible to generate a small but useful ELF signal through ionospheric heating. According to HAARP officials, this ELF signal "will be more than eleven million times weaker (smaller) than the Earth's background field and about one million times weaker (smaller) than the level where researchers have reported biological effects in the literature." The field is so weak that it may only be detected with sophisticated instruments.

> *HAARP has also been blamed for major power outages in the western United States, the downing of TWA flight 800, and mysterious diseases such as the Gulf War Syndrome and Chronic Fatigue Syndrome.*

Could HAARP impact the weather?

According to the HAARP website, "The HAARP facility will not affect the weather. Transmitted energy in the frequency ranges that will be used by HAARP is subject to negligible absorption in either the troposphere or the stratosphere—the two levels of the atmosphere that produce the earth's weather." HAARP's transmissions do interact with the near-vacuum region of the ionosphere. However, the "downward coupling from the ionosphere to the stratosphere/troposphere is extremely weak, and no association between natural ionospheric variability and surface weather and climate has been found, even at the extraordinarily high levels of ionospheric turbulence that the Sun can produce during a geomagnetic storm. If the ionospheric storms caused by the Sun itself don't affect the surface weather, there is no chance that HAARP can do so either."

How long do the effects of ionospheric heating last?

The HAARP website says, "Since the ionosphere is, inherently, a turbulent medium that is being both 'stirred up' and renewed by the sun, artificially induced effects are quickly obliterated. Depending on the height within the ionosphere where the effect is originally produced, these effects are no longer detectable after times ranging from less than a second to 10 minutes." Once again, local changes to the ionosphere resulting from HAARP are many orders of magnitude less than those global changes caused by variations in the Sun's energy output. According to the HAARP Environmental Impact Statement, there are no significant impacts to the ionosphere, and therefore, no mitigation measures are required.

Can HAARP create a hole in the ionosphere?

According to the HAARP website, "No. Any effects produced by HAARP are miniscule compared with the natural day-night variations that occur in the ionosphere. Several ionospheric layers completely disappear naturally over a whole hemisphere during the evening hours. HAARP can't come close to producing this effect, even in the limited region directly over the site."

What effect will HAARP have on the Earth's magnetic field?

According to the HAARP website, HAARP's transmitter "becomes useless during a geomagnetic storm. During these common solar induced events, the natural variations reach a level that is more than 10,000 times stronger than any variation that HAARP could produce . . . The Earth's static magnetic field, in turn, is more than 1,000 times stronger than the variations that occur during a magnetic storm and more than 10,000,000 times stronger than the variations that HAARP could produce."

Bibliography

The following books and articles provide additional information on this subject. Most of the noted articles are available on EBSCO host databases.

Allen, Gary. *None Dare Call It Conspiracy*. Cutchogue, N.Y.: Buccaneer, 1976. Print.

Barkun, Michael. *A Culture of Conspiracy: Apocalyptic Visions in Contemporary America*. Berkeley: U of California P, 2003. Print.

Benson, Michael. *Who's Who in the JFK Assassination: An A-to-Z Encyclopedia*. New York: Citadel, 1993. Print.

Berlet, Chip. "Siren Song—Conspiracy!" *New Internationalist* Oct. 2007: 12. Print.

Bethune, Brian. "Cracking the Da Vinci Code." *Maclean's* 20 Dec. 2004: 34–36+. Print.

Blakeslee, Nate. "Alex Jones Is About to Explode." *Texas Monthly* March 2010: 114–117+. Print.

Boyd, Herb. "The Man and the Plan: Conspiracy Theories and Paranoia in Our Culture." *Black Issues Book Review* March/April 2002: 38–40. Print.

Bratich, Jack Z. *Conspiracy Panics: Political Rationality and Popular Culture*. Albany: State U of New York P, 2008. Print.

Bugliosi, Vincent. *Reclaiming History: The Assassination of President John F. Kennedy*. New York: Norton, 2007. Print.

Burnett, Thom, et al. *Conspiracy Encyclopedia*. New York: Chamberlain Bros/Penguin, 2005. Print.

Carey, Thomas J., and Donald R. Schmitt. *Witness to Roswell: Unmasking the Sixty-Year Cover-Up*. Franklin Lakes, N.J.: New Page, 2007. Print.

Carpenter, Mackenzie. "Sept. 11 Conspiracy Theories Thrive, Despite All the Evidence." *Pittsburgh Post-Gazette* 4 Sept. 2011. Web. 14 Dec. 2011.

Cockburn, Alexander. "From Flying Saucers to 9/11." *Nation* 9 Oct. 2006: 9. Print.

Cook, Andrew. "Lone Assassins." *History Today* Nov. 2003: 25–31. Print.

Critchlow, Donald T., John Korasick, and Matthew C. Sherman. *Political Conspiracies in America: A Reader*. Indianapolis: Indiana UP, 2008. Print.

Dice, Mark. *The Illuminati: Facts & Fiction*. San Diego: Resistance, 2009. Print.

Dunbar, David, and Brad Reagan. *Debunking 9/11 Myths: Why Conspiracy Theories Can't Stand Up to the Facts*. New York: Hearst, 2006. Print.

Eisner, Will. *The Plot: The Secret Story of the Protocols of the Elders of Zion*. New York: Norton, 2005. Print.

Estulin, Daniel. *The True Story of the Bilderberg Group*. Waterville, Ore.: Trine Day, 2009. Print.

Fenster, Mark. *Conspiracy Theories: Secrecy and Power in American Culture*. Minneapolis: U of Minnesota P, 1999. Print.

Fraser, Stephen. "Phantom Menace?" *Current Science* 94.14 (2009): 8–9. Print.

Friedman, Stanton T. *Top Secret/MAJIC: Operation Majestic-12 and the United States Government's UFO Cover-Up*. New York: Marlowe, 2005. Print.

Gartner, John. "Dark Minds. When Does Incredulity Become Paranoia?" *Psychology Today* Sept./Oct. 2009: 37–38. Print.

Gilson, Dave. "The Truth Is Out There: 9/11 Conspiracy Theorists." *Mother Jones* Sept./Oct. 2008: 95–97. Print.

Goldberg, Robert Alan. *Enemies Within: The Culture of Conspiracy in Modern America*. New Haven: Yale UP, 2001. Print.

Greaney, T. J. "Thrill of Conspiracy Theories No Secret." *Columbia Daily Tribune* [Missouri] 22 July 2010: A2. Print.

Griffin, David Ray. *The New Pearl Harbor Revisited: 9/11, the Cover-Up, and the Exposé*. New York: Olive Branch, 2008. Print.

Hari, Johann. "Conspiracy Theories: A Guide." *New Statesman* 16 Dec. 2002: 27. Print.

Hasan, Mehdi. "It's Time to Lay the Sharia Bogeyman to Rest." *New Statesman* 13 June 2011: 16. Print.

Henderson, Cinqué. "Myths of the Unloved: The Paranoid Style of Black Politics." *New Republic* 25 Aug. 1997: 14–15. Print.

Hodai, Beau. "Alex Jones and the Informational Vacuum." *Extra!* Feb. 2011: 14–15. Print.

Hofstadter, Richard. "The Paranoid Style in American Politics." *Harper's* Nov. 1964: 77–86. Print.

Holland, Max. "The Assassination Tapes." *Atlantic Monthly* June 2004: 82+. Print.

———. "The Demon in Jim Garrison." *Wilson Quarterly* Spring 2001: 10+. Print.

Jacobsen, Annie. *Area 51: An Uncensored History of America's Top Secret Military Base*. New York: Little, Brown, and Company 2011. Print.

Jacobson, Mark. "The Ground Zero Grassy Knoll." *New York* 27 Mar. 2006: 28-35+. Print.

Kaiser, David. *The Road to Dallas: The Assassination of John F. Kennedy*. Cambridge, Mass.: Belknap, 2008. Print.

Knight, Peter, ed. *Conspiracy Nation: The Politics of Paranoia in Postwar America*. New York: New York UP, 2002. Print.

Kreyche, Gerald F. "Paranoia May Be Justified After All." *USA Today* [magazine] May 1999: 82. Print.

Lane, Mark. *Rush to Judgment*. New York: Holt, 1966. Print.

Linse, Pat. "Did We Go to the Moon?" *Skeptic* 9.1 (2001): 97–104. Print.

MacKenzie, Debora. "Power to the Paranoid." *New Scientist* 15 Oct. 2005: 21. Print.

Mailer, Norman. *Oswald's Tale: An American Mystery*. New York: Random, 1995. Print.

Mallon, Thomas. "A Knoll of One's Own." *Atlantic Monthly* June 2007: 106+. Print.

Manchester, William. *Death of a President*. New York: Harper, 1967. Print.

Marcel, Jesse, Jr., and Linda Marcel. *The Roswell Legacy: The Untold Story of the First Military Officer at the 1947 Crash Site*. Franklin Lakes, N.J.: Career, 2009. Print.

McLynn, Frank. "History Isn't Always a Cock-Up: Conspiracy Theories May Sometimes Be Right." *New Statesman* 20 Sept. 1999: 25–27. Print.

Meyssan, Thierry. *9/11: The Big Lie*. New York: Carnot U.S.A., 2003. Print.

Molé, Phil. "9/11 Conspiracy Theories." *Skeptic* 12.4 (2006): 30–42. Print.

Newton, Michael. *The Encyclopedia of Conspiracies and Conspiracy Theories*. New York: Facts on File, 2006. Print.

"The 9/11 Conspiracy Nuts." *Nation* 25 Sept. 2006: 12. Print.

Olmsted, Kathryn S. *Real Enemies: Conspiracy Theories and American Democracy, World War I to 9/11*. New York: Oxford UP, 2009. Print.

Oren, Michael B. "Quiet Riot: Tin Foil Hats in Harvard Yard." *New Republic* 10 Apr. 2006: 9–10. Print.

Patoski, Joe Nick. "The Two Oswalds." *Texas Monthly* Nov. 1998: 135+. Print.

Peppard, Alan. "'The Lost JFK Tapes: The Assassination' Takes Viewers back to 1963." *Dallas Morning News* 22 Nov. 2009. Web. 14 Dec. 2011.

Peters, Justin. "Paranoid Style." *Washington Monthly* Dec. 2004: 13–14. Print.

Pipes, Daniel. *Conspiracy: How the Paranoid Style Flourishes and Where It Comes From*. New York: Free Press, 1997. Print.

Polak, Allan D. "Salt, Toothpaste, and the CIA." *Skeptic* 11.1 (2004): 64–71. Print.

Poor, Kim. "Carl Sagan, Where Are You? The Moon Hoax." *Ad Astra* Nov./Dec. 2001: 38–39. Print.

Posner, Gerald. *Case Closed: Lee Harvey Oswald and the Assassination of JFK*. New York: Random, 1993. Print.

Ray, John. "How Skeptics Confronted 9/11 Conspiracy Advocates." *Skeptic* 14.2 (2008): 16–17. Print.

Self, Will. "Armageddon out of Here." *New Statesman* 22 Feb. 2010: 57. Print.

Shermer, Michael. *The Believing Brain*. New York: Holt, 2011. Print.

———. *Why People Believe Weird Things*. New York: Holt, 1997. Print.

Starobin, Paul. "The Radical Right Returns." *National Journal* 2 Oct. 2010: 4. Print.

Steiger, Brad, and Sherry Steiger. *Conspiracies and Secret Societies*. Canton, Mich.: Visible Ink, 2006. Print.

Swann, Julian. "Conspiracy Theories." *History Today* May 2001: 5. Print.

Tuckett, Kate. *Conspiracy Theories*. New York: Berkley, 2005. Print.

Vankin, Jonathan, and John Whalen. *The Eighty Greatest Conspiracies of All Time*. New York: Citadel, 2004. Print.

Web Sites

The 9/11 Truth Movement
http://www.911truth.org/

The 9/11 Truth movement is the leading counterpoint to the official 9/11 narrative. One of the main goals of the organization is "to expose the official lies and cover-up surrounding the events of September 11th, 2001 in a way that inspires the people to overcome denial and understand the truth." Visitors to the organization's multimedia web site can view the evidence and hear the arguments employed by Truthers to support their case.

Debunking 911 Conspiracy Theories
http://www.debunking911.com/

This web site is devoted to countering the contentions of the 9/11 Truth movement. The collapse of WTC 7, the alleged molten steel found in the rubble, the explosive "squibs" during the collapse of the Twin Towers, and other supposed anomalies noted by Truthers are explained in detail.

The 9-11 Commission Report
http://www.gpoaccess.gov/911/

Headed by former New Jersey governor Tom Kean and former Indiana congressman Lee Hamilton, the 9-11 Commission was charged by President George W. Bush with investigating the 9/11 terrorist attacks on the United States. The commission's thirteen-chapter summation, *The 9-11 Commission Report: Final Report of the National Commission on Terrorist Attacks upon the United States*, is available on this web site.

National Archives: JFK Assassination Records
http://www.archives.gov/research/jfk/

This site gives visitors full digital access to a host of government documents, including the Report of the President's Commission on the Assassination of President Kennedy, otherwise known as the Warren Commission Report, as well as the Report of the Select Committee on Assassinations of the US House of Representatives, which in addition to reinvestigating President Kennedy's murder, also examines the 1968 assassination of Martin Luther King, Jr. A host of background information is provided, including multimedia material and data on the Bay of Pigs incident in Cuba. Links to the John F. Kennedy Presidential Library and other web sites of interest are available as well.

The Sixth Floor Museum at Dealey Plaza

http://www.jfk.org/

The Sixth Floor Museum is housed on the sixth and seventh floors of the former Texas School Book Depository building overlooking Dealey Plaza in Dallas, Texas, where Lee Harvey Oswald allegedly fired the fatal shots that killed President Kennedy. Visitors to the web site can learn about the museum's latest exhibits and permanent collections, and shop for memorabilia.

Index

✣

About the Editor

A Connecticut native, Paul McCaffrey was born in Danbury and raised in Brook-field. He graduated from the Millbrook School and Vassar College in Dutchess County, New York, and began his career with the H.W. Wilson Company in 2003 as a staff writer for *Current Biography*. He has worked on The Reference Shelf series since 2005, personally editing a number of titles, among them *The News and Its Future, Hispanic Americans, Global Climate Change,* and *The United States Election System.* As a freelance author, he has written several biographies for Chelsea House. He lives in Brooklyn, New York.